The Practice of Managerial Leadership

Second Edition

The Practice of Managerial Leadership

Second Edition

Nancy R. Lee

Library of Congress Control Number: 2012905556
ISBN: Hardcover   978-1-4691-9082-2
                   Softcover   978-1-4691-9081-5
                   eBook   978-1-4691-9083-9

Image reproduced from Jaques, Elliott. *Requisite Organization: A Total System for Effective Managerial Organization and Effective Managerial Leadership for the 21*st* Century*. Baltimore: Cason Hall & Co. Publisher, 2006. Reprinted with permission. All rights reserved. www.casonhall.com

Print information available on the last page.

Rev. date: 08/30/2017

To order additional copies of this book, contact:
Xlibris
1-888-795-4274
www.Xlibris.com
Orders@Xlibris.com
549792

CONTENTS

This book is dedicated to Elliott Jaques, friend, mentor, visionary.

It is also dedicated to my husband Fred Mackenzie and my two sons, Greg and Paul, all three of whom have provided me with the love and support that has enabled me to do Requisite Organization consulting for more than twenty-five years.

Acknowledgments

I want to thank my many colleagues and clients who have helped me to understand, explain and utilize Elliott's concepts, especially Charlotte Bygrave, Tim Burke, Sandi Cardillo, Janet Langford Carrig, Kathryn Cason, Rebecca Cason, Sir Roderick Carnegie, Steve Clement, Linda Gloe, Carol Dolan, Betsi English, Sabrena Hamilton Mayhan, Tim Hart, Sherrye Hutcherson, Katie Jones, Fred Mackenzie, Fran Marshall, Chris Osborn, Joe Privott, Carolyn Rose, Susan Schmitt, Terry Seigel, Ken Shepard, Thad Simons, Mark Van Clieaf, Betsy Watson, Tova White and Ken Wright.

I appreciate the time Dr. Elliott Jaques spent editing the material in Chapters One through Five so that it accurately represented his ideas.

Nancy Lee
Longboat Key, Florida
2017
nmrlee@aol.com
RequisiteOrganization@gmail.com

Preface

Shortly after he returned from his service as a psychiatrist in the Canadian Army in World War II, Elliott Jaques became one of a pioneering group of psychiatrists and psychologists at the Tavistock Institute in London. Their military experience led them into innovations in organizations.

Jacques was consulting in the Glacier Metals Company when an employee asked him why it was that workers like him were paid by the hour while the executives drew an annual salary. That question aroused Jaques' curiosity and led him to start investigating the possible replies. His search led to a 50-year creative quest that became a major re-thinking of human capability and organizational structure.

Jaques' investigation took him into many parts of the world. A major learning experience was his consultation with Rio Tinto Zinc, a mining company in Australia. The chief executive of that company, Rod Carnegie, quickly grasped the import of Jaques' inquiry. Together they fostered extensive consultation in that company which resulted in a systematic refinement of Jaques' thinking and the profitable reorganization of that minerals giant.

Meanwhile he was also consulting with private and governmental organizations in Great Britain and did extensive work with the United States Army. Together these efforts, his writings, and the stimulation of working with companies in different countries fostered his conceptualization of human effort in organizations.

His thinking was a monumental reformulation of the basis of human capacity and organizational structure, reflected in twenty books and scores of articles.

Jaques not only posited eight different levels of conceptual thinking among human beings but also elaborated the curves of that thinking over an adult lifetime. In turn, his conceptualization gave rise to a new logic for organizational structure, an area that had previously had no logic for organizational leadership and accountability.

His work early on aroused my own curiosity and I invited him to join me in weeklong seminars I was conducting for the Levinson Institute. I also introduced him to several of the companies I was working with in the United States and South America. Executives quickly discovered his sophistication about their organizational lives. However, it soon became apparent that their re-thinking would have to go beyond slogans, clichés and traditional practices to become familiar with Jaques' formulations. Once they grasped his creative logic, they recognized that his thinking was far beyond what was in the management textbooks.

Jaques, with the help of his wife, Kathryn Cason, and the author of this book, Nancy Lee, continued to refine his thinking about levels of conceptual ability and even began to extend his thinking to understanding how animals differed in their capacity to grasp complexity.

Because his work required his audiences and his readers to make a radical change in their customary thinking about organizations and managers, many were reluctant to undertake that change for themselves and others and gave up on the possibility of introducing his concepts into their organizations.

In short, Jaques' work requires readers to take the necessary time to grasp his innovation. It also requires radical change in how executives are chosen and companies are organized. Like all new thinking his work necessitates testing the applications in one's own organization.

But grasping complexity need not be an overwhelming task. In this book Nancy Lee, herself an organizational consultant long immersed in Jaques' conceptualization efforts, has made his thinking much easier to grasp. That, in turn, should make this volume highly useful to executives, consultants and graduate students who seek to make organizations more effective.

Harry Levinson, Ph.D.
Chairman Emeritus, The Levinson Institute
Emeritus Harvard Medical School, Clinical Professor of Psychology

Introduction to the Practice of Managerial Leadership

The material in this book describes the comprehensive set of concepts, principles, practices and procedures called Requisite Organization. These ideas are logical and consistent and were developed over more than fifty-five years by Dr. Elliott Jaques and his colleagues in fifteen countries through continuing consulting research work in many types of organizations. The ideas have been tested and put in practice in organizations throughout the world.

Dr. Jaques chose the term 'requisite' to describe this integrated theory of how organizations work best because requisite means 'as required by the nature of things'. The ideas contained in Requisite Organization theory and practice flow from the nature of things—the nature of people, the nature of work and the nature of the relationship between the two.

Organizations exist to get work done in order to achieve their goals. Achieving organizational goals requires an organization that is appropriately structured, competent individuals at each organizational level, and procedures and practices that facilitate the work. This book deals with organizations that employ people—managerial hierarchies where accountability is delegated down through the organization from the owners/board members. People are employed within these managerial hierarchies as individuals (not as teams or as partners) to do the work required.

The material that follows is largely focused on the role of the manager because that is where most of the guidelines are needed in order to accomplish the work of the organization. It is the work of managers that determines the results achieved with the available resources. Requisite practices enable decisive, accountable, value-adding managerial leadership throughout the organization. There is also information on the roles and accountabilities of non-managerial subordinates. Each employee needs to understand fully his or her own role and the organization's structure and practices. All of the principles in Requisite Organization are intended to enhance trust between employees in the organization and employees and the organization.

Trust and understanding are further enhanced in Requisite Organization by the explicit definition of commonly used business terms. These terms are generally ill-defined and ambiguous. Clearly describing requisite practices and procedures in a consistent language that everyone understands provides clarity about what should be done and how to do it.

This book is written for managers at all levels in organizations. It is meant to introduce the material contained in Dr. Jaques' books, *Social Power and the CEO* and *Requisite Organization: A Total System for Effective Managerial Organization and Managerial Leadership for the 21st Century*. The reader is urged to read both of those books.

The second edition of this book includes extensive material on Requisite compensation and the Requisite process of succession management and talent pool development. There is a section at the end of the book that contains a number of individual articles on Requisite topics. These articles are useful in introducing Requisite concepts and in providing education on Requisite Organization.

Chapter One describes the Basic Concepts of Requisite Organization. Chapter Two deals with Human Capability, Chapter Three describes

Working Relationships and Chapter Four discusses the Organization Structure required to establish work and functions at the right level in the organization. Chapter Five describes Managerial Leadership Practices, Chapter Six describes how to establish fair and requisite Compensation, and Chapter Seven discusses Succession Management and Talent Pool Development. Chapters Eight and Nine describe the implementation of requisite concepts and practices in two organizations. In Chapter Ten I describe insights I have gained in more than 25 years of using Requisite Organization theory as the basis of my consulting practice.

Dr. Jaques edited the first five chapters of this book for accuracy in explaining his ideas. In Chapters Six and Seven written for this second edition, I have sought to describe Requisite Compensation and Requisite Talent Pool Development in such a way that Dr. Jaques would have approved. These seven chapters are intended to describe Requisite concepts, principles and practices comprehensively for managers at all levels.

A Requisite glossary is included at this book. There are also additional definitions I developed over the years that help bring clarity to strategic planning and to process design and implementation.

The reader can contact me to reproduce any of the material in this book for educational purposes, with the exception of the Potential Progress Data Sheet referenced on the copyright page. This reproduction may be done as long as there is no charge made for the use of this material. Please contact me at nmrlee@aol.com, or requisiteorganization@gmail.com to receive this permission and let me know the content you wish to reproduce.

The theory and concepts in this book are set out as a series of propositions to be considered. In my experience the use of these Requisite Organization principles and practices results in increased productivity and profitability and a socially healthy organization that provides employees the opportunity to use their capability as fully as possible in an environment conducive to personal growth.

Chapter 1

BASIC CONCEPTS OF REQUISITE ORGANIZATION

"Having a comprehensive system of concepts and principles to explain and guide organization functions, structure and processes makes it possible to teach your managerial leaders what is expected of them at every stage in their careers and to train them to apply this teaching effectively."

Dr. Elliott Jaques

The practice of managerial leadership based on Requisite Organization concepts sets out a systematic and science-based approach to management. These concepts, developed by Dr. Elliott Jaques, provide a comprehensive and coherent theory with an integrated set of principles that enables organizations and the people who work in them to be fully effective.

The use of Requisite Organization concepts enables organizations to:

- establish the correct number of layers in the organization
- establish roles that contain the appropriate work

- place roles in the right layer
- fill each role with a person capable of handling the work in the role
- provide clarity of roles and the relationships between roles
- assign tasks appropriately
- designate clear accountability
- establish effective management practices
- provide value-adding managerial leadership
- enhance productivity and profitability
- provide a socially healthy workplace

Many of the concepts that form the foundation for understanding how to achieve a requisite organization are introduced in this chapter. The first section explores organizations in which people are employed and defines the managerial hierarchy. The second section describes the all-important relationship between managers and subordinates. The third section deals with the complexity of tasks and the level of work in roles.

ASSOCIATIONS AND MANAGERIAL HIERARCHIES

More than 90% of those who work in the U.S. and most modern industrial societies do so in organizations that employ people, yet until Dr. Jaques' work there was no precise definition of what these employment organizations are. It is essential to have a clear understanding of employment organizations in order to structure the roles and role relationships in them effectively and to take advantage of the differing levels of capability that people possess to carry out the tasks necessary to achieve the goals of the organization.

Associations

Organizations that employ people are one type of association. An association is a social institution where the members of the group come together for a common purpose. There are voluntary associations such as companies, trade unions and clubs, in which individuals have chosen to become members. There are also non-voluntary associations such as nations, states and cities, whose citizens do not have free choice of membership.

Employment Organizations

In an employment organization the owner or the association of shareholders, through an elected governing board called the Board of Directors, hires a chief executive officer (CEO) for the organization. This person, in turn, employs other people to produce the organization's products and services. The CEO is held accountable by the Board of Directors for the output of the employees. The resulting organization of employed individuals lacked a specific name until Dr. Jaques named it the '**managerial hierarchy**'.

The rights and obligations of those involved in a managerial hierarchy are defined in the legal charter of the organization. It is, therefore, useful to review an organization's charter and to understand the information it contains.

Managerial Hierarchy

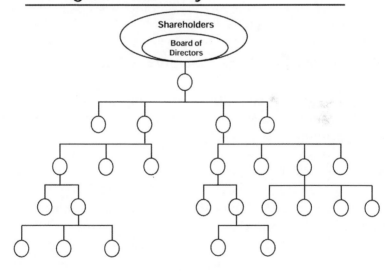

The Managerial Hierarchy

In a managerial hierarchy people are employed as individuals and have managers. The system of manager-subordinate roles that is developed from the CEO down through the organization is a hierarchy of working relationships. This hierarchy is a system of roles in which an individual in a higher role (manager) is held accountable by his/her manager (or in the case of the CEO by the Board of Directors) for the output of persons in immediately lower roles (subordinates).

A managerial hierarchy is a vertical organization for getting work done, with clearly specified accountabilities and authorities. In a managerial hierarchy, managers hold immediate subordinates accountable for using their best judgment and commitment in striving to get the assigned work done, as well as for the results of the work of their subordinates if they are managers. In this way work and accountability cascade in successive layers and a system of organizational layers is formed.

Many people have trouble with the word 'subordinate' as it has some connotation of lower or inferior. However, subordinate is used in requisite work since there is no other precise word available in the English language. In fact, everyone in a managerial hierarchy is the subordinate of someone else, including the CEO who is subordinate to the Board of Directors. Hence all employees are subordinates, and some are managers as well.

Definitions of Manager, Accountability and Strata

Some of the precise definitions that aid in understanding and establishing fully effective managerial hierarchies are those for manager, accountability and strata.

Manager

The definition of manager is someone who is accountable for the results of the work and the working behavior of others. The operant phrase here is 'accountable for'. People can 'report to' any number of others about any number of things, but in order for an organization to function properly it is essential to be totally clear about who is 'accountable for' what.

The lack of clear accountability by whom, for whom and for what breeds politics, buck-passing, excuse generating and game playing and makes for dysfunctional organizations. In a requisite organization managers are held clearly accountable for the results of their subordinates' work, for sustaining a team of subordinates capable of doing the work of the unit they manage, and for carrying out specified, common sense leadership practices.

Accountability

Accountability is a situation where an individual can be called to account for his/her actions by another individual or body authorized to do so. Managers in managerial hierarchies are persons who have subordinates and who can be called to account for the results of the work of their subordinates by their own manager.

Strata

Dr. Jaques gave the term 'strata' to organizational layers. He selected the term because it describes and connotes a layer that is a band similar to a stratum of rock. The words stratum and strata will be used throughout the book interchangeably with layer and layers. **In a requisite organization strata comprise a series of layers in the organization, with specified work of differing levels of complexity done in each stratum.**

Other Types of Associations

There are other types of associations for common purposes including partnerships, churches, colleges and universities, doctors and hospitals and political organizations. The chief characteristic distinguishing these organizations from the managerial hierarchy is that their primary output is not generated by means of manager-subordinate relationships. Only the administrative work of such associations is accomplished using the managerial hierarchy.

Partnerships

Partnerships are associations where a group of partners, often professionals such as lawyers, accountants or architects, decide they are going to work together. They form a partnership company, and the partners produce the output. They may employ technicians such as paralegals or draftsmen and also support staff to help them get their work done, but the primary work of the partnership is done by the partners, who do not have a manager-subordinate relationship.

Churches

Churches are another kind of association. Clergy are not employees of this association but rather are very special, ordained members. There are employees of the church, however, who are the people hired in a managerial hierarchy to do administrative work.

Colleges and Universities

In a university or college, tenured professors are members of the university association. They are not employees, and the heads of academic departments are not managers because they are not accountable for the work of the professors in their departments. Universities do, however, have employees and managers in administrative areas in a managerial hierarchy who support the work of the professional educators.

Doctors and Hospitals

Doctors are generally not employees of hospitals to which they bring their patients for treatment. They are not subordinates of the hospital president or administrator. The situation is different in a health maintenance organization (HMO) and other similar groups where the doctors are employees of the organization.

Government Organizations

In a nation/state/city that is democratic all citizens/members are equal, and they elect a government. It is this government that employs people in a managerial hierarchy. In the U.S. they are called civil service employees.

Family-owned Organizations

There are also family-owned organizations that are managerial hierarchies but where there are interpersonal issues that generally need to be taken into consideration and dealt with in addition to the normal concerns of a hierarchical organization. For example, some members of the family may be part owners, others part owners and employees, and others employees only. Things become even more complex where one family member is the manager of other family members.

Understanding the Differences

Most management theorists have not identified, nor do they distinguish, these different types of organizations from one another or from the managerial hierarchy. This results in broad generalizations that are frequently misleading. It also results in recommendations for structuring organizations that are often inappropriate and counterproductive.

Dr. Jaques defined the differences. This book focuses on his work with managerial hierarchies. He also did extensive work in defining principles relating to the other types of organizations described above that are beyond the scope of this book.

Purpose of Requisite Organization Theory

The aim of Requisite Organization theory is to discover and describe how to structure and staff managerial hierarchies and institute practices that will enable them to achieve the results determined by the owner or Board of Directors. The use of the principles in this theory enables employees to use their capabilities to their fullest extent, releasing human creativity and enabling the organization to do business with efficiency and competitiveness.

Creativity and innovation depend not upon downplaying or trying to eliminate hierarchy (which is inappropriate because that is how organizations are legally established), but upon the development of requisite organizations that enable employees to work together harmoniously and effectively.

Organizations are Systems with Process and Structure

Systems are made up of both the **processes**—the way things happen—and the **structure** in which things happen. Managerial organizations, like all systems, are a result not just of processes, which are the focus of most organization theory, but also of structure. Organizational structure is defined as a system of roles and role relationships that establishes the boundaries within which people relate to each other.

A foundational concept of Requisite Organization theory is that there is a requisite (right and natural) way to structure organizations based on the nature of work and the nature of people.

In a managerial hierarchy, organization structure must be looked at separately from staffing considerations and from organizational processes. In creating an effective organization, the first step is to define the structure by determining what roles are needed to get the required work done and at what level the work needs to get done. Decisions about structure and whom to place in given roles are often intertwined, instead of first defining a role and the work to be done in that role and then determining who should fill it, to the detriment of the organization and the people in it.

In the concepts and principles of Requisite Organization, Dr. Jaques described both the structure and the processes for successful and humane managerial hierarchies. The complete requisite managerial system he set forth in a clearly defined, logical and scientific way is described in detail in this book.

In an organization that is requisite the right people are placed in the right roles and are able to do the right work at the right time.

Organization Structure (Roles and Role Relationships)

Organization structure is made up of roles and role relationships within which people work together. These role relationships establish the boundaries within which people relate to each other.

All personal relationships go on within boundaries, even spouse/spouse, parent/child or teacher/pupil relationships. Without the background of expectations that are built into roles and role relationships, people do not know how to behave toward each other. Role relationships set the external framework of mutual accountabilities and authorities that govern the behavior between the incumbents of the roles.

Far from restricting freedom, having clear-cut role relationships established that are understood by those involved is the foundation for setting limits. These limits give real freedom within which to act because the parties involved know what is expected of them. For example, persons with drivers' licenses (a limit) are free (within required limits such as having necessary minimum vision, being sober, etc.) to hurtle several tons of metal down roadways (limits) at high speeds (again, with limits). Without such limits, no driver would have any real freedom.

Role clarity with the limits defined and understood, coupled with clear accountability and authority, builds individual confidence and esteem and generates trust in the system. Requisite organization structure of roles and role relationships is discussed in detail in Chapter Four.

Organization Processes (Practices and Procedures)

Organization processes consist of practices and procedures that enable the organization to function effectively. In a requisite organization key processes include such things as context setting, task assignment, coaching and appraisal. These processes are dealt with in depth in Chapters Three and Five.

THE MANAGER-SUBORDINATE WORKING RELATIONSHIP

The most important relationship in a managerial hierarchy is that of manager and subordinate.

Managerial Accountability

Managers are persons in a role in which they are held accountable not only for doing their best personally but also for the results of the work and the results of the working behavior of their subordinates. Managers hold this accountability because they control the resources available, decide priorities, assign tasks and integrate the work of their unit.

Contrary to much management theory, managers cannot delegate all of their work. They have substantial work to do that is their own, including the work of managing others and of integrating the work of their unit.

Managers are accountable for selecting qualified subordinates who are capable of performing the work required of them and for overall unit/ department results. They are accountable for building and sustaining an effective team of subordinates and for carrying out the required management practices as well as for their own personal effectiveness.

Managerial Accountability

Managers are accountable for:

- Results of the work and working behavior of subordinates

- Building and sustaining an effective team of subordinates and the work of the unit

- Their own personal effectiveness

- Exercising managerial leadership

Managerial Authority

In order to be held accountable for their work as managers, by their own managers, there must be certain minimum authority with regard to immediate subordinates, including vetoing appointments, deciding on a subordinate's removal from role, assigning tasks and conducting appraisals. Without such authority managers cannot be held accountable for the results of their subordinates' work.

Veto Appointment

Managers cannot be held accountable for the work of someone whom they do not believe can do the work required. Therefore, a manager needs to be able to veto the appointment of such a candidate. A manager does not need to be the person who chooses the slate of candidates for a position; that is done by the manager's manager.

A manager is not to be forced to accept someone as an immediate subordinate whom s/he judges cannot do the work in the role. It is usually the more competent managers who are asked to take on subordinates who have not performed satisfactorily, in order to help the organization handle a difficult problem. This is not a requisite practice.

Decide on Removal from Role

Managers need to be able to decide to remove immediate subordinates from their roles whom they judge are not performing at the minimum level of work required. Managers do not need the authority to discharge these individuals, since they are employed not by the manager, but by the organization. If a given subordinate's work continues to be unacceptable after the manager has discussed the problem with the person and provided substantial ongoing coaching, the manager needs to be able to tell his or her own manager that s/he no longer will keep this person as an immediate subordinate. It is then up the manager's manager (with the help of Human Resources) to see if any suitable place can be found in the organization. It is the manager's manager who determines the need for separation from the company if no appropriate role is available.

Assign Tasks

Managers decide what tasks they will give subordinates to do. The manager's manager is not to by-pass the manager and give assignments, nor tell the manager what types of task to give subordinates or how to do specific tasks. That is up to the manager and is the manager's work.

The essence of the manager-subordinate relationship is the clear specification of the tasks to be carried out. Managers are also accountable for coaching their subordinates and providing them with ongoing feedback so they know how well they are doing.

Appraisal and Merit Increase

It is up to managers to judge how well subordinates are doing their work. Managers have the authority to decide, within policy, how much merit increase each subordinate receives. Leaving decisions regarding merit increase to managers higher up or to committees seriously undermines the immediate manager's authority and his/her ability to exercise effective managerial leadership. Each manager must be able to decide the personal effectiveness appraisal of immediate subordinates and decide merit pay within policy. The operant word here is 'decide': it is not 'recommend'.

Managerial Authority

Managers have the authority to decide:

- To veto any candidate they do not believe can do the work of the role

- Assignment of tasks

- Evaluation of subordinates' effectiveness

- To initiate removal from role

Leadership

Leadership is a function of role. Some roles carry leadership accountability and some do not. Dr. Jaques designated the inseparability of the managerial role and the leadership accountability it carries by the term '**managerial leadership**'. All managerial roles in all functions in all organizational strata carry direct leadership accountability with regard to subordinates.

Leadership is not made up of mysterious personality characteristics and charisma. There are not natural leaders who have certain inner qualities different from other people who do not have these qualities and, hence, are not leaders. Leadership is grounded in role and in the work of that role. The critical issues with respect to managerial leadership are an understanding of the managerial role and a knowledge of how to do the necessary work in the role of manager.

Managerial Leadership

Managerial leadership is the process whereby the manager sets the purpose or direction for his or her subordinates and enables them to move along together in that direction with competence, full commitment and enthusiasm, dealing with obstacles they meet on the way.

Managers have the accountability to carry out established management practices with regard to their subordinates. This means that managers set direction and context for subordinates. They make decisions about whether subordinates will do their work independently or as part of a team. Managers provide direction in such a way as to ensure that they get their subordinates' full cooperation both with the manager and with each other. Managers need to win their subordinates' confidence in the managers' ability, in the managers' method of working and in the tasks they set.

Managers in roles in each stratum need to have the necessary capability to exercise effective leadership in relation to immediate subordinates. They need to be capable of doing the work in one layer higher than their immediate subordinates in order to carry out their managerial accountabilities such as providing necessary context setting, delegating tasks appropriately and making judgments of the personal effectiveness of their subordinates. Managers need to be able to integrate the work of their subordinates to achieve the assigned output of their unit. **Organizations achieve their results through managerial leadership.**

Misconceptions about Managerial Work

Managerial work is somehow felt to be contrary to the idea of effective leadership. There is sometimes a feeling that managerial work is autocratic, one-way down, and controlling. These are misconceptions.

The essence of leadership accountability is for managers to enable all of their subordinates to work together in such a way that each person can get on with his or her own work, knowing where all relevant others are going. In this way, everyone moves along together and the desired outcomes are achieved. A requisite managerial hierarchy enables the managerial leaders and the subordinates to move along together to achieve the organization's goals.

Subordinate Accountability and Authority

The manager-subordinate relationship is a two-way working relationship. Subordinates, too, have explicit accountability and authority. Subordinates are accountable to work to accomplish the tasks they are assigned and to bring to bear their full capability in working to achieve those tasks. The basic nature of the employment contract is that employees will always try to do their best to carry out tasks assigned by their manager. Subordinates are accountable to continue to develop knowledge and skills needed in their role.

If a subordinate is doing his or her best, there is nothing more s/he can do to affect the results. The results are determined by the prevailing conditions and the decisions the manager makes in assigning tasks and resourcing them. That is why the manager is held accountable for the subordinate's results, rather than the subordinate.

Subordinates are accountable to provide their managers with ideas and useful suggestions as to how the work can be done more effectively, to inform them about changes in prevailing conditions and to advise their managers if what is being assigned to them seems wrong or doesn't appear to fit the circumstances.

Subordinates are accountable to inform the manager if circumstances change while they are working to complete their tasks and if results cannot, in their judgment, be achieved as specified or if it is possible for even greater results to be achieved. This must be done in time for adaptive action to be taken. They are also to seek special consideration from the manager if they are unable to work at their best for a given time due to a personal situation. This ensures that the manager is aware of what is going on and can adjust assignments as appropriate. There should be no surprises.

Subordinates' Accountability and Authority

Subordinates are accountable to:

*   Bring their full capability to the workplace every day in doing the work to achieve their assigned output

*   Seek special consideration from manager if unable to do so

*   Continue to develop knowledge and skills needed in their role

*   Provide managers with:
    *   feedback about how things are going
    *   information on changes in circumstance
    *   useful suggestions
    *   ideas to improve processes

Individual Contributors

There is an important category of employees called individual contributors. These are people who work to complete the final output themselves. They can be found at any level in the organization, depending upon the complexity of the role they occupy and the tasks that they are assigned. Individual contributors may work alone or may have one or more persons assigned to them to assist in completing their work. In the latter case, the individual contributor is also a manager.

The role of Chief Economist in a bank is an example of an individual contributor role. This role would typically be immediately subordinate to the CEO of the bank.

Individual Contributors

Individual contributors:

- Are people who do their own work and who complete the final output themselves

- May have subordinates to assist in producing their output; in this instance they are also managers

- Can be found at any level in an organization except that of CEO

WORK, TASKS AND ORGANIZATIONAL LAYERS (STRATA)

Companies employ people to get the work of the organization done—work such as production, marketing, sales, accounting and so on. Yet until Dr. Jaques defined the term, there was no precise, generally understood definition of what '**work**' is. The lack of a clear understanding of what work is leads, all too often, to the situation where organizations become structured not for getting their work done, but for providing pay levels and career progression. Organizations then become structured in the form of grade levels for establishing status and pay brackets which leads eventually to the structure being decided upon not by accountable managers, but by human resource staff and job classifiers. Furthermore, the ability of a particular individual is often taken into account and **the level or grade of a position is often raised to fit that person, rather than the organization structure being established on the basis of the work that needs to be done in the role.**

Such practices result in less than optimally functioning organizations and, in particular, cause a proliferation of unnecessary layers. It is the negative result of this excessive layering, with its attendant impact on productivity and morale, that so many organizations address in their efforts at downsizing staff in order to survive in today's highly competitive environment. To correct the expensive and wasteful situation of having unnecessary layers, organizations are also eliminating layers of management. Unfortunately downsizing occurs and organizations are flattened without any comprehensive model of how they should be restructured and why.

In the absence of a specific definition of what work is, it is difficult, if not impossible, to specify clearly the work needed to be done in the organization, to decide how many layers are needed, in what layer work needs to be done and what roles and layers are no longer necessary.

Definitions of Work, Task and Role

The word **'work'** has many different meanings. Consider the following sentences: "That was difficult work doing the work I was given at work today. In my work I often have a lot of challenging things to do."

Here are four different uses of the word 'work'. The first connotes the effort applied, the second means tasks or assignments and the third indicates place of employment. In the second sentence the word work is used in a fourth way to indicate the role occupied.

In Requisite Organization practice the use of the word 'work' is limited to one meaning: **Work is the exercise of judgment and discretion in making decisions while carrying out assignments.**

There is also a precise definition for 'task' in requisite organization. **A task is an assignment to produce a specified output**. Tasks have a specified quantity and quality, and a targeted completion time. Tasks are carried out with allocated resources and within specified limits (policies and procedures). A manager assigns a task and the subordinate works to complete it.

Both tasks and the work that needs to be done to achieve the tasks are distinguished from the 'role' someone occupies. **A role is a position in the organization**. Tasks are assigned to someone who is occupying a role in the organization. Using these definitions, the illustrative sentences above would be more clearly stated as: "That was difficult work doing the task I was given in my role of manager at the insurance company." The words 'work', 'task' and 'role' are used throughout this book with the above definitions.

Work

The exercising of judgment in carrying out goal-directed tasks requires that the person understands the output to be achieved. The person either has been given a pathway to follow or has to plan a pathway to get to the goal. In either instance, the person has continuing decisions to make and problems to solve.

If an employee is given a report to write and has been given three months by his manager in which to write it, what does that person have to do? He will have to decide what he is going to do, how he is going to do it, and how much of his time will be needed on different aspects of carrying out the task. Then more decisions are needed about exactly where and when to start, what references to look up, what literature to read. Next, decisions have to be made about what material to use and how to use it. All the time he is deciding whether to do this part of the task right now or do some other tasks that he has also been assigned.

Work consists of solving problems on a continuing basis. Organizations pay their employees for using their judgment in making the decisions necessary to carry out the tasks they have been assigned.

Task

Managers need their subordinates to work to produce certain outputs. They communicate a task (often calling it an assignment, goal or project) having in mind some kind of output that is expected to be generated when the task is completed—a report to be written, a research program to be completed, a table waited on, some calls on customers to be made, a sale to be closed. Output can be a finite product or a service rendered. Output, whether a product or service, is both visible and observable.

There are a number of parameters to each task that a manager must clearly specify including the quantity and quality desired, available resources and when the task needs to be completed. Any variance from normal policy or procedures also needs to be described.

Quantity (Q)

There is always a quantity involved in an output, hence the quantity needs to be specified or understood in the assignment of the task. It may be one, ten, or ten thousand. Examples of task quantity include: installing the windows in 10 cars; painting the trim on 100 specially ordered dinner plates; selling 10,000 barrels of oil.

Quality (Q)

The manager specifying output always has a quality in mind. There are quality standards to be met. Too low a quality and the output is unsatisfactory; too high and more resources are used than necessary. The output needs to be provided within certain quality standards, and these standards must be set in terms clear enough that everyone knows what they are. If a subordinate is to produce a given quantity to that quality, it is necessary to ensure that the quality required is understood.

Resources (R)

Tasks need to be assigned in terms of resources—the amount of money that can be spent, how many people can be used, what equipment and materials are available. To continue the example of the report that needs to be written, the manager assigning the task further states that certain books on the subject will have to be reviewed and a literature search carried out. She tells the subordinate that there is a budget of $900 to cover research expenses and provides the use of the summer intern to compile the bibliography.

Time (T)

What is often not specified, but always exists in the mind of the manager, is the outside time limit by when the task must be completed. This is the 'when' of a task. A task is not only a 'what' but is a **'what-by-when'**, something that is to be completed by a targeted time. The completion time that is targeted by the manager should be made explicit when assigning a task or the manager should be confident that the subordinate understands the target completion time.

The time the manager has in mind when assigning the task, by when s/he needs the task to be completed, is called the 'target completion time'. The manager plans this target completion time to fit with the other tasks that the manager needs to get done toward achieving the unit's goals. One of the reasons for making the time explicit when assigning a task is that the subordinate can discuss with the manager any problems anticipated in meeting that timing, given the resources, quantity and quality specified.

In the example of the assignment to write a report, the manager stated that the researcher had three months to complete it. The manager did not want it in six months, but specified that it be completed in three months. The manager further expected the subordinate to work on this report along with other ongoing work in such a way that the report would be completed on time as well as all of his other assigned tasks.

There is an important point here that needs to be understood. If the manager assigns a task that is to be completed in three months, it is a different task than if the subordinate is given one month to do it, and again different if the time specified for completion is six months. Some people have difficulty with this point and think that it cannot be a different task just because the time allowed is two months less or three months more. But it is a different task, and the subordinate will have to make different decisions and behave differently.

With six months to do the report, the person assigned the task may choose to spend a lot of time at the beginning preparing very carefully, ensuring that all possible references have been discovered and reviewed. With only one month to do the report, the subordinate will decide to do much less research and the literature review may have to be much more cursory. The employee will have to decide priorities with regard to the work he has to do on other tasks in quite a different way, because of the allotted time he has been given to complete the report. Depending upon how much time he has to spend on the report, he will have to decide what can be set aside for now and what cannot, in working to complete all of his assignments on time.

Policies and Procedures

Organizations have company-wide and department policies and procedures. It is a manager's job to familiarize subordinates with these and see that they are adhered to in working on tasks. For example, the report must be no longer than 50 pages and must be bound in accordance with the standard procedure.

QQTR

A task, then, can be defined as a quantity (Q) of things within given quality (Q) limits to be produced by a target completion time (T) within specified resource limits (R) or QQTR. Although quality standards, resources and policy and procedure limits are not always explicitly stated, they always exist and are implicitly assumed by both manager and the subordinate. If no target completion time is understood, it is difficult to plan and organize to get the task done.

The manager and subordinate can discuss any of these parameters in order to agree on an outcome that is satisfactory to the manager and that the employee believes can be accomplished as assigned. This is part of the two-way manager-subordinate working relationship.

All tasks are to be done on time and to quality and quantity parameters with specified resources following policies and procedures.

Task Assignment

Each assigned task has a:

Quantity	Q
Quality	Q
Target Completion Time	T
Resources	R

$$\boxed{\text{QQTR}}$$

All tasks are to be done on time and to quality and quantity parameters with specified resources following policies and procedures

Context Setting

The manager needs to provide context for the subordinate by showing how the completion of this task fits with the other work that is being done and by describing the larger outcome the manager is seeking. "Hank, I need this report completed no later than three months from now since I have to put it together with the material that Sue and Jose are doing in order to advise the president on a recommendation to the board." It is this kind of context setting that enables subordinates to move along together with the manager.

As the task proceeds, clear context setting and specification of QQTR enable the subordinate to evaluate the situation and make good decisions. If the original time frame or the resources provided were not realistic, the subordinate must advise the manager as soon as possible so that the manager can re-evaluate the task, the target completion time, and the resources needed. Or, if there should be a change in circumstances, the subordinate can come back to the manager and discuss the situation. If the subordinate can finish the task sooner than requested, the manager, once advised, can plan accordingly. By having this information, the manager can modify priorities and determine the results that will be achieved by the work of subordinates.

This type of feedback enables tasks to be done on time or revised as required. It also enables full use of employees' time and talent. It eliminates the game-playing often brought about by such practices as management by objectives, where subordinates often only agree to end results which they are absolutely sure they can achieve or where they intentionally overestimate the time needed for completion. The manager needs to know what actually can be achieved if subordinates use their full capability. Requisite practices enable honest estimates and continuing feedback as to progress. Realistic estimates and continuing communication and feedback in assigning tasks and working on them builds trust between managers and subordinates.

LEVEL OF WORK AND TIME SPAN OF DISCRETION

Comparing roles within an organization or between organizations has always been very difficult, if not impossible. There has been a great deal of concern in recent years about providing equal pay for comparable work. But how is comparable work to be measured? There has been no accurate way of talking about comparable work with regard to how complex the work is. This is an example of the problems caused by a lack of clear definitions of the word 'work'. In talking about comparable 'work', the word 'work' is often used in seeking to determine comparability both in the sense of the tasks involved in a role, and in the sense of what a person must do in order to carry out the tasks.

Level of Work

Dr. Jaques used the term **'level of work'** to talk about the complexity of what needs to be done in a role in order to carry out the tasks that are given to that role. It is evident that the level of work varies from role to role, but how can this be thought about or described, and what is it that is being described? The level of work of a role is commonly talked about as the 'size of a position', 'how big one position is compared to another', 'how big a role someone has', 'the amount of responsibility in a role,' 'the weight of the responsibility felt in a given role'.

These ideas of more complex or more difficult or higher levels of work do not refer to more work in quantity but to work that is greater or lesser in scope. Although everyone has a sense of what these ideas mean, until Dr. Jaques developed and specified the concepts and definitions of Requisite Organization there was no clear, unequivocal language to describe or to discuss them.

Job evaluation schemes seek to measure differences between the level of work in roles, but they are unsuccessful. Current job evaluation measures are cumbersome, subjective and unreliable because they do not have a precise definition of what they are measuring. They do not have a clear concept of what it is about the work that varies in size. They, therefore, lack an objective method of measurement.

There is, however, a method of comparing the level of work in roles in managerial organizations that was discovered by Dr. Jaques as the result of the consulting research he was doing in organizations. This measurement is called the '**time span of discretion**'. It is also referred to simply as '**time span**'.

In order to carry out this measurement it is necessary to note the distinctions between two types of roles:

- *Multiple-task roles,* in which the manager assigns numbers of short and longer term tasks, to be worked on simultaneously, and
- *Single-task roles,* in which the employees have only one task at a time to be completed before starting the next.

In both cases, employees must balance efforts to assure that they are working both quickly enough and well enough to meet time, quantity and quality targets.

Time Span of Discretion

Every task has a time by when the manager wants it completed. Even when managers say they do not have such a time frame in mind, upon questioning it becomes evident that there is always a maximum time in their mind by when a task should be completed. It is possible to observe and study the time span (the target completion time) that a manager has in mind when s/he assigns a task. Extensive research by

Dr. Jaques and his colleagues has shown that the target completion time of the longest tasks a manager assigns to a role turns out to provide an objective measurement of the level of complexity of the work of that role. Time span measurement is covered in depth in Dr. Jaques book, *Time Span Measurement,* which is available from www.casonhall.com.

Time Span in Multiple-Task Roles

In a discussion with the immediate manager of a particular role, a trained observer can discover which of the multiple tasks being assigned to that role have the longest target completion time. No one other than the immediate manager can provide this information because it is his or her decision. These longest assignments give the longest time that the manager must rely on the judgment of the subordinate. This is because the subordinate can borrow against completion times of these assignments, in balancing pace against quality—that is, doing well enough, quickly enough.

Consider the case of a subordinate who has been given five tasks that need to be finished by the end of the day, another two that must be done next week and yet another that needs to be finished in two weeks. If the last task is the longest task the subordinate has to deal with, the time span of that role is two weeks. That is the measure of the level of work of that role and places it requisitely in a specific stratum in the organization.

Subordinates are given longer and shorter task assignments and are given additional task assignments from time to time. The longest task assigned is not necessarily the most difficult or most complex task in a role. However, it is the longest task(s) that a manager gives a subordinate that provides the measure of level of work in that role. This is because the subordinate must be capable of juggling the planning of and completion of all other tasks assigned to him/her in that role within the time frame of the target completion time given for the longest task.

Time span is an objective fact, since it is derived from an objective decision of the manager. Time-span measures cannot be falsified because managers are committed to the target completion times they set, and the effectiveness of these decisions can be checked by their managers.

The longer the time span of a role, the higher the level of complexity of the work in that role. Any two roles with the same time span, regardless of occupation, have the same level of work.

Time Span in Single-Task Roles

In addition to roles that have multiple tasks that must be balanced against one another, there are roles that have single-task assignments. There may be a number of sub-activities involved in carrying out the task, but the full task itself must be completed before moving on to the next task. An example is the work of a batch-work machine operator who must complete each batch in its given order and by a specified completion time. Another example is a document clerk who must complete each document in order and by the designated completion time. Most single task roles are first-line work.

There is an important difference in one-task-at-a-time roles and multi-task roles. In the latter, employees can borrow against time needed to complete other tasks if they cannot get any individual task done in a timely fashion as assigned. The manager may not know if the subordinate is doing this until some of the longer tasks fail to be completed.

In the roles where one task at a time must be done, the manager will know right away if the task is not completed on time, but may not know for some time if the quality of the work is up to standard. For example, an operator may be working quickly enough, but the manager will not know if the output is of good enough quality until some of it arrives at the first point where the quality is checked. In this example the employee is, in effect, borrowing against the minimum acceptable quality of work in the role in order to appear to get the work done as assigned. In single-task roles the time span is measured by the length of time it takes to determine if the work of a subordinate is just marginally sub-standard.

Origins of Time-Span Measurement

The evidence that, by itself, the time span of a role measures the level of work in that role comes from a number of sources. First is the accidental finding in 1953 by Dr. Jaques that individuals working at the same time span stated the same total compensation to be fair and just for their work, regardless of occupation, actual pay, or any other factors. These findings have been confirmed in 15 different countries since that time. Second is the consistent finding that if the time span of a role is increased through the assignment of tasks of longer duration, the incumbent feels the weight or level of responsibility to have increased. Finally, there is the finding that time-span measurement reveals a universal basic structure of organizational strata for employment organizations. This last point is discussed in detail later in this chapter.

In the 1950's, Dr. Jaques was working in the United Kingdom at the Glacier Metal Company with a group of junior staff who were concerned with fairness. They asked him if he could help them get away from job evaluation jargon and find a direct way of measuring work so that the work one was given to do determined pay and status, rather than pay and status being based on one's social status and accent. After months of seeking a method of measurement to no avail, the group suggested to Dr. Jaques that it might have something to do with time, since the higher one went up in the system the longer was the period of time used to describe pay. Workers' pay was described in terms of hourly rate or a daily rate, then the next level up had weekly pay, managers got monthly salaries and pay for senior executives was talked about in terms of annual compensation.

While exploring this issue, Dr. Jaques found that the target completion time of the longest task or tasks assigned to a role seemed to indicate a difference in the complexity of the work in that role relative to other roles. He also discovered that there appeared to be a consistent and universal amount of pay that was felt to be fair for each of the different role strata and levels within the strata, as established by time-span measurement.

There appeared to be an important connection between the weight of responsibility in a role, the level of work in that role, and what people considered as reasonable pay for what they were given to do. (Responsibility in this instance is defined as something one is depended upon or trusted to carry out.)

People working in roles having the same time span talk about similar amounts of pay as being fair for work they were doing. This finding, which is referred to as **'felt fair pay'**, has proven to be consistent throughout the years regarding relative pay for various levels of work, in different types of organizations and in many countries.

THE REQUISITE PATTERN OF ORGANIZATIONAL STRUCTURE

A pattern of work emerged that became the basis for evolving a requisite management structure for management hierarchies based on the discovery of time span of discretion and the proposition that time span gives a measure of level of work. This discovery was further confirmed by the finding that people appear to have a fairly universal sense of fairness of total compensation for given levels of work.

Dr. Jaques found a consistent pattern. Persons in roles with a time span below three months will describe as their 'real' manager whoever is in the first role that has a time span above three months. There may be shift supervisors or other levels and titles in between in roles that have time spans below three months, but the subordinate worker will not consider any of these people as their actual manager. They, of course, are not aware of the time span, but rather are aware of who is actually able to give them guidance and direction.

This pattern continues in a regular and predictable fashion with the next breaks occurring at one year, two years, five years, ten years and twenty years. These are critical boundaries between strata. Individuals working effectively in a role with a time span of more than three months but less than a year will typically name the first person with a time span of more than a year as their real manager, no matter how many apparent levels of management there are in between.

To have effective managerial leadership, a structure of layering must be set up with the first stratum—operators/clericals—in roles with time spans between one day and three months with the first-line managerial layer falling between three months and a year. The next layer of roles, typically that of department managers, has time spans between one and two years. Managers of functions are found in roles having time spans between two and five years, business unit presidents between five and ten years, corporate vice presidents between ten and twenty years and finally the chief executive with a time span somewhere between twenty and fifty years.

Stratum and Time-Span

Stratum	Time	Role
VII		Corporate CEO
	20 Years	
VI		Executive Vice President
	10 Years	
V		Business Unit Manager / General Manager
	5 Years	
IV		Functional Manger
	2 Years	
III		Unit Manager / Middle Manager
	1 Year	
II		First Line Manager / Specialist, Analyst
	3 Months	
I		First Line Employee / Clerical, Office, Factory
	1 Day	

The time span of any given role that falls within one of these strata will fall somewhere within the range of that stratum. For example, one role in Stratum I (one day to three months) can measure one week and another role can measure one month. A role in Stratum II might measure six months and another measure ten months. **The objective 'measure' is the longest target completion time of a task that a manager actually assigns to a specific role**. Wherever it falls is the level of work of that role within a specific stratum.

There is sometimes the mistaken understanding of this measure where the time span of the role is thought to encompass the **range** of that stratum, so that a marketing director role at Stratum IV would range in time span (longest task assigned) from two to five years. This is not the case. The time span of the longest task in a role determines the **specific level** within a stratum where the role needs to exist. For example, this marketing director role in a Stratum V business unit may be at three years or it might be at four years six months. There would be a substantial difference in the complexity of these two roles. Another example is that of a business unit president role with the time span of six years compared to a business unit president with a time span of nine years. Though both roles head business units they are of a very different complexity. The compensation that is felt to be fair for the weight of responsibility in these roles is also quite different. Furthermore, the time horizon required of the role incumbents for these roles is different and needs to at least need to match the time span of the role.

The Requisite Strata Required

The findings described earlier with regard to time span and to 'felt fair' pay led Dr. Jaques to conclude that a business unit needs no more than five strata, a corporation consisting of more than one business unit needs no more than seven strata and a mega-corporation that is composed of several large corporations needs no more than eight strata.

These findings mean that multi-billion dollar companies employing perhaps 20,000 or 30,000 employees can operate effectively with only seven layers, from the CEO down to the shop or office floor. Where there are additional layers, one or more people will fall into the same layer and provide no value-added for the organization. In fact, there is value-subtracted, and this practice is counter-productive.

Not long ago many, if not most, large organizations had 12 or even 15 layers. It is no coincidence that in the face of tough global competition one of the first cost-cutting measures in many organizations was to eliminate unnecessary layers to become more effective and efficient. Still many organizations today have 9 or more layers. Yet, organizations have a sense that there is no added value in many of these layers but, as was mentioned earlier, the difficulty is that decisions are often made in flattening or 'delayering' without any conceptual theory. This damages both organizations and their employees.

ROLE COMPLEXITY AND TASK COMPLEXITY

The complexity of a role can be objectively measured using time span. With the use of time span measurement and the requisite compensation practices it is possible to compare roles accurately and to establish comparable compensation.

Role Complexity

The time span of and the complexity of a role, as measured by the longest task in the role, determines the level within a Stratum at which the role should be placed. The longer the time span of a role, the higher the level in the organization the role needs to be positioned. There is, furthermore, an observable and consistent relationship between the total compensation for a given role that is felt to be fair and the complexity of that role.

Task Complexity

It is not yet known how to measure the complexity of a task. Although differences in task complexity cannot be objectively measured, it is possible to describe these differences. Managers, in fact, generally have quite a clear idea of the differences in the complexity of tasks. They are aware both of the differing complexity of tasks and the differing ability of their subordinates to carry out assignments. Managers use that knowledge every day in their planning and assigning of tasks and work.

What does the complexity of a task mean? How is the complexity of a task understood and described? The complexity of a task cannot be looked at in terms of the result that is to be achieved, that is, in terms of the output. Where is the complexity of a task if it is not in the output?

The complexity is found in what has to be done in order to get to the output. The complexity is in the pathway to the goal, in what needs to happen on the way to the goal. In studying gravitational force on a free-falling object, there is no use studying the state or condition of the object after it has hit the ground. That is the result. What needs to be observed is the process, what is happening as the object is falling.

Differences in task complexity can be observed in the differences in the process involved in working to achieve a goal.

The complexity of a task is a function of the complexity of the work involved in doing that task. Task complexity can be studied and understood by looking at the pathway to a goal and describing the work involved—what should be done to arrive at the goal, what judgment must be used, what decisions must be made. It is important to understand work in terms of its complexity and that as one goes higher up in work systems, the complexity of the problems to be solved increases.

Stratum I Complexity: Direct Judgment

In Stratum I, the manager assigns a task and describes the pathway to follow, telling the subordinate about the obstacles that can be expected and what should be done to overcome each one, if and when encountered. Work in this stratum requires direct action and problems are dealt with as they are encountered. This is called **direct judgment**.

The subordinate does not have to anticipate difficulties. When subordinates encounter an obstacle, they use information provided by the manager to try to solve the problem. If the problem cannot be solved as the manager has described, or if other obstacles are encountered that the manager has not anticipated, the subordinate goes to back to the manager for direction as to what to do. The time span of roles in this stratum ranges from one day to three months. This means that a role at low Stratum I might have a one day task as the longest task in the role, a role at mid Stratum I might have the longest task at ten days and at a very high Stratum I might have a task or sequence of tasks as far out as almost three months.

An example of Stratum I work could be found in a commercial organization that makes photocopies, and the copies are not coming out dark enough. The copy machine operator has followed the manager's instructions about what to do in this event, which is to change the toner cartridge. If this does not fix the problem, the operator has to go back to the manager to ask what to do next.

Stratum II Complexity: Data Accumulation and Diagnosis

Individuals capable of working at Stratum II are able to use diagnostic judgment in accumulating information and putting that information together to solve problems along the pathway toward a goal. This is the level of first-line manager and of individual-contributor analyst roles. At Stratum II someone has to be able to anticipate the relevance of particular items, to recognize what pieces of information are important in solving a problem and what are not. These tasks require **diagnostic accumulation and diagnosis**. The time span of roles in Stratum II ranges from three months to one year.

An example of diagnostic accumulation is the work of police detectives in solving cases. Clues are discovered and accumulated (or rejected as misleading or irrelevant) in order to reach a conclusion. Another example is an analyst's preparation of a report where information must be gathered and conclusions arrived at, with numerous decisions made along the way about what to include and what to leave out.

Stratum III Complexity: Constructing Alternative Pathways

Someone working in Stratum III has to be able to think out several pathways and choose the best one to follow. If the chosen pathway turns out not to be proceeding as planned, s/he needs to be able to change to one of the other pathways. This is called **serial processing**. This is the stratum of middle managers in the organization, and the work requires the ability to construct and to use alternative plans. The time span of roles in this stratum ranges from one year to two years.

An example of task complexity at Stratum III would be someone who is reorganizing the machine department in a factory. She has considered gradually training her operators section by section. She has also thought about training all her operators at one time. In considering both possibilities, and perhaps even a third or fourth way of approaching the problem, she weighs the pros and cons of each pathway and makes a choice. If the chosen pathway does not succeed as anticipated, she then selects another pathway to follow. Stratum III tasks require **constructing alternative pathways**

Stratum IV Complexity: Parallel Processing and Trading Off

Stratum IV is the functional manager stratum where a person does not deal with just one pathway at a time, but manages numerous pathways in relation to each other. This is called **parallel processing**. It is the kind of work that involves critical path analysis and where PERT charts are used. Assignments of Stratum IV complexity require that numbers of interactive projects be undertaken and adjusted to each other regarding resources and timing as work proceeds to keep the total program on target. Tasks of Stratum IV complexity require **Parallel Processing and Trading Off**. The time span of roles at this stratum ranges from two to five years.

An example of the type of work at Stratum IV is found in the role of a general sales manager who has several subordinate regional sales managers working at Stratum III overseeing Stratum II sales representatives. All their work and the available resources and changing conditions have to be balanced on a continuing basis to reach the company's sales goals.

Stratum V Complexity

At Stratum V, typically the role of business unit president, the person in the role must deal with a unified whole system. The tasks in Stratum V roles require the use of direct judgment, but the information that now should be used is at a higher order of complexity than the information used in roles at Strata I through IV. There are a wide variety of issues that have to be worked on in the context of the relationship between the business unit and the outside marketplace. This is where profit and loss accounting takes place. There are financial, human resourcing, production, technology and product research issues to be dealt with which interact with each other. The business unit president must handle problems like shortage of raw materials, strikes, rising costs, new product issues and so on, playing the whole range of complex variables against each other. The time span of this stratum ranges from five to ten years.

Stratum VI Complexity

The roles of corporate executive vice presidents in large corporations are at Stratum VI. Here again is a diagnostic accumulation type of work but at a higher order of information complexity. Executive vice presidents are dealing not just inside the corporation but with issues involving the whole world-wide environment. Problems have to be anticipated that are concerned with external political, economic, and societal issues. The time span here ranges from ten to twenty years.

Stratum VII Complexity

The Stratum VII corporate CEO puts Stratum V business units out into society. This involves dealing with the complexity of financial market issues, of balance sheet value of the business units, of issues of major competitors and of what is happening in the world on a continuing basis. The time-span in this stratum is from 20 to 50 years.

Stratum VIII Complexity

There are some very large organizations, such as General Electric, that are made up of a number of Stratum VII corporations. The time frame here appears to range from 50 to 100 years. This type of mega-corporation has not been studied in detail.

Orders of Complexity

There is an increase in complexity of work and tasks as one moves up to higher and higher strata in the company. Discontinuous change in the complexity of the work required to complete the tasks assigned to a role occurs at each stratum. These changes are not gradual but appear as if one moved from one step to quite a different step—from one way of processing information to a different way.

There are distinct differences in how information is used in making decisions as one's complexity of information processing matures and one can fill a higher role in the organization. There appears to be a very basic relationship between the fact that there is a requisite structure for managerial hierarchies based on the complexity of tasks and the roles where those tasks are assigned and the need for higher and higher levels of problem-solving capability. This is based on and required by the nature of work, tasks and human capability. The proposition set forth by Dr. Jaques is that there is a universally occurring natural (requisite) structure of managerial layers that is a direct expression of the discontinuous categories of complexity of information processing (CIP) found in human beings. These differences in human capability in processing information is explored in Chapter Two.

Chapter 2

HUMAN CAPABILITY

"The managerial hierarchy is a direct expression of the hierarchical structure of human capability."

Dr. Elliott Jaques

The basic Requisite Organization concepts and definitions discussed in Chapter One, including managerial hierarchies, roles, work, tasks and structure, provide a clearer understanding of organizations in which people work. In Chapter Two the people who work in these organizations, these managerial hierarchies, are considered regarding human capability and its use in working to produce desired results. The focus here is on an increased understanding of people at work, the differences in their capability to get tasks of differing degrees of complexity done and the maturation of this capability over time.

Requisite Organization principles and practices provide a total system of management, of organization structure and of how people work together. The use of this system results in effective organizations and effective circumstances for individuals to be able to use their full capability in their work.

THE NATURE OF HUMAN CAPABILITY APPLIED TO WORK

One of the most important basic human needs is to have the opportunity to use one's full capability; work is essential. Work gives individuals the opportunity to test and understand themselves in terms of their capability for making judgments and dealing with problems. When people do not have the opportunity to use their full capability they are very often dissatisfied, unmotivated and frustrated.

Until Dr. Jaques' research there was no straightforward, generally agreed upon, definition of work outside the science of physics. This lack of definition has made it difficult to understand human capability as applied to human work. As set forth in Chapter One, the requisite definition of human 'work' is that it is the use of discretion and judgment in making decisions in carrying out a task. When the word 'work' is used in this book it will refer to this definition.

Any satisfactory measure of potential capability in work requires two things: first, a measure of level of work; and second, a method of determining an individual's potential to work at a given level. The measurement of level of work was described in Chapter One in terms of the longest task or task sequence in a role as the measure of the complexity of a role, referred to as the time span of discretion.

Potential Capability and Applied Capability

The reason there is a structure in managerial hierarchies that is requisite is because of the way people use information in making decisions when they are engaged in working, in problem-solving. Therefore, to understand these organizations, it is necessary to understand human capability and its development. There are two different aspects of human capability relevant to work in organizations. They are 'potential capability' and 'applied capability'.

Potential Capability

Potential Capability is the maximum level at which a person could work, given the opportunity to do so and provided s/he values the work and has the opportunity to acquire the necessary skilled knowledge.

This is the level of work that people aspire to and feel satisfaction when they are able to achieve it.

It is important to understand each person's potential capability for work at any given time since that is what determines the highest level at which someone could work if he or she valued the work and had the necessary skilled knowledge. This provides a benchmark in seeking to use a given person's capability to the fullest for the good of the individual and of the organization.

Managers can and do judge each of their subordinates about their current potential capability and it is one of their important accountabilities. In fact, they would not be able to keep themselves from doing so.

There are two different aspects of potential capability. The first is *Current Potential Capability (CPC)*, which is the highest level at which someone could work **right now** if they had the necessary skilled knowledge and valued the work. The second is *Future Potential Capability (FPC)*, which is the maximum level at which someone could be capable of working **at some specified point in the future,** say five or ten years from now. Managers are generally able to judge both current and future potential capability with reasonable accuracy for subordinates with whom they have been working for six months or more.

For example, Jeff, a Stratum III manager, has a subordinate named Janice. Jeff's judgment of Janice's current potential capability is that she could currently work at his level if she had the required skilled knowledge. When considering Janice's future potential capability, he judges that she will probably be able to work at the next level up in the organization in about four or five years and that she possibly might be able to work one level further up toward the end of her career. Whether she will be able to fill any specific roles at those levels will be determined by her valuing the roles and gaining the necessary skills and knowledge.

Applied Capability

Applied Capability is the capability someone has to do the work in a specific role. Applied capability is always related to a specific role.

There are three critical aspects of applied capability. First, the work must be *valued* by the person. If someone is not interested in the work s/he is doing, it is difficult to be committed to the work and to apply his or her full capability. Second, the person must have the necessary *knowledge and skills* to carry out the work or s/he will not be able to do it, no matter how much s/he wishes to do so. Finally, a person must have the *complexity of information processing* to handle the complexity of the work. Tasks, and the work required to accomplish them, vary in complexity and people vary in the complexity of information processing that they possess to apply to these tasks.

There is an important difference between the Current Potential Capability that someone has at a given time and the amount of Applied Capability the person uses or applies in a given task or role. Current Potential Capability is often more than the capability that someone is applying at the present time. A person's full potential capability for work may not being reached because there is something out of line, for example the skilled knowledge may not be complete or s/he may not value that task sufficiently.

Values

The more a person values an activity, the more initiative s/he will take in carrying it out. The more intensely something is valued, the more strongly will it be pursued. 'Value' in this sense refers to how much individuals are committed to the role they occupy as well as the tasks and the work which make up the role. This must include not only the work content of the role, but also the value of having the role to work in. An indication of valuing the work of a role is demonstrated by employees understanding and accepting the requirements and obligations of the role and demonstrating the relevant behavior.

An example of placing someone in a role she does not value occurs when an outstanding sales person is made a regional sales manager, but she does not value managing other people. She values being an outstanding salesperson, rather than being a manager and doing the work required of a manager. It will be difficult under these circumstances for her to apply her full capability to the new managerial role she has been given.

There is a proposition in requisite work that individuals do not need to be motivated or stimulated by external incentives and that people are spontaneously proactive and energetic when they do things they value and when they have work for which they have the necessary capability. Managers need not try to encourage output by providing incentives. Instead they need to provide conditions in which the work itself has inherent value to the people performing it. The core of what has been called motivation is actually the value someone places on something. Most people value the opportunity for work that uses one's full capability. Indeed, they need to be free of de-motivators, to be free from conditions that inhibit their desire to gain the satisfaction from fulfilling work.

In order for people to apply their full capability they must value the work they are doing and the role they occupy. All employees should explore their own values in the light of the work they are given to do. Managers must be aware of and discuss with their subordinates the kinds of work they value and what is required by the roles they occupy.

Skilled Knowledge

Knowledge is what one has learned. It can be articulated and shared. To work effectively in each role, a person must have a certain background, training, education and/or experience. An engineer must know the principles of physics and how to use them. An accountant must know accounting rules and procedures. However, it is not enough simply to have the required knowledge: it is also necessary to know how to apply the knowledge. Skill is the ability to use the knowledge one has. It is necessary to become skilled in using the knowledge that one has and this occurs through experience. For many roles, there are also certain educational requirements and qualifications.

Complexity of Information Processing

A person's complexity of information processing (CIP) is the complexity of mental activity a person uses in carrying out work. CIP determines the maximum level at which that individual could work at any given time in his/her maturation and development, if s/he valued the work and had the necessary skilled knowledge. Each person's complexity of information processing (CIP) is innate. The ultimate level of CIP that can be reached in one's lifetime is determined genetically, just as is one's ultimate height.

Complexity of information processing can be thought of as mental capability. It has to do with such things as:

- the number, rate of change and ease of identification of factors in a situation that can be dealt with
- the ability to pattern, order, categorize and generalize information. CIP provides the ability to do a given level of work based on its complexity. It is reflected in employees' judgment and decision making capability
- the ambiguity and complexity of factors/information that can be managed and anticipated into the future and how far into the future this can be done. This includes the ability to foresee and anticipate problems and hence avoid or resolve them

How far in the future individuals can conceptualize is called their '**time horizon**'. In selecting someone for a specific role it is necessary for their time horizon to at least equal the time span of the role, the role complexity as described in Chapter One.

Managers can judge the level of their subordinates' complexity of information processing as: at or above their own level; just right to be an immediate subordinate; or two or more levels below their own. This last judgment provides the feeling that there is a need for one or more managers in between that subordinate and the manager making the judgment.

Managers are unable to stop themselves from making these judgments. They are a necessary part of knowing what and how to delegate to get the work of their unit done. Managers make these judgments based on experience working with their subordinates, handing off assignments and seeing the results. It takes three to six months of experience with a new subordinate to feel comfortable with judging his/her level.

Managers can also generally judge at what point in the future subordinates might be able to work at the next level up and at what level the person may be able to work ultimately in their career.

Productivity, profitability and employee satisfaction are substantially increased when work/tasks are at the right level in the organization, roles are staffed with individuals capable of doing the work of their role and employees are able to use their full capability.

Complexity of Information Processing (CIP)

Complexity of Information Processing provides the ability to do a given level of work.

CIP has to do with:
- The number of factors that can be dealt with
- The rate of change of these factors
- The ability to categorize factors
- Ambiguity of factors that can be managed
- The ability to foresee problems and avoid or manage them
- How far in the future an individual can conceptualize

Decision Making

There is an important underlying proposition in Requisite Organization theory with regard to how people make decisions. It is that people do not make decisions through the use of knowledge that can be fully articulated prior to making those decisions. Knowledge and the skilled use of knowledge differ from decision-making and it is important to understand the distinction.

If someone can describe all the reasons in making a choice prior to doing so, that person hasn't made a decision: s/he has made a calculation. Decision making has to do with the moment of choice. People do not fully know what choice they have made until they have made it. Knowledge of all reasons for decisions and choices is always retrospective. People can only determine all reasons why they decided after they have made the decision. The process of choosing is at the non-verbal level and is a continuous and on-going function not only in humans but in all living organisms. Dr. Jaques discusses this concept in detail in his book entitled *The Life and Behavior of Living Organisms*. It is the complexity of this internal process that determines a person's potential capability.

Other Measures of Ability

None of the types of measurement presently in use, such as IQ, clinical assessments or evaluations done in assessment centers, deals effectively with a person's ability to work at a particular level in an organization. Because the concept of human work does not have a widely understood and agreed definition and no tests have ever been validated against the ability to do work, organizations have no way to measure the differences in levels of work.

Measurement of IQ determines something quite different from that being considered in Current Potential Capability. IQ does not give any indication of someone's ability to do work in employment organizations.

Measurements done in assessment centers depend on the capability of the people on the team doing the assessing. Clinical judgments vary according to the clinical experience and ability of the person making the judgment.

With the clear and explicit definition of work—as the use of discretion and judgment in carrying out tasks—and the discovery of the time span of discretion measurement to differentiate the complexity of work in roles, it has become possible to talk about differing levels of work and the differing ability of people to carry out that work.

Personality Characteristics

Personality can be defined as the totality of traits and characteristics that are peculiar to a specific person. It has been commonly assumed that someone's basic personality characteristics are extremely important with respect to getting different kinds of work done. There are endless lists of personality traits such as being reflective, thoughtful, mature, dedicated, calm, energetic, and charismatic that are considered useful or even necessary in various aspects of work-related behavior. For example, salespeople should be gregarious, scientists should be reflective.

However, the concern in managerial systems needs to focus on whether a person is sufficiently free of extremes of behavior that interfere with getting work done (which is called 'negative temperament' in requisite work) rather than on an endless list of personality characteristics that are ambiguous and ill-defined.

The issue, for example, is not how mature a person is, but whether a person is so immature that it is difficult for that person to do his/her work. It is not how sociable someone is, but whether that person is so abrasive that it is difficult for him or her to work with others.

Negative Temperament

Temperament is defined as the method of behaving or reacting that is characteristic of a person. Where there are interpersonal stresses between individuals in the workplace and evidence of negative temperament, the first thing to look for is any organizational faults that may be making it difficult for employees to work together effectively. It is only when managers are sure the organization's structure and practices are satisfactory that it is time to look at possible temperamental problems in the individuals working there.

If a negative temperamental problem (-T) is determined to exist, it is a problem to be handled by the individual, but outside the organization. It is not the organization's business to work with employees in modifying their behavior. It is, however, a manager's accountability to tell subordinates if their behavior is causing problems and the consequences of not making needed changes. There is implicit in the employment agreement the understanding that employees demonstrate the behavior required to get work done. If their behavior is unacceptable it is the accountability of employees as adults to seek whatever help they need externally. The employer can provide time off or other assistance in doing so.

For example, Stan was a highly-qualified employee who held both a doctoral degree in Physics and an MBA. He had a great deal of knowledge that was useful to the company for which he worked. However, he was extremely argumentative. He became confrontational whenever someone disagreed with his point of view. His behavior disrupted his work and the work of those around him—his manager, his subordinates and his colleagues. His manager discussed this behavior with him in terms of what was expected, but Stan, over time, did not make the necessary changes. Finally, the manager determined he needed to deselect Stan from the unit, and he advised his manager that Stan was too disruptive to continue as his subordinate. It was arranged for Stan to leave the unit and subsequently the organization, to the relief of his co-workers.

Another example of negative temperament is avoidance. By this is meant avoiding doing some of the crucial managerial tasks such as making the decision to request the removal from role of an employee who is not able to do the required work. This situation often goes on for months or years because both the manager and the Manager-once-Removed hesitate to address the situation. This is neither a good situation for the subordinate involved nor for the organization. Also avoiding being fully honest and truthful in appraising performance is another common example of avoidant behavior, often because it is uncomfortable for the manager to do so.

There are many people today, experts, academics and consultants, who consider that the prime route to modifying and improving organizations is by changing the behavior of the people involved. They attempt to do this through team building techniques, or by trying to resolve interpersonal conflicts between individuals through individual counseling, group discussions and other behavior modification methods. These attempts by an organization to change a person's behavior are counter-productive. An individual's personality or personal style is not the organization's business if the person performs his or her work satisfactorily and does not cause problems for other people with whom s/he interacts.

The Maturation of the Complexity of Information Processing

As was described earlier, everyone's complexity of information processing (CIP) is innate to him or her and unfolds throughout life. It is inborn. The maturation process of each person's complexity of information processing cannot be speeded up or enhanced by special educational procedures or occupational opportunities nor impeded by less favorable social, educational or occupational opportunities. These experiences are far less important for individual maturation in potential capability than are the problems that must be solved in living everyday life.

Each individual's maturation of CIP proceeds from infancy through to adulthood and on to old age. It is a natural unfolding. Evidence shows that individuals mature in predictable patterns and that this maturation continues throughout life, with the result being that the growth of potential can be plotted. People's ideas about 'felt fair' compensation also increase along with their growth of potential when they are in appropriate roles.

Mode

Dr. Jaques gave the term '**Mode**' to the trajectory of this maturation and its ultimate result. For example, Janice who was mentioned earlier is currently judged by her manager to be able to work is a role now at Stratum III, at Stratum IV in 4 or 5 years' time and possibly to have the future potential capability to work at Stratum V toward the end of her career. Hence, she appears to be a Mode V. Whether or not she will be able to do any specific role at these levels will depend upon her gaining the required skilled knowledge and her valuing the work of any role for which she might be considered. These kinds of judgments of current potential capability (Stratum III in Janice's case), anticipated development and ultimate Mode (V in Janice's case) are very useful in considering the talent pool available in any given organization. This topic will be dealt with in greater detail in Chapter Seven on Succession Management and Talent Pool Development.

Development and Maturation

Maturation is different from development. Development refers in a general way to change through time where the eventual outcome cannot be foreseen at the beginning, such as a person's emotional development or the development of a professional practice. Maturation by contrast is predetermined and predictable.

At any given stage in a person's maturation, there is a maximum level at which that individual has the current potential capability to work at present and his or her ultimate potential (Mode). That maximum level and its rate of maturation is innate: it is genetically established just as is height. Maturation of potential capability is not affected by education or the amount of knowledge the person may acquire or by any particular experiences. An exception, however, is that a person's maximum potential might be stunted in infancy by extreme negative factors such as severe malnutrition or debilitating illness. Such a person as s/he matured in potential capability would appear as a damaged or handicapped higher level individual.

An individual's potential capability is an innate property of that person. By contrast, values (commitment) and knowledge can be taken up by individuals or not. Values can and do change with circumstances. Knowledge can increase, be forgotten, can be combined or can be stored for use later. A person's knowledge or values may often be confused with potential capability in the sense of someone's being judged to be ignorant or to be knowledgeable in various matters pertaining to work, or 'unmotivated' or 'highly motivated' about certain work. The understanding or judgment of someone's current level of complexity of information processing is different from knowing about what work the individual values or the skilled knowledge that the person possesses.

Fairness in Employment

The idea that individuals' current and ultimate potential mental capability can be determined is a controversial proposition that seems to run counter to ideas of fairness in democratic countries and the belief that individuals ought to be able to reach any level, depending on where they want to go. This is referred to as the Horatio Alger fantasy.

In fact, it is obvious to most people that some individuals have greater capability than others and greater future potential as well. Managers can readily discuss the present capability of their subordinates as well as predict with a reasonable degree of accuracy how much potential each has for handling increasingly complex work. Managers do this all the time.

The issue is not whether, in industrial societies, people should all have the opportunity to develop to whatever level they choose. It is rather that many managerial hierarchies have not found ways of ensuring that the people who work in them have the opportunity for work consistent with their potential capability. Because of the way in which most organizations are presently structured, many people do not have the opportunity to realize their full potential, with the attendant loss both to these individuals and to the organizations employing them.

Fairness in employment cannot be based on the wishful thinking that all persons can achieve anything they wish, but by understanding people's actual level of potential (all people, not just that of the dominant group) and ensuring that they are given the opportunity for work at their true level of potential, regardless of gender, color, age and ethnic background. Individuals, of course, must put forth the effort to acquire the necessary skilled knowledge for roles that use their potential capability.

Everyone will benefit when organizations ensure that individuals are assigned levels of work in positions equal to their levels of current potential capability and ensure that, as people grow in capability, they are provided with opportunities for greater and greater levels of work whenever this is possible. This situation not only provides fairness for the employees involved but also provides for the maximum use of capability in the company.

Complexity of Information Processing and Organization Strata

When Dr. Jaques discovered the discontinuity in organizational structure that showed up in time-span measurement, he postulated that there must be some kind of discontinuity in the way people work, a qualitative difference that corresponded with the different strata.

Through the years, he found that there was indeed a difference in the way people process information when they are engaged in goal-directed behavior.

Dr. Jaques, in collaboration with Kathryn Cason, determined that there are four different ways in which people can be observed processing information, and they named these **declarative, cumulative, serial** and **parallel**. The differences in these four methods are observable when people are engaged in a discussion in which they are fully engrossed.

Declarative Processing

A person using **declarative** processing explains his or her position by bringing forward a number of separate reasons for it. Each reason is stated on its own, and no connection is made with any of the other reasons that may be mentioned. For example, "Here's one of the reasons for my idea and here's another reason. I can give you several others as well". To the observer, the use of information has a declarative quality and the points that are made lack unity or a sense of being connected. Each of the reasons stands alone in support of the conclusion. There is an 'or-or' quality about this type of processing. The conclusion is supported by this reason or that reason or yet another reason.

Cumulative Processing

A person using **cumulative** processing explains his or her position by bringing together many different ideas none of which is sufficient alone to make the case, but do so when taken together. For example, a detective might argue, "If you take this first point and put it together with this second fact and then the third clue, it becomes clear that the thief must be working inside the company." The reasons are accumulated and explicitly connected; there is a clearly stated relationship between them. This type of processing has an 'and-and' quality, that is, the position is supported by this reason and that reason and another reason.

Serial Processing

A person using **serial** processing explains his/her position by constructing a line of thought consisting of a sequence of reasons, each one of which leads on to the next, thus creating a chain of linked reasons. For example, "I think we should do A because it will lead to B and B will cause C to happen, and C will enable D to occur and that is what we want to have happen." This method of information processing has both a serial quality and a conditional quality in the sense that each reason in the series sets the conditions that lead to the next reason. That is, if this happens then that will happen which will lead to something else happening. Serial processing has an 'if-then; conditional quality—if this happens then that will happen.

Parallel Processing

A person using **parallel** processing explains his or her position by examining several positions, each arrived at by means of serial processing. These statements almost have the sense of the person arguing with him or herself. The several lines of thought are held in parallel and are linked to each other. Reasons or points are selected from these parallel sequences, and a new sequence is described that supports the position chosen.

An illustration of this process is, "We could do A which would then lead to B and we could get to end X. Or, we could do M, which would lead us to N, and we would arrive at another desired end, Y. Or, we could do S which would cause T and we could then achieve Z. But we might get a better outcome, W, by modifying the plan A with M and adding S. The person combines reasons or points from one or more chains to reach a desired conclusion. The nature of this, the most complex type of information processing, is bi-conditional, meaning that only if particular consequences could be met would another series of conditions be put into place. It is the kind of processing needed to carry out critical path analysis in which progress in a number of processes has to be controlled in relation to others. There is a quality of 'if…then, but only if…' in this way of reasoning.

Four Methods of Processing Information

Declarative Reasoning by one or more unconnected arguments (or…or)

Cumulative Reasoning by two or more linked arguments (and…and)

Serial Reasoning by chains of two or more cause and effect sequences (if…then)

Parallel Reasoning by cause and effect sequences that are linked and interwoven (if…but only if…then…)

Orders of Complexity of Information Processing

Dr. Jaques' research has shown that there appears to be no other methods of processing information and that these four methods just described recur at higher and higher orders of complexity of information processing. These propositions about successively higher orders of information complexity are supported by the experience of most people in their observation that different individuals live in what almost seems to be different worlds. Persons of differing levels of complexity of information processing placed in the same situation and faced with a common problem will perceive different sets of important features. And those sets of information will not only differ in content, but usually also differ markedly in the amount of information obtained from observing and thinking about the situation. Each person will differ in the amount of information s/he is able to take into account. This is why people capable of working at higher levels in an organization are commonly described as being able to handle masses of detail rapidly.

The first and second orders of information complexity belong to the world of childhood. The third and fourth orders of information complexity, called **symbolic verbal** and **abstract conceptual**, apply to the levels of work in the adult employment world from the shop or office floor to the top executives of large corporations.

Childhood Order of Information Complexity – Tangibles

In childhood, the kind of information used is tangible. In early childhood, the objects are concrete and in the present. There is no sense of future or past. This is the world of infants up to the age of about two or three. The things being discussed can be pointed to, for example, this book or that orange. A task stated at this concrete level of information complexity would be, "Take the ball." The objects are clear and unambiguous. This is the world of action. Apes and chimpanzees can operate in this world; only human beings mature into the higher levels of processing information.

The second order of complexity involves related sets of tangibles. This is the world that children mature into when they start telling stories and when they can draw stick figures. An example is 'I took the egg from the refrigerator and put it in the pan of water'. 'Apples and pears are fruit.' Children mature from this order into the third order at varying ages from perhaps as early as 8 to 10 on into late adolescence depending on their individual rate of development.

We grow through and use these four methods of processing information and these two orders of information complexity in our own childhood development. Children mature from declarative up through parallel first in individual tangible items and then in sets of tangibles. In adolescence or early adulthood most, but not all, individuals will move into the adult order of information complexity, Symbolic Verbal.

Symbolic Verbal Order of Information Complexity

In the business world people need to be able to deal with each other without having to point to concrete examples of the things they have in mind. This order of information complexity deals with intangibles and allows work to be discussed, instructions to be issued, factories to run, new products designed, problems discussed with customers, and all the activities carried out that make it possible to manage a business unit and communicate from the shop/office floor to management levels. The variables in this order of information complexity, **Symbolic Verbal**, can be broken down into many concrete things and actions. Examples of symbolic verbal concepts include profit and loss, income tax, labor relations. sales, marketing and human resources. The first four strata of organizations (Stratum I through IV) reflect the four methods of information processing, from declarative to parallel.

Abstract Conceptual Order of Information Complexity

From the level of the business unit president to corporations made up of many business units, or in the case of mega-corporations made up of other large corporations, ideas are used that are abstract and conceptual in nature. Some people mature into handling information in this way. And once again the four methods of information processing repeat themselves if one can use higher and higher levels of information complexity. **Abstract Conceptual** concepts are used by those with the complexity of information processing to handle the types of problems encountered at corporate levels in large corporations. Here the intangible concepts are constantly changing and exist in sets. It is the area of true strategy as compared to the tactics needed to implement the strategy. Here the four methods of processing information range from the ability to head a complex business unit to being able to run a mega corporation, made up of several large corporations. Some examples of abstract conceptual concepts are balance sheets, treasury policies, the Pacific Rim, the European Union. Embedded in each of these concepts are numbers of symbolic verbal concepts.

Universal Order of Information Complexity

This is the world of **universal** ideas and language used in handling problems of whole societies, developing lasting philosophies or ideologies and bringing about revolutionary developments in scientific theory. The variables here are of a complexity well above those that are required for handling problems of corporate life. Those few corporate leaders who mature into this fifth order world tend to leave the corporate world and take on global missions. Examples of this are personal interest and participation in worldwide problems such as seeking to eradicate virulent diseases, concerns about changes in the environment and what might be done.

Information Processing and Organizational Strata

Order of Complexity	Stratum	Time Span	Method of Processing
Conceptual Abstract	VIII	50 Years	Parallel
	VII	20 Years	Serial
	VI	10 Years	Cumulative
	V	5 Years	Declarative
Symbolic Verbal	IV	2 Years	Parallel
	III	1 Year	Serial
	II	3 Months	Cumulative
	I	1 Day	Declarative

Managerial Leadership and Information Complexity

A major proposition in Requisite Organization is that managers need to have one level of complexity of information processing higher than their subordinates to provide effective managerial leadership. They will be able to conceptualize in a longer time frame to manage the work of the unit and will have the capability to assist in solving problems faced by their subordinates.

The chart above illustrates the recursive nature of four methods of information processing. Persons capable of working in roles at Strata I and V are declarative processing, at Strata II and VI cumulative processing, at III and VII serial processing and at IV and VIII parallel processing.

At Strata I through IV the method of information processing is used with Symbolic Order of information complexity described above. At Strata V through VIII the same methods of processing information are used but with the Abstract Conceptual order of complexity.

A manager who is capable of cumulative processing (Stratum II) can provide leadership for those who declarative processing (Stratum I) by providing a connected picture of the various aspects of the situation.

A manager who serial processes (Stratum III) can anticipate future consequences for subordinates at Stratum II who serial process. A manager who parallel processes (Stratum IV) will be able to consider the multiple pathways used by their subordinates at III in parallel to each other and interweave them or trade them off as necessary. At Stratum V a manager again uses the declarative method of information processing but at the higher order of Abstract Conceptual to consider various parallel pathways of the subordinate at Stratum IV.

Where there are individuals managing others of the same level of CIP over layering occurs. Over layering increases the cost of management and reduces productivity and morale. It may occur in any layer in the organization. When managers have subordinates who are of the same capability it is referred to as role compression or a 'jam up'. Jam ups cause frustration and subordinates often have to go around their immediate manager to someone more capable to get problems solved.

When managers are more than one level of CIP higher than subordinates they often need to spend their time doing a substantial amount of the work that would ordinarily be delegated. In these instances, subordinates often don't fully understand the managers task assignments or are unable to complete them satisfactorily. These situations are referred to as role gaps or a missing layer. In an organization that is requisitely structured each subordinate has a manager one level of Complexity of Information Processing higher. Compression and gaps are eliminated by requisite layering and role filling.

Distance from Manager to Subordinate

III	Manager / Manager	Manager	Manager
II	Manager / Manager	Manager	
I	Supervisor / Subordinate	Subordinate	Subordinate

| Role Compression "Jam Up" | Requisite "Just Right" | Role Gap "Missing Layer" |

Research in the Complexity of Information Processing

The results of extensive research on observations of these different methods of information processing and the different orders of information complexity are described in a book co-authored by Dr. Jaques and Kathryn Cason, entitled *Human Capability* which is available from www.casonhall.com. Their research demonstrates that it is possible to observe objectively and reliably the manifestation of current potential capability. The authors of *Human Capability* recommend that this type of observation only be used in an organization that is undertaking the application of requisite principles.

Chapter 3

WORKING RELATIONSHIPS

"If you establish sound rules and specify sound working relationships between roles, you lay the basis for constructive behavior."

Dr. Elliott Jaques

This chapter deals with the relationships that enable the work of the organization to get done including:

- Task Assigning Role Relationship between managers and subordinates
- Teams and Team Working
- Cross-Functional Working Relationships
- The Role of the Manager-once-Removed

All of these working relationships take place in the context of the proposition that **it is a basic underlying accountability of all persons in work-related roles in a managerial hierarchy to do their best to get along with one another.** This is part of the general accountability of all employees in managerial hierarchies to give their best efforts each day in their work.

THE TASK ASSIGNING ROLE RELATIONSHIP
BETWEEN MANAGER AND SUBORDINATE

The essence of the vertical manager-subordinate relationship is the delegation of tasks to be carried out. Dr. Jaques termed this all-important relationship between managers and subordinate Task Assigning Role Relationships (TARRs). Managers make decisions about how they want the work in their unit to get done. In order for the work to be performed and the output to be achieved, managers must plan the work, set context for their subordinates and then clearly delegate the assignments.

Managerial Planning

To assign tasks appropriately, managers first have to plan how they want to get the work of their unit done. Managers cannot delegate this work to subordinates, asking them to come up with plans and planning alternatives. Managerial planning is not the work of planning departments or of subordinate planners: it is the manager's work.

In an organization that is requisitely structured, managers can understand the situation more fully, to plan in more comprehensive ways than their subordinates and to envisage possibilities that subordinates are not able to see. Subordinates know when their manager has the ability to do this and when s/he does not.

Subordinates can help their manager by adding details to the plans and by examining possibilities that the manager has outlined, but the final planning decisions are the manager's.

Managerial Planning

Managers plan how to get the work of their unit completed

Managers are not to delegate planning to subordinates; subordinates can help in detailing the manager's plan

Managers discuss planning options with subordinates whenever possible and seek input and suggestions

Managers make the planning decisions

Planning is ongoing managerial work

Setting Context

Delegating tasks consists of more than simply telling subordinates what to do. Managers need to communicate background information on a continuing basis, for it is this context that provides the setting in which subordinates can make informed decisions in collaboration with each other without having to come back to the manager.

Managers set context for their subordinates by providing them with the big picture within which they are working. If the context set is too narrow, subordinates feel constrained, restricted, tightly reined in and frustrated by micro-management. This is usually the case when the manager is not one level of complexity more capable than his/her subordinates.

If the context set is too broad, subordinates feel disorganized, lost, lacking direction. They feel their manager is too distant and is someone whom they cannot understand, someone who leaves them unclear about exactly where they are going and who expects them to understand too much. This is what happens when a manager is more than one level of capability higher than the subordinate. (An exception is the case of personal assistants, who may sometimes be two levels lower in complexity than their manager, since they are in an individual contributor role that exists largely to assist with the manager's work.)

The optimum conditions for context setting are those provided by a one-step difference in complexity of information processing between manager and subordinate. Cumulative processors (those who add pieces of information together to resolve a problem) can set the right context for declarative processors because they can make connections that pull together the separate, unconnected items of information used by the declarative processor. Serial processors can set context for cumulative processors by providing a chain of causal consequences within which their subordinates' cumulatively organized judgments can flow. Parallel processors can set context for serial processors because they can provide the connecting framework between multiple pathways.

The Context Trio

There are three aspects to setting full and clear context: first, managers need to let their subordinates know about the manager's goals and problems; second, they need to let subordinates know about the problems and goals of the manager's manager; and, finally, they must keep their subordinates informed about each other's assignments. These three aspects of context can be thought of as the 'context trio'.

In setting context, managers keep subordinates informed about the managers' own goals and challenges. Subordinates should be clear about the problems their managers have and areas in which the managers need their assistance in order to get various tasks and project work completed. Managers should inform their subordinates about these same issues regarding the manager's manager, providing the larger picture. From time to time, managers should provide this information in a three-level meeting that includes both their immediate subordinates and the subordinates of their subordinate managers. (In requisite work subordinate managers' subordinates are referred to as Subordinates-once-Removed or SoRs.)

Managers also provide information so that their subordinates understand each other's assignments, enabling them to work knowledgeably together. Having information about each other's relevant tasks helps subordinates work to together as an effective managerial team. Setting regular and sufficient context saves a great deal of time both for managers and subordinates.

Setting Context

Managers are accountable for setting context for their subordinates on a regular basis by:

- Providing the larger picture within which they are working

- Letting subordinates know about issues and problems of the manager

- Informing subordinates about each other's work

Task, Work and Role

Specific definitions of work, role and task were introduced in Chapter One. They are reviewed here because these concepts underlie effective delegation of tasks. A **task** is an assignment to produce a specific output. The words task and assignment are used interchangeably. **Work** is what a person has to do to carry out a task; it is the use of judgment to overcome obstacles encountered en route to the completion of that output. A **role** is a position in the organization where tasks are aggregated and an individual is placed to carry out those tasks.

Specifying Tasks

As was discussed in Chapter One, when delegating a task a manager must specify or ensure that the following are understood by the subordinate: quantity (Q); quality (Q); time by when the task is to be completed (T); available resources (R); and. relevant policies or procedures. Managers often neglect to state explicitly by when they need a task or assignment completed, yet they do have a maximum time in mind since they must coordinate and integrate all the assignments of their unit. A useful reminder for managers when delegating tasks is to specify clearly each aspect of QQTR (Quantity, Quality, Target Completion Time and available Resources).

Outputs have Value

When managers set tasks for their subordinates they are transmitting their own values; they are indicating that they value the results of the work they have assigned. What is required of subordinates is that they accept their manager's valuing of the assigned task, even if the subordinate does not value the task or the results of the assigned work. The expectation is that employees will treat the work they have been given to do with the same value that is placed on that work by the manager and by the organization. This is not the same as a subordinate valuing a role as a whole. All roles usually contain tasks that one would rather not do but are part of the whole and must be completed.

Delegation

The art of delegation is to understand the nature of the work needed to complete a given task and then to delegate that work to the right level in the organization. Work should not be delegated to too low a level. Managers can specify when they do not want a task delegated further down. Delegating tasks to too low a level is costly—the work takes longer, more resources are used than necessary and the quality is lower, if the tasks get completed at all.

In a recurring fad sometimes referred to as 'empowerment', the idea is to push work as far down in the organization as possible. True empowerment consists of delegating work to the correct level, thus providing people with challenging work that they can do in their own way. Delegating a task to the right level, with an appropriate amount of resources, results in the task being completed at the desired time, in the desired quantity and of the right quality, by a satisfied employee.

Manager's Integration of the Unit's Functions

Managers do not delegate all their functions and processes. They can delegate part of their work to subordinate roles in the tasks they assign, but they must add value to each of them. The manager adds value by setting sufficient context and by solving problems the subordinate cannot solve. The weaving together of the work and functions of the unit remains with the manager as well. It is the manager's accountability to integrate the work of the unit.

For example, a business unit head can delegate production, marketing and selling functions but retains the accountability for adding value by providing the over-arching context and the decisions that meld all of the functions together.

Types of Delegated Tasks

Managers get work done in three ways. They do it themselves, they get help from subordinates or they delegate the task completely to a subordinate. Thus, there are two different types of delegated tasks. The distinction between them is useful to both managers and subordinates and if necessary need to be clarified when assigning a task. Managers can delegate a task as a direct output of the person to whom the task has been assigned or the manager can delegate a task that is part of completing the manager's own output.

Direct Output

Direct Output (DO) is a tangible or intangible finished product or service that will be provided to someone (either within the organization or outside it). When a service or product is handed off, it becomes direct output. The person who has been delegated the direct output decides when the finished output is good enough. The finished product or service does not have to be reviewed or approved by that person's manager. First-line work is largely direct output. Direct output can, however, come out of the managerial hierarchy at any level. Managers can and do produce direct output themselves rather than delegate all the unit's tasks to subordinates.

Delegated Direct Output

Managers can fully delegate tasks to their subordinates. This is **Delegated Direct Output (DDO)**. Some of the tasks a manager assigns to subordinates can be delegated further down through the organization to whatever level is appropriate to have the work completed. When managers delegate tasks to subordinates, part of their planning is to think about the level at which the work needs to be completed and to specify when they do not want the work to be delegated further down.

For example, a vice president of human resources wants a workshop to be prepared on interviewing techniques. She decides to delegate the task to the director of management development with specific instructions that the director is to prepare the material himself and not delegate the design of the workshop to a subordinate trainer.

Direct Output Support and Aided Direct Output

Both managers and subordinates have direct output work. Managers do not delegate all their tasks to their subordinates. Managers have some work they must do themselves. When managers are the ones to complete a task, they often need direct output support.

When a subordinate provides the manager with **Direct Output Support (DOS)**, the manager is producing **Aided Direct Output (ADO)**. These two ideas always go together; that is, any time someone is receiving direct output support that person is in the process of producing aided direct output.

This occurs, for example, when the unit manager who must turn in the annual departmental budget asks first-line managers in the unit for budget estimates for their sections. These go to the unit manager who is producing the unit budget and thus the manager is producing aided direct output. The first-line managers are doing direct output support work.

When assigning tasks, clarity is enhanced when the manager specifies if the subordinate is assisting with manager's work by providing Direct Output Support or if the task is Delegated Direct Output and the task is delegated to the subordinate to complete.

Individual Contributors and ADO/DOS

The individual contributor role was described earlier as anyone who is mainly engaged in producing direct outputs and is the person who signs off on these outputs. An individual contributor does not delegate his/her work but may get some of it done as aided direct output through subordinates who provide direct output support. If individual contributors need help in getting their work done and are provided with people to help them, they then become managers of those individuals. Most of the work of these subordinates goes back to the individual contributor.

A chief scientist, for example, doing her own research work and sending the result of that work out is doing direct output work as an individual contributor. This person has subordinates to assist her in doing parts of the work, helping her to produce the output. She is the manager of these people, but she is the one who completes the work, determines its quality and decides when it is ready. Another example is project engineers who produce designs for the manufacturing department. The engineers have subordinate technicians to help them work on detailed portions of the design. The work of the subordinates goes back to the project engineers who integrate it into their work and it becomes part of the engineers' final product. The engineers are producing work with ADO and the technicians have DOS tasks.

Managers Complete Tasks in Three Ways

They do it themselves

They complete it with the help of subordinates

They delegate it to a subordinate

INTEGRATING WORK ACROSS FUNCTIONS

One of the most vexing problems in organizations is the smooth integration of work across functions. This has become increasing crucial as much work needs to be done 24/7 and throughout the world. There are many ways in which cross functional integration takes place.

These include the manager's integration of the unit's functions and processes and the work of the manager's immediate subordinates who do so as part of their required collateral relationship which is explained in detail later in this chapter.

This integration also takes place between individuals who have different managers. Requisite principles clearly spell out the accountability and authority of six different types of relationships that can be assigned to these roles to clarify how roles can productively relate in this regard. There is also a seventh relationship that exists between all the immediate subordinates of each manager. These seven relationships called Cross Functional Working Relationships (CFWRs) are described in detail in this chapter. Teams of individual working on specific assignments are also essential to integrate work across functions.

TEAMS AND TEAM WORKING

A 'team' in requisite work can be defined as a group of people who work together to achieve a specific output for which there is an accountable manager. Teams and team working are essential for any organization to work effectively across functions.

There are three types of teams in requisite organization: project, coordinative and managerial. Project teams have an accountable manager for whom they produce an output. This, like the manager-subordinate relationship, is a task-assigning relationship. Coordinative teams consist of several people representing different functions whose work needs to be synchronized. The third type consists of all of a manager's immediate subordinates, who can be thought of as a managerial team.

Project Teams

All requisite project teams, sometimes called ad hoc teams or task forces, need to have a manager for whom the work is carried out and who is accountable for the output of the team. Project teams are resources that managers use to help them solve problems or accomplish tasks.

The accountable manager specifies the tasks regarding the target completion time and the quantity and quality desired and also secures and provides resources for the team. Project teams may be made up of people chosen from a manager's own unit, or people selected from across several units when cross-functional expertise is needed. The manager accountable for the project team may or may not appoint a team leader. When the work of the project team is completed the team is disbanded.

Project Team Members

Individuals are requested to participate on a team by the team's accountable manager. An estimate of the time required is provided since the manager of the team member may need to modify some of that person's task assignments. By agreeing to make any given subordinate available for work on a team, the immediate manager of that person demonstrates that s/he values the work of the team.

If subordinates find that the time needed for the work of a team they are on is interfering with their ability to get the work done on their usual assigned tasks, they discuss this with their immediate manager and resolve the issue.

Team members are to bring their full capability to bear on the work of the team. They are to attempt to resolve any team and departmental conflicts with the team, the team leader and the team's accountable manager. Any conflicts that cannot be resolved are to be referred to the team member's immediate manager who then discusses it with the team's accountable manager.

Project Team Output

Teams are often formed to provide direct output support (DOS) to the accountable manager who has decided s/he needs the help of several people who may be within his or her own unit, or from across several units. It is also possible for the accountable manager to delegate direct output to a team. If this is done, the accountable manager must appoint a project team leader so that there is a single designated person who is accountable for the team's direct output.

Individual contributors may also need a team to provide them with direct output support. The individual contributor then becomes the manager accountable for the output of any team that s/he forms. An individual contributor would not delegate direct output to a team. Output of individual contributors is their own.

Project Teams

Are created to solve a specific problem or complete a task

Have a manager accountable for the **team's** output Generally exist to provide support for the work of the accountable manager

May have a project leader appointed by the accountable manager

Are disbanded when the project is completed

Coordinative Teams

Project teams differ from coordinative teams because the coordinative team leader does not have task-assigning authority. Coordinative teams are used in situations where the work of a group of people representing a number of functions must be coordinated over a period of time. This type of team is described below in the section on cross-functional working relationships on coordinative accountability and authority.

Managerial Teams

Because the use of the concept of a 'team' is so pervasive in organizations, a manager's subordinates can be thought of as a manager's team. They are permanently part of the manager's team by virtue of the role they occupy. There are several types of managerial teams including:

- all of a manager's immediate subordinates
- three stratum teams made up of immediate subordinates and subordinates-once-removed
- all of a manager's subordinates at all levels

No Team Decisions

In working together as a team, subordinates are actively encouraged to express their opinion, to explore pros and cons and to engage in debate with the manager or project team leader and with each other. But, if there are decisions to be made, the accountable manager or the accountable project leader makes them.

In a managerial hierarchy, decisions are made by individuals. People are employed as individuals, not as groups, and are held accountable for decisions as individuals. There are no group decisions and no self-managed teams in a requisite organization. Consensus is desirable but not essential. The manager decides.

Team Summary

All teams have a manager accountable for the output of the team

The accountable manager may appoint a team leader

There are no team decisions; decisions are made by the accountable manager

Effective team working is essential for cross-functional work flow

CROSS-FUNCTIONAL WORKING RELATIONSHIPS

Managerial organizations need an extensive network of lateral relationships between persons who cannot directly assign tasks to each other. These are people in roles who are immediate subordinates of the same manager or who are subordinates of different managers. The designation of cross-functional working relationships describes the exact nature of the relationship and clarifies the authority and accountability of each role involved with respect to certain specified activities or situations.

Cross-Functional Working Relationships Exist Between Roles

Cross-Functional Working Relationships (CFWRs) are established between roles, not between people. Frequently, what has seemed to be a clash of personalities disappears when role relationships are clearly spelled out. Employees know where they stand with each other, they know who is accountable for doing what and who has the authority to do what in relation to other roles. Establishing these relationships between roles enables disagreements and problem resolution, often caused by insufficient resources, to move up in the organization to a level where the issue can be resolved. For example, the task may need to be changed or more resources may need to be provided. Dr. Jaques also called this type of lateral role relationships Task Initiating Role Relationships (TIRRs) as distinguished from the vertical Task Assigning Role Relationships (TARRs) that exist between manager and subordinates.

Establishing Cross-Functional Working Relationships

The Manager-once-Removed establishes CFWRs as a means of integrating the work of the organization across functional areas. Immediate managers, and often the individuals currently filling the roles, are consulted and can suggest which CFWR might be most effective in a given situation, but it is the MoR who makes the decision.

Where the relationship needs to be specified between roles at different levels in the organization, the type of CFWR is decided by the first cross-over manager. A cross-over manager is the first common manager of the roles involved. The MoR or the cross-over manager communicates decisions about cross-functional accountability and authority to the individuals concerned and their immediate managers. In the illustration below E is the Manager-once Removed between roles A and B that have different managers. E is also the first cross-over (common) manager between roles C and D. It is E who makes the decision as to what CFWR is to exist between the roles involved after discussing the situation with the individuals involved.

Designated cross-functional working relationships can be expected to change as conditions change and as the work in roles change. They need to be reviewed from time to time to determine if different CFWRs are needed.

Cross-Functional Working Relationships

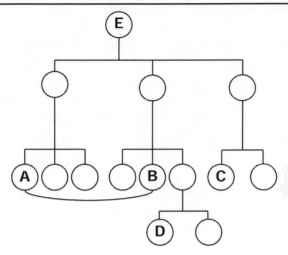

Exploring CFWRs

If the person in a cross-functional working relationship who needs to initiate a task or take an action is designated as person A and the person who must respond is designated as B, here are some of the questions that arise in thinking about and determining what kind of accountability and authority to assign to integrate work:

> Can A advise B?
> Can A try to persuade B about something?
> Can A tell B to delay doing something?
> Can A tell B to stop doing something?
> Can A tell B what to do?
> Does A need a service from B to complete an assignment?
> Does A need to get Bs to work together toward a common goal?
> Can A report higher in the organization if B does not cooperate?

The Seven Cross-Functional Working Relationships

There are seven different cross-functional working relationships. The first is the Collateral Relationship and is the only one that exists between all immediate subordinates of a given manager. The other six CFWRs exist between roles at one or more remove from the cross-over manager. These are called Advisory, Monitoring Auditing, Prescribing, Service and Coordinative. These six relationships exist between roles that are subordinate to different managers.

Four of the CFWRs are related in nature and carry an increasing amount of accountability and authority. These are Advisory, Monitoring, Auditing and Prescribing. The remaining two CFWRs are called Service and Coordinative. Service accountability and authority is the most common CFWR. Coordinative accountability and authority is used when it is necessary for someone to integrate the work of several other persons.

Brief descriptions of the seven CFWRs are given below. Because these relationships are so critical to integrating work across functions, more detailed descriptions of each are also provided later in the chapter along with examples.

Collateral Relationship

The Collateral Relationship is the foundation of effective cross-functional working. Colleague subordinates of the same manager frequently have work that impinges on each other's, yet they are not accountable for each other's work. In this relationship, each of the subordinates has the accountability and the authority to try to persuade the other regarding their respective needs. In the collateral relationship people cannot tell each other what to do, but their common manager can expect them to work things out in a satisfactory way. They are not to fight about who is right. If they cannot agree they then attempt to resolve the issue as they believe their manager would want the situation handled. If they cannot come to a mutually agreeable solution that they think would be satisfactory to their manager, they go <u>together</u> to discuss the issue with their manager.

Advisory Relationship

Persons who have advisory accountability and authority are held accountable by their managers for providing information to designated individuals. The advisees are required, by their own managers, to keep the advisor informed about their work and to listen to the advisor's advice. Individuals whose roles have advisory accountability and authority are not held accountable as to whether the persons being advised act on their advice. It is the accountability of each individual's manager to see that the advice is used appropriately.

Monitoring Relationship

In a Monitoring Relationship, the monitor has the accountability and authority to be kept informed about the relevant activities of the person being monitored. A, the monitor, can try to persuade B to change what s/he is doing if A is not satisfied with what is happening in the area that s/he has the accountability to monitor. If A is still not satisfied, A can ask B to delay taking action. A then takes the matter up with his/her manager, who decides with B's manager what is to be done. The matter is resolved between the respective managers, and B's manager tells B what s/he should do. Taking the matter up higher is part of A's accountability and authority. If A does not do so, it is assumed A is satisfied with what B is doing.

Auditing Relationship

Auditing accountability and authority usually occurs only when there is some kind of serious threat, perhaps with regard to safety, environmental or financial issues. It is not enough, for example, for the persons with accountability in areas such as legal and regulatory merely to be able to try to persuade others to do something in critical areas. In addition to being informed about their work, the auditor is also accountable for requiring designated persons to stop doing something that s/he judges to be out of line with prescribed boundaries and where serious consequences may result. If they disagree, the matter is taken up to their respective managers.

Prescribing Relationship

This is the strongest lateral working relationship and is only used when health and safety issues are at stake. It is sometimes necessary for person A not only to tell person B to stop doing something but also for A to tell B to take a different kind of action to avert a serious outcome or disaster. This is called prescribing accountability and authority and usually is held by someone who is an expert in a particular field or discipline.

Service Relationship

There are always two parts to the service relationship, the service-getter and the service-giver. They are authorized, respectively, to request and to provide the service in question. If the service-giver cannot provide the needed service for whatever reason, the service-getter must take the matter higher to his or her own manager. This generally happens when there is a shortage of resources that must be resolved by the relevant managers.

Coordinative Relationship

With coordinative accountability and authority, the coordinator A, has the authority to bring together the people whose work s/he is coordinating and to try to persuade them to take a suitable course of action. Coordinative accountability and authority is used where there is a group of people who need to be coordinated in some kind of action or process and need to be called together from time to time. This accountability and authority is given to leaders of coordinative teams.

Collateral Accountability and Authority

Collateral accountability and authority occur in the work of two or more immediate subordinates of the same manager, and who must interact in a manner of mutual accommodation. As has already been mentioned, **this is the only cross-functional working relationship between immediate subordinates of the same manager**. The obligation of immediate subordinates of the same manager to work together brings about critical integration of the work within each manager's area, starting with the immediate subordinates of the chief executive officer. It is this accountability and authority that prevents what is often referred to as 'stove piping' or 'siloing' where managers of different functions or areas do not cooperate.

Each of the colleagues in a collateral relationship has the accountability and authority to:

- try to persuade his/her colleague to take appropriate action that could facilitate the task with which they are involved and increase its effectiveness
- solve problems based on the context set by the manager
- accommodate the other's needs as far as possible
- refer to their mutual manager any significant problems that cannot be resolved

All immediate subordinates of a manager have collateral accountability and authority regarding each other and cooperative collateral relationships are required.

Example The CEO is the common manager of the vice president of sales and the vice president of production in a business unit. The sales vice president has the authority to try to persuade the production vice president to produce more, even though the production unit is up to capacity and scheduling this additional production will drive up costs because of overtime. The president must be able to rely on these two colleagues to try to find a solution they know she would want them to have. It may satisfy neither of them, or it may satisfy one and not the other, but the president can expect them to work things out in a way that will be satisfactory to her. They can neither tell each other what to do nor stop each other from taking any particular action, but they can try to persuade each other. Only if they cannot come to the kind of solution that they think would be satisfactory to the president do they go together to discuss the situation with her.

Advisory Accountability and Authority

In the advisory relationship, the person giving the advice (the advisor or expert) has the accountability and authority to:

- take the initiative in approaching the advisee and presenting ideas or information that may be useful

- take the time to explain to the advisee where and why the ideas may be useful
- be kept informed about the activities and problems of the advisee

There are clear limitations to an advisor's accountability and authority as follows:

- if the advisee does not accept the expert's advice, then the matter must rest there as far as the advisor is concerned. The expert will proceed no further.
- the advisor must not report the advisee's reaction to his/her advice to any other person. It is for the advisees' managers to judge how effectively subordinates are using advisory resources.

If an expert needs to have stronger authority than this, the advisor should instead be given monitoring accountability and authority. In the monitoring relationship, the monitor can instruct the person in the role being monitored to delay an action until the matter is brought to a higher level in the organization.

Advisory accountability and authority is a way to ensure that the best use is made of resident experts. With their advisory role relationship clearly spelled out, experts can take the initiative in offering their expertise in the form of unsolicited advice to specified others. However, it is essential to define precisely who is authorized to take the initiative to give advice to whom and about what.

In addition, subordinates have advisory accountability and authority in relation to their own managers. If a subordinate thinks of something that might be important to his or her own work or to the manager's work, the subordinate is accountable for advising the manager.

Example: The corporate CEO gives the corporate economist advisory accountability and authority to meet with each of the organization's business unit presidents to give them advice about relevant economic issues as well as information about what she thinks they ought to take into account when doing their work. The economist has the authority to go to see the specified individuals to provide them with information and they should listen. However, it is the accountability of their manager, the corporate EVP, to ensure that each BU president notes the advice and uses that information appropriately.

Monitoring Accountability and Authority

Monitoring accountability and authority is needed in situations in which it is necessary to ensure that employees are adhering to policies and maintaining adequate standards by subjecting what they are doing to critical review. Examples of this are financial limits, technical standards and interpretation of policy.

A person operating in the monitoring capacity has the authority to:

- be informed about the activities and issues of the people being monitored
- discuss possible improvements with them and/or their managers
- try to persuade them to modify their present practices and procedures where necessary and, if not satisfied, to get them to delay until the matter is referred to the relevant managers
- recommend new policies or standards where required
- report sustained or significant deficiencies to his or her own manager

The monitoring component does not give authority to:

- permanently stop people from doing something
- instruct people to change their present practices and procedures
- judge the personal effectiveness of the person being monitored and report on him/her personally
- set new policies and standards

Monitoring involves persuasion but, unlike the advising role, the matter can be taken higher to the monitor's manager when the monitor is not satisfied with the results of the persuasion. If there is disagreement and the monitor chooses not to exercise his/her authority, then it means the monitor does not consider the disagreement to be serious and is prepared to accept accountability for letting the matter rest.

Example A development specialist has perfected a chemical cleaning process and has been given monitoring accountability and authority for ensuing that it is used effectively in a given unit. The specialist has the authority and accountability to go to the appropriate first-line managers in the unit, to stay informed about how the use of the new process is proceeding and to decide if the cleaning work is taking place in a satisfactory way. If the specialist is not satisfied he can try to persuade the person controlling the new cleaning process to make the necessary modifications.

The person being monitored may say, for example, "Look, this is too costly, I really can't do it this new way. This is the best I can do." If the specialist is not satisfied, he is accountable for taking the matter to his manager to see if there is some way to use the procedure properly. The person being monitored knows that this is what the specialist must do.

Auditing Accountability and Authority

Auditing accountability and authority is used to maintain the quality of the organization's processes and products.

A person in an auditing role has the authority to:

- have access to the work of specified others
- inspect the work in accordance with corporate procedures
- stop someone from doing something that is outside acceptable limits

If the auditor decides that the work being inspected is outside the rules, regulations, policies, tolerances or other limits governing it, the auditor has the authority to instruct the other person to stop doing the work unless and until it can be brought within the organization's agreed standards.

The auditor/inspector does not have the authority to:

- instruct the other person on what to do (if that is necessary then the accountability and authority must be that of prescribing)

- judge the effectiveness of the person being audited and report on him or her personally

If the person whose task is being audited disagrees, he or she must nevertheless stop and then refer the issue to his/her own manager.

Auditing accountability and authority has more force than that of monitoring. It is used for situations that might develop into an emergency or to deal with critical issues such as an environmental, legal or financial threat or where someone is operating near the margin of safety in a situation or is just over that margin.

Example A boiler operator has set the boiler pressures so close to the margin of safety that the safety officer believes the boiler may explode. The safety officer has been given auditing accountability and authority for these situations. In addition to having the authority to try to persuade the boiler operator to make modifications in the pressure he uses, the safety officer can also tell him to stop operating in the way she believes to be unsafe, until they have both discussed the matter with their managers and the managers have discussed the situation with each other and resolved the issue.

Prescribing Accountability and Authority

Prescribing accountability and authority is the strongest of all cross-functional accountability and authority. Here person A can require person B to do something and B must do it. B can raise questions afterwards if s/he is dissatisfied with A's prescription. When there is a difference of opinion between A and B and A has prescribing authority, then A makes the decision. B must do as A instructs.

Wherever there is danger that a catastrophe could result either from failure to conform to established limits or from interpretation of those limits, or in the event of an emergency situation, it is necessary to provide experts to make external checks on the work being done and for these experts to have prescribing accountability and authority.

Example In an organization that moves a dangerous chemical by
truck throughout the country one role has been designated
prescribing accountability and authority in the event of an
emergency. If a road accident occurs the individual in this role
is notified and all persons working for the company must do
exactly as he instructs until the emergency is under control.

Service Accountability and Authority

Service-getting and service-giving accountability and authority
are the most widespread cross-functional working relationships in
most organizations. Clearly establishing the service component of
relationships so that services are provided smoothly substantially
increases work and organizational effectiveness. This requires that
everyone is clear about the specific services they can get and the services
they must give, and about how to act appropriately if they are unable
to get or to give the authorized services. Service-getters need to have
clearly specified what services they are authorized to get, and from
whom, and service-givers need to know what services they must provide
and to whom.

The service-giver cannot decide that s/he will not give an authorized
service but has the authority to determine if s/he cannot do so by
the time requested. For example, s/he may not have the necessary
resources to provide the service. When a service-giver cannot provide
the service within the time requested by the service-getter, s/he must
report the difficulty to his/her manager, who then resolves the problem
and negotiates any delays or reduction of service with the manager of
the service-getter.

The service-getter who is confronted by sustained difficulty getting
the service required in a timely fashion is accountable for taking the
matter to his/her own manager. The service-getter's manager then
can negotiate an improved and consistent service provision with the
manager of the service-giver.

When the limits of service-giving and service-getting are clearly spelled
out and understood by all parties, wasteful and costly service and
interpersonal difficulties can usually be avoided.

Example A first-line manager (FLM) is authorized by her manager to get services from the maintenance technician. The technician has the accountability and authority to provide maintenance services to specified first-line managers. The maintenance technician does not have the authority to tell the FLM he cannot provide the service. He does have the authority to tell the FLM he cannot provide it right away and to tell her by when it can be done. The FLM is not to try to persuade the technician do it by when she needs the work completed. If she is unsuccessful in getting the service she requires in a timely fashion, she refers the matter to her manager, who discusses it with the manager of the technician.

The FLM is not reporting about 'bad' service, but is taking the matter higher in an effort to postpone the maintenance until the technician can do it, to get more resources allocated to maintenance or to be given the authority to seek maintenance services elsewhere. The matter is referred up a level to the respective managers of the roles where the problem can be resolved.

Coordinative Accountability and Authority

Coordinative accountability and authority is useful as a means of arranging for a number of people to work together who are not subordinate to the same manager. The function of the coordinator is to persuade a group or team of people from different functions to work together in a joint undertaking. The coordinator and the individuals whose efforts are to be coordinated are specified by their own managers.

The coordinator has the accountability and authority to:

- propose how tasks should be approached
- keep the group informed of progress in carrying out the tasks
- help overcome setbacks and problems encountered

To carry out these functions, the coordinator has the authority to:

- try to persuade the others to act together to implement plans for action

- arrange meetings
- obtain necessary information from team members
- take issues and disagreements to his/her manager if persuasive efforts fail to settle the problem

A coordinator does not have the authority to issue overriding instructions when there are disagreements. If a coordinative team member is not participating as fully as needed, the leader/coordinator reports the problem to his/her manager, who takes up the issue with the manager of that function. The manager with functional accountability for the issues resolves any problems that the coordinator in unable to resolve.

Example New sales territories have been laid out and some national accounts have been identified. The shifting of accounts should be done in a smooth fashion. One regional manager is assigned coordinative accountability and authority in regard to implementing these changes. This regional manager will get all the sales representatives involved together and persuade them to time their actions in a coordinated fashion, and will help coordinate the common courses of action that seem best for the customer and the company.

Summary of Cross-Functional Working Relationships

Except in the instances of monitoring, auditing and prescribing the person in the role with the specified accountability and authority is not held accountable for what the other person does. Person A, with the designated accountability and authority, can initiate activity but the other person, B, has the authority to decide whether to accept the instruction or initiation. The manager of A, the initiator, is accountable for the A's work in relation to the other person, B. B's manager is accountable for B's work and outputs.

In monitoring accountability and authority persons in the monitoring roles are held accountable only if they believe the situation is problematic and they do not discuss it with their manager. In prescribing and auditing accountability and authority, the auditor can tell person B to stop doing something and the prescriber can tell B what to do, or what action to take to avert some kind of serious event. The instructions to delay or to do something must be carried out by B, who can refer questions to his/her own manager afterwards. Prescribing and auditing accountability and authority are generally specified only for serious circumstances. Ordinarily one would want to provide monitoring accountability and authority, or even, where appropriate, the lesser advisory type of accountability and authority.

Authorities and Accountabilities in Cross-Functional Working Relationships

Prescribing	Auditing	Monitoring	Coordinative	Service	Advisory		Collateral
✔				✔		A can instruct B to do something	
	✔					A can instruct B to stop and B stops	
		✔				A can instruct B to delay and B delays	
✔	✔					A and B disagree; A decides	
✔	✔	✔	✔		✔	A can be informed about B's work	
	✔					A can have access to persuade B	✔
				✔		A can have access to explain to B	✔
			✔			A can call coordinative meeting with B	
✔	✔	✔	✔	✔		A can report higher about B	

THE ROLE OF THE MANAGER-ONCE-REMOVED

Dr. Jaques identified the significant relationship between managers and the subordinates of their subordinates. The managers in this relationship are referred to as Managers-once-Removed (MoRs) and the subordinates' subordinates are referred to as Subordinates-once-Removed (SoRs). This three-level relationship is essential for effective resource allocation, communication, individual development and fairness. Specific aspects of the MoR's accountability and authority with regard to SoRs are described in the remainder of this chapter.

Manager and Manager-once-Removed

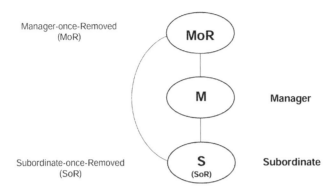

Assign SoR Roles

Managers-once-Removed decide *how many* subordinate roles at the SoR level there will be and at *what level* within the stratum these roles are positioned, because these are major resourcing decisions. MoRs do not leave it to their immediate subordinates to decide how many subordinate roles they shall have and where those roles will be positioned. Immediate managers have the authority to decide *what* tasks they assign to their subordinates' roles. MoRs are not to give assignments directly to SoRs without consulting with the immediate manager since those individuals are that manager's resource.

Decide SoR Cross-Functional Working Relationships

As described above, the MoR has the authority to make the final decision on cross-functional working relationships to integrate the work flow across functional areas.

Talent Pool Development and Succession Planning

To compete successfully in the marketplace, it is necessary to ensure that an organization has enough available, trained, and capable people to do both current work and anticipated future work. Immediate managers deal with their subordinates' ongoing work, evaluate how effectively they are performing in their role and coach them so that they can fill their roles more effectively, but it is the Manager-once-Removed who looks at all of his or her SoRs to see who has the potential capability to move up, when and if opportunities are available.

There has been a widespread belief that every good manager ought to select his or her successor. This procedure has serious problems. What if an MoR's subordinate selects a successor who is not satisfactory to the MoR as an immediate subordinate or the MoR does not believe that person can work at that level. Managers are not required to have as a subordinate someone they do not believe can do the work the role requires. MoRs have accountability and the authority for evaluating their SoRs' current and future potential and for judging promotability. This is done in consultation with the immediate manager. It is not a manager's accountability to select a successor.

Individual Development

In a requisite organization, Managers-once-Removed are accountable for establishing development plans for their Subordinates-once-Removed. MoRs are the persons who are most directly concerned with the talent pool and the long-range development of their SoRs.

In a process, Dr. Jaques called **mentoring**, MoRs work with each SoR individually regarding that person's work future and career development, training and education, beyond that needed in his/her present role. SoRs formally discuss their aspirations and career opportunities in the company with their MoRs, not with their immediate managers. Immediate managers are concerned with their subordinates' continuing growth and development in their current role.

Transfer Decisions

MoRs determine when they want individual SoRs transferred as, perhaps, part of their career development or to fill a role that has become vacant. The MoR discusses this with the SoR's immediate manager before making a decision. An immediate manager can recommend a transfer when s/he sees the person might be suitable for a role, but the MoR makes the decision.

Deselection and Dismissal with Cause

When a manager finds that a subordinate is not able to do the work of the role, the MoR works with Human Resources to try to find the person an appropriate role within the organization. The MoR determines the issue of separation from company employment of a Subordinate-once-Removed if it should become necessary.

If an immediate manager finds it necessary to recommend the dismissal of an immediate subordinate for serious negligence or some flagrant breaking of rules and regulations, the MoR has the accountability for seeing that the dismissal decision and the process follow the proper legal procedures and are within policy. Regarding these difficult people issues, an MoR needs to ensure that, in his or her judgment, procedures are being handled fairly.

Provision for Appeal

SoRs have the authority and must have the opportunity to tell their MoR when they want to appeal their immediate manager's judgment because they feel they are being unfairly treated. An example would be an SoR who believes he is being more harshly treated than some of his colleagues. This opportunity for appeal is an important condition that gives people a sense of fairness and justice.

Equilibration

Managers-once-Removed are also accountable for ensuring even treatment of their SoRs by their immediate managers. In requisite work this is called **equilibration**. MoRs judge if their SoRs are getting reasonably equitable treatment from their managers, and MoRs have discussions with their immediate subordinate managers in this regard as necessary.

Ensure Effective Managerial Leadership

MoRs are accountable for using management practices and for ensuring that their immediate subordinate managers use them as well. MoRs work with and observe the way in which their immediate subordinate managers are handling their subordinates, the manager's SoRs, both as individuals and in team working so that they have a good sense of their effectiveness in managerial leadership work.

Manager-once-Removed Accountability and Authority

Resource the Work Unit

Provide Context Setting and Ensure Effective Managerial Leadership for SoRs

Manage SoR Development beyond Current Role

Three-Level Managerial Team Working

As was mentioned earlier, from time to time MoRs hold meetings between their individual immediate subordinates and their SoRs. When the three levels are all together, the MoR can give the group a sense of where the business is going, discuss corporate policies, and review problem areas. These meetings allow MoRs to observe their SoRs, observations that are necessary for the MoR's career development and mentoring accountabilities. These three-level meetings also provide an opportunity for people to get to know each other and an atmosphere that strengthens collaborative effort and facilitates the cooperativeness of employees with each other.

Chapter 4

ORGANIZATION STRUCTURE & FUNCTIONAL ALIGNMENT

"The first step in getting a good organization is to establish the right number of layers."

Dr. Elliott Jaques

There are certain functions that can be generalized for all managerial hierarchies. This chapter examines the major functions that are necessary at given levels of organizations, providing a framework for how work should be organized and roles should be established.

FUNCTIONS IN AN ORGANIZATION

Function refers to a type of work or cluster of activities that is required by the objectives of an organization. Functions are particular kinds of work, including the mainstream business activities of procurement, production, marketing, selling distributing and product service development as well as services to other parts of the organization such as human resources, legal, accounting and so on. The **alignment** of functions refers to the process of grouping functions to provide the best fit in a role or in a department.

The first step in aligning functions and establishing a requisite structure is the articulation of the organization's vision and mission by the owners or board of directors. Based on this, the CEO, working with the senior management team, provides direct personal leadership in deciding the corporate goals and objectives and the strategy for achieving them.

Determining corporate strategy includes deciding what functions are needed and at what level of complexity the work needs to be done, hence the stratum in which the functions should be placed. For example, if corporate research and development work has a 15-year perspective, the work needs to be done in a role at Stratum VI. However, if the work only needs an eight-year time frame, it can be established in a role at Stratum V.

Strategic planning includes determining which functions the organization needs, aligning functions in an effective manner, and establishing those functions in the right stratum, based on the level of work the CEO determines is required to carry out the function. This provides the basis for establishing a requisite organization structure functions appropriately aligned.

An organization structure that is requisite is a system of roles and role relationships. The essential functions in those roles enable the organization to operate as required by the nature of the work to be done and the nature of the human beings involved.

BUSINESS UNITS

In corporations that contain multiple business units there are two main groupings of functions, those that are corporate and those belonging to the individual business unit. The first grouping, functions needed at the corporate level, includes operations, corporate development work and corporate services. The second group of functions are those of the smaller, typically Stratum V, business units within the corporation. These include six mainstream business functions of production, marketing, selling, procurement, delivery and product development/

enhancement as well as three supporting functions: services, resource sustainment and resource enhancement.

Having Stratum V business units within a Stratum VII corporation generally appears to be the most effective way of structuring large organizations. This may be related to how far into the future finite planning can be carried out. It appears that about seven years forward is the longest period over which people are capable of planning and carrying out finitely budgeted projects and that this period is the longest outreach for systematic predicting and forecasting. Beyond ten years a conceptual approach is needed in which the future is constructed rather than forecasted. This phenomenon may underlie the fact that Stratum V business units with a five to ten-year time-span seems to be the ideal level to establish a single unified whole business system.

However, sometimes the time frame of what has to be done in Stratum VII corporations makes it necessary to do the work in business units established at Stratum IV or VI. The same functions are required in these business units.

Some businesses need to be conducted in one large business unit because of the nature of the product or the market place, such as oil refining or automobile production. (In these instances, it becomes even more critical to establish very clear cross-functional working relationships and coordinative teams.) The existence of a single corporate business unit does not eliminate the need for the Stratum VII corporate functions necessary to maintain a national/global perspective on social, political, economic, values and technological changes that are occurring. The CEO should also continually seek the opportunity to devolve the single large business unit into smaller Stratum V business units, if possible.

When a business unit operation is stand-alone and not part of a larger corporation, the most complex work of the company may be at Stratum IV, III or even II, rather than at Stratum V. For example, in small shops the owner may do all the mainstream business functions except for having some assistance in direct selling.

As the CEO role is located higher and higher because of the outreach of the strategic direction, more and more functions need to be differentiated where the CEO can delegate the essential activities. Some of the functions can be outsourced such as legal, HR or IT rather than establishing subordinate roles.

STRATUM VII CORPORATIONS

A Stratum VII corporation generally requires several functions whose purpose is to oversee groups of business units and to enhance their asset value while maintaining a profitable balance sheet for the business as a whole. The Stratum VII CEO must do the strategic work necessary to enable the Stratum V business units to operate successfully and at the same time must ensure the future business development of the corporation by finding or internally developing new business opportunities and adding and divesting business units as necessary.

Working with the senior leadership the CEO develops the organization's competitive strategy, keeps the consequences of that strategy under review and networks nationally and internationally to keep strategy in line with worldwide developments. The CEO gives his/her own direct personal leadership to the process of deciding the corporate strategic thrust.

Other functions of the CEO include ensuring that the business is financially strong, has essential information, planning and control systems and has the necessary human resources throughout the corporation both for the current needs and to staff the constantly-evolving organization.

The corporation's Stratum VI roles are established to help the CEO carry out his/her work in performing the functions just described. The number of Stratum VI roles that are necessary is a matter of the CEO's judgment. These Stratum VI corporate roles may have subordinates in Stratum V and IV depending upon the requirements of the work.

Stratum VII Corporate Functions

VII	Corporate Functions		CEO 20+ Years		
VI	**Strategic Staff Work** (finance, human resources, technical resourcing, general counsel, public affairs). Assist president & stratum colleagues in the development of corporate strategic thrust, policies, & methods of implementation.	Corporate Policy Audit and Control	**Business Operations** One or more portfolios of business units	Corporate New Business Development Development of longer-term corporate business advances	Corporate Services Economies of scale with respect to, for example, legal accounting information technology, training, recruitment, insurance, property
V	**Business Unit Functions**		**Business Unit President 5 – 10 Years**		

		Mainstream Business Functions					
Staff Specialist Support (Production, technical, human resources, business analysis)	Production	Sales/ Marketing	Product/ Service Improvement Current	Continuous Improvement Functions		Business Unit Services (Accounting, Maintenance, Personnel, Administration, etc.)	Corporate Functions Finance Controller Budgeting

Corporate Operations Vice Presidents

To the extent that there are groupings of business units, one or more corporate operations executive vice president roles are required at Stratum VI, each with a portfolio of business units. These corporate executive vice presidents operate in a ten- to fifteen-year thrust, setting context for their business units that are typically operating in five- to seven-year time span. The corporate executive vice presidents are accountable for the results of their subordinate business unit presidents.

How business units are grouped is a matter of corporate strategy, determined by the requirements of the marketplace. Strategic groupings of business units are temporary in nature and can be altered in response to changing business circumstances. Business units may be grouped for reasons of common markets, common geography, common production or common products.

The Stratum VI operational executive vice presidents generally do not require many support staff roles. They may need a small personal staff, but the emphasis is on the executive vice presidents doing their own work, both within the organization and in the outside world, of adding value to the work of the business units by sustaining conditions in which they can function effectively and by developing the Stratum V and IV corporate talent pool.

Corporate Development Officers

Corporate development work is concerned with keeping abreast of developments worldwide and developing or acquiring new products or new production technology that can be used either to transform existing businesses or to create new ones. Corporate development also seeks to discover new business investment opportunities. The CEO may want to have a corporate development role at Stratum VI to help carry through this long-term development work.

There are two different aspects of the work of this role. One is concerned with worldwide networking to keep abreast of developments and of businesses that might potentially be of commercial significance for the organization. The other is directed toward the development of new technological knowledge within the corporation.

If laboratories, for example, are needed for research and development work, they would be subordinate to a Stratum VI corporate development officer. These corporate laboratories would not be concerned with the products that the organization is currently providing (that work belongs to the individual business units), but with the development of those products that the CEO judges are going to be necessary strategically in ten, fifteen or more years.

Commercial analysis and negotiating staff are needed by the corporate development officer to analyze potential opportunities and secure them for the corporation. The decision to go ahead with any given proposal is determined by the CEO and the corporate executives with sanction by the corporate board.

New Ventures

It is the work of the new ventures function to make the new business opportunities operational within the corporation. The new ventures executive vice president, with the help of a few Stratum V and IV subordinates, builds the starting teams for new units. The selection of the president for the new business unit would be done jointly with the operational executive vice president who will be the eventual recipient of the new unit. When the new business is established and operational, it is handed over to the operational executive vice president. New ventures development work requires close collaboration between the new venture function and the operational executive vice president with whom the business will be placed. The handover process is a gradual one.

Corporate Services

Experience has shown that the provision of services such as legal, accounting, information technology and similar functions can often be combined effectively at the corporate level, resulting in substantial economies. These service functions are not part of the corporation's strategic thrust work, nor are they part of the business operation or future business development work. The issue of centralization versus decentralization applies to these service functions.

The CEO may decide that it is preferable to outsource some services. This is sometimes the case with information technology work, for example. Or the CEO may judge that to have an effective service, direct accountability within the corporation is required. The optimum balance of providing the services from a central source, allowing business units to provide for themselves or to buy them from outside will vary with changing circumstances such as cost and availability of external services and of competent staff.

Internally provided services can be grouped and run like a business unit, providing services as needed. An executive vice president role for corporate services is sometimes needed, and such a role may be advisable if necessary services are extensive. The persons engaged in corporate services to business units should not be the same people who help the CEO with strategic work. Trying to do this as well as trying to run services at the same time generally does not work well because the focus of the roles are very different.

Headquarter Strategic Staff Functions

There are five functions that relate to the organization's competitive strategic thrust that usually need to work directly for the CEO to support his/her work. These include economic, human and technology resourcing, public affairs and corporate counsel. These five functions are distributed in up to five roles at the executive vice president level.

These are policy development positions whose work is largely direct output support work for the CEO. Those who fill these specialist roles, providing the CEO with strategic advice, should be individuals who like this kind of intellectual work and who do not especially value having large departments to manage. Persons who value managing large departments can be given departments in business units or in services instead. These large units do not belong in the strategic thrust area.

Corporate Chief Financial Officer

A Stratum VII CEO generally has a chief financial officer at Stratum VI who may have a small subordinate group of Stratum V's and IV's doing financial analysis and keeping in contact with the financial world. This helps the CEO's strategy development by translating that strategy into financial terms. This function also includes networking in world financial markets.

The CFO is not accountable for bookkeeping and accounting services but is concerned instead with economic resourcing and keeping track of financial conditions from a worldwide perspective. Accounting work belongs in corporate services.

Chief Human Resources Officer

A staff officer is needed to help with the organizational development of the corporation, with policies in this area and with the talent pool development in the context of long-term corporate strategic plans and societal changes. Again, this role should consist of an individual with just a few subordinates.

The human resources specialist role is not concerned with personnel services such as recruitment, training, benefits, and salary administration. These services are requisitely done by corporate services or by Human Resources functions within the business units.

Technology Advisor

The person in this role is concerned with the interplay between the commercial consequences of scientific developments and the general trend of new products and production technologies as well as the strategic shape of the future corporation. S/he must develop policies on the technology development work within the corporation.

This function may seem similar to the new business opportunities development role, but the differences in focus make it inefficient to place the work in one role. The technology advisor provides direct output support to the CEO regarding technology, in close daily interaction with other headquarter colleagues. This is an individual contributor role that should have, at most, a few direct output support subordinates at Stratum V and IV.

Public Affairs

This function involves dealing with governments, networking with other large-scale institutions with respect to possible common interests around strategic issues, and working with customer/client marketing relationships that must be managed 12 to 15 or more years into the future.

General Corporate Counsel

This role is concerned with strategic consequences of long-term legislative developments and seeks to ensure representation of corporate requirements in new legislation or other government or legal developments.

STRATUM V BUSINESS UNITS AND ROLES

At Stratum V, the level of many business units, there are certain functions that arise whether the business units are freestanding

Stratum V companies or Stratum V subsidiary companies in larger corporations. The key function of a business unit president is to integrate the interplay between product development, production and marketing/sales in relation to the marketplace, while giving sufficient priority to resource enhancement.

When the business unit is part of a larger corporation, the Stratum V president role serves as an essential connection between the individual business unit operation and the corporate work at Stratum VI and VII. One of the reasons that Stratum V appears to be the highest level at which business work ought to be carried out may have to do with the nature of human capability and the fact that Stratum V is the level where people begin to move into borderline areas of the level of complexity of corporate work.

At Stratum V the person has the capability to understand and deal with corporate strategic concepts but is not very far away from the more concrete concerns of Stratum IV general manager level.

Business Unit Functions

Mainstream Business Functions
- Procurement/Production/Delivery
- Sales/Marketing
- Products/Service Improvement

Staff Specialist Support Functions
- Technical
- Human Resources
- Business Analysis

Service and Audit Functions
- Accounting
- Maintenance
- Personnel Administration
- Audit

Finance and Control Functions
- Finance
- Controller
- Budgeting

Stratum V Mainstream Business Functions

The six mainstream functions are procurement, production, sales, marketing, delivery and product/service development. (The term product is subsequently used to indicate both products and services.) These are the functions that make up the operational spine of the organization. Too often organizations are not clear about the functions that are central to their business and confuse them with support and service functions.

Profit and loss accounting takes place at the business level and has to do with providing products that the marketplace will want: producing or procuring them, selling them to the marketplace and understanding the market in order to continually improve the product. The primary concern of an individual business is with the expenses for providing products to the marketplace and the total revenues from that provision to achieve a profit.

These mainstream functions can be aligned in as many Stratum IV roles as are required for the volume of the work. Each of these functions then extends vertically down through Stratum III, II and I as necessary. In some organizations information technology has replaced some or all the Stratum I roles and even some Stratum II roles.

Production and Procurement

Companies provide products for their customers in several ways. Products can be manufactured by the company or can be secured from another organization. Some companies manufacture their products and procure the materials to do so, while others need a procurement function that buys the finished products for resale.

An example of a large Stratum IV unit would be a factory of 2000 people headed by a Stratum IV general manager. This factory might have 10 units, each employing 200 people. There would be staff specialists assisting the general manager in the areas of human resources, technology and programming as well as accounting and property and equipment maintenance functions. There would also be ad hoc teams engaged in special projects to seek improved methods of production, production-flow control and organization structure and staffing.

Marketing and Selling

A business organization must be able to deal with the marketplace and provide everything that goes into selling to individual customers. It is necessary to understand what the customer wants, negotiate sales and provide customers with given products at an agreed price.

Marketing is concerned with customers collectively. Marketing functions include market research to determine market needs/desires and promotional campaigns to influence customers to choose the company's products. Marketing also involves continual analysis of pricing structure, distribution, activities of competitors and providing advice to the business unit president based on these analyses.

Sales is concerned with individual customers. Selling includes working with individual customers, helping them decide which product to choose, getting them to buy, arranging for delivery and payment terms and maintaining regular contact with them.

Many organizations sell directly to customers. These may only need a small sales organization if they are dealing with a few very large customers, or they may need a large sales organization if selling to a large diversified market is required. Some organizations need to have a sales force selling to customers throughout the country or in many countries throughout the world while others may sell through distributors, dealers and wholesalers. In many instances selling takes place through a combination of sales channels.

Marketing functions may be mixed with selling or set up separately, depending on organizational requirements. Neither marketing nor selling is senior to the other although one may be more dominant because of the nature of the business. Sales may be more important, for example, where the production of components is for wholesalers and, therefore, marketing has little relevance. Marketing will likely be dominant in mass retailing where such things as advertising, store and shelf layout, special promotions and packaging are major buying influences.

Confusion sometimes exists in organizations about who 'decides' or who 'owns' prices, discounts, advertising and promotion, customer mix and the like. The CEO of the organization is the person who makes the policy decisions in these areas and who holds the final authority on pricing policy decisions. No other role 'owns' these decisions. Specific decisions are made within marketing and selling in accord with the policies set by the CEO.

Product/Service Development

A product improvement and development role is not always necessary. It may be possible to do the improvement and development of the company's products and services as part of the marketing function. If it is services that are being provided to the marketplace, a development organization may not be needed. However, in this instance a marketing general manager will likely be needed at Stratum IV who can carry out market research, who seeks to understand the changing requirements in the marketplace, and who redefines and redevelops the kinds of products or services that are being provided.

A business unit president who is operating in five- seven- or nine-year thrusts must have subordinates who can help him/her understand the ever-changing two-, three-, or four-year market requirements and who are capable of doing the development work to ensure that the company is able to cope with the shifting market.

If the company is producing a technical product, there may need to be a Stratum IV product development role with subordinates to help in doing the work. For example, there may be a physical product needing redesign in order to improve it in relation to the evolving market.

Where there is a separate product development function it is preferable to designate it by that title rather than calling it research and development. Research often implies a focus on 'fundamental science' rather than the commercial focus required of this function in a business unit setting. The product development function should be in continuing contact with customers and the marketplace. It should also work closely with production, marketing and sales so that their requirements are all taken into consideration.

Product development work for a Stratum V unit should not be confused with the Stratum VI corporate development work. The Stratum VII CEO is concerned with the ten- to fifteen-year business thrust, anticipating what is likely to happen in that period of time, what big competitors are doing, and what scientific and technical breakthroughs are likely to occur. This corporate role involves an understanding of what new products are necessary to modify the nature of the corporation's business units.

Business unit presidents are accountable for ensuring that their existing products are being improved through redesign, development and modification so that the products the business unit is providing are in line with changing market needs.

Business Unit Services

The operational functions of a business unit are the functions by which the business gets done (procurement, production, marketing, selling, distribution, product/service improvement) In addition to these six mainstream business functions there are also necessary resource sustainment, resource enhancement and service functions in support of the operational functions. There is staff specialist work in support of the work of the business unit president as well.

The business unit president may need to provide services such as accounting, human resources, maintenance, information technology, legal counsel and administration for the operational areas. What services are provided and how they are organized in the service unit are dependent upon the requirements of the organization. It is important to keep in mind that the business is not set up to provide internal services: it is set up to deal with its customers, providing them with products at a profit to the company.

Resource Sustainment Services

There are three main areas where activities may be necessary for a Stratum V business unit to sustain the existing resources. These are finance, general services and maintenance/repair. These services may be grouped under one Stratum IV general manager or be separate if the services are extensive.

Financial Auditing and Services

The financial services provide auditing activities and maintain purchase and sales records, pay accounts, do billing and carry out other activities associated with financial accounting. The accounting function must carry auditing authority to ensure that expenditures fall within the policy limits. However, cost accounting activities generally are carried out by a programming specialist because it is part of advisory work to the BU CEO.

General Services

General services may include administrative services such as purchasing, property administration, security, information technology and personnel services such as recruitment, interviewing, procedures, training and personnel records.

Repair and Maintenance Services

Repair and maintenance services may require site workshops at Stratum IV or at Stratum III. If the need for these services is not extensive they may be included under general services.

Stratum V Staff Specialist Functions

The business unit president may need the following staff specialists to assist him or her in business programming, human resources and technology.

Business Analysis/Programming Specialist

Business programming involves modeling the interplay between the functions of the organization, or exploring various decisions to help compare possible courses of action. The business analysis function is called programming. This staff specialist helps the president analyze business plans and priorities by modeling actual and potential markets and sales, production capacities and costs, sales and labor flows, competitor activities and price structure, transportation facilities and costs, work-in-progress and finished goods stock levels and other inventories, cash flows, capital costs, interest rates, foreign exchange and resource flows affecting business strategies and business success. This ongoing analysis helps to drive long- and short-term business unit planning and the development of new options and helps to optimize the balance between current profitability and longer term development, change and survival.

This Stratum IV role calls for a combination of knowledge and skills in operation research, cost accounting, and process statistics. It requires substantial business knowledge and an understanding of the interdependencies and interactions of product development, material procurement, production, distribution, marketing and sales.

The programming specialist helps the Stratum IV general managers optimize their own programming priorities in relation to the business unit CEO's plan. The role carries coordinative authority to attempt to sort out differences in priorities and resource demands that may arise between various functions of the unit.

Human Resource Specialist

At Stratum IV the HR specialist helps the president analyze human resource requirements and plans. This assistance includes providing the human resources needed to achieve the strategic plan, monitoring the talent pool and organization development work. It also involves tracking developments in human resource practices, maintaining contact with the corporate human resource policy changes, and recommending human resource policies to strengthen leadership effectiveness and reinforce a constructive climate. The human resource specialist helps the Stratum IV general managers stay within human resource policy in the management and leadership of their people and can educate the general managers in this respect on behalf of the BU CEO.

Human resource work needs a practical understanding of the business of the organization, of all of the work involved and a theoretical and practical understanding of managerial hierarchies and how human nature and capability are expressed in them.

Technology Specialists

Information technology and production technology are concerned with finding ways of optimizing current methods to reduce cost and improve quality, service and delivery. The Stratum IV technology specialist helps the president to ensure the development of technology to achieve continual cost reduction, quality control, increased output and adaptation to requirements for the production of new products.

This work requires ongoing searching for information about new methods being developed in the technical field to keep abreast of competitive opportunities. The technical specialist monitors the methods being used, continually re-evaluating them and coming up with ideas for improvement. The new ideas may be in the form of designs for improvements to existing methods or of proposals for development projects to be carried out by task forces. If a project team is formed, the technology specialist monitors its progress. On behalf of the president this specialist may also contract to get work done with corporate technology areas or with outside suppliers. Issues of information security are a continuing concern.

Resource Enhancement

The business unit CEO has the accountability to enhance the value of the human and physical resources at his/her disposal. This function is usually carried out by special project teams established under Stratum IV project managers. Examples might be task forces set up to implement a major reorganization or to introduce new production technology.

Stratum IV General Managers

Stratum IV general managers of production, sales and marketing and product development may need Stratum III specialist staff in programming, personnel and technology.

For example, a Stratum IV production general manager will often need a programming specialist to act as factory production controller, to help him/her plan, schedule and follow the progress of the factory work flow. This person coordinates the flow of production between units, between suppliers and production, and between production and services such as maintenance and repair. Technology specialists may be needed to keep the general manager up-to-date on the latest information technology advances or advances in production technology.

The human resources specialist assists the production manager by analyzing and planning human resource requirements and developments. These activities include planning for personnel changes needed because of changes in the type of work or in technology, planning for recruitment and retirements, monitoring and coordination of human resource practices of colleagues at Stratum III, maintaining contact with business unit human resources on HR policies and recommending any changes needed for improvement.

STRATUM III MUTUAL RECOGNITION UNITS (MRUs)

In organizations where there is extensive first line work as in a factory where the direct output is at Stratum I, mutual recognition units (MRUs) generally need to be established. MRUs are groups of up to 200 or 250 people with a maximum of 300.

The reason for the maximum of 300 is the discovery that up to that number it is possible for the Stratum III MRU manager to carry through his or her function (service providing, manufacturing or production) in a unit in which everybody can recognize everyone else. That mutual recognition is lost when numbers get above the 300 level.

For many years, it was thought necessary to have so-called small factories because they seemed to work better than large ones. That does not appear to be necessary. What seems to be important is that factories or large-scale service organizations be organized at Stratum III in mutual recognition units. The Stratum III MRU breaks the Stratum IV general managerial organization, where there are large numbers of employees, into units that are small enough for people to recognize each other and there is a feeling that everyone is working in the same place. This provides a sense of cohesiveness in the shop and office services floor areas that gives a sound basis for effective managerial leadership at the first line managerial level in relation to operating, clerical and service-providing personnel. These MRUs have a Stratum III MRU manager with first line managers at Stratum II and then Stratum I operators and clerks.

MRU Specialist Staff

The MRU manager may need programming and service specialists, especially if it is, for example, a production department. The MRU will not need an HR specialist because the maximum number of subordinates does not provide enough work for such a full-time role.

With regard to programming it may be useful for the MRU manager to have specialist staff such as technicians at Stratum II who can help with scheduling, technical, or manufacturing process problems as they come up. It must be absolutely clear, however, that production accountability is in the operational managerial line.

A Stratum II technology staff specialist may be needed to assist the Stratum III unit manager to sustain unbroken production flows by providing on-site methods for overcoming unforeseen obstacles and by preventing such obstacles by anticipating them.

First Line Units

In many organizations, or in specific units of an organization, first line employees produce much of the output. In organizations that have first line units, a large percentage of the employees are found in Stratum I roles. Because these units have a large impact on the organization, its human resources, its output and its bottom line, the factors involved in managing first line units are dealt with extensively in this chapter.

Managing these units effectively can substantially:

- improve the work environment
- enhance employee satisfaction
- increase productivity and profits

A first line unit is composed of a first line manager (FLM) and all of his/her subordinates. In the following sections the role of the first line manager is described along with the accountability and authority of this role. Issues in managing first line units when shifts are necessary are also discussed. The material focuses on Stratum I first line work with the First Line Manager at Stratum II, since this is where most first line work is found.

This unit is also referred to as a mutual knowledge unit (MKU) where everyone is able within reason to know each other. Research and experience has shown that this unit can sometimes consist of as many as 70 people depending upon such considerations as the output required, the location of the employees and type of assistance the First Line manager has.

Three Common Problems Found in First Line Units

Three common problems are frequently found in organizations that have first line units:

1. First line employees do not have <u>one</u> clearly designated manager.

    They may have a 'supervisor' who has only partial managerial accountability and authority. This person is usually not Stratum II capable, but rather is a more experienced or higher level Stratum I. Sometimes there is no Stratum II manager at all, with the first full managerial role found at Stratum III. In situations where shifts are required, a Stratum II manager is sometimes assigned to the day shift with 'supervisors' handling the 2nd and 3rd shifts. Often there are 'supervisors' on each shift with 'their people'. However, no one is accountable for the area or activity as a whole.

The result is that in many organizations first line employees are given assignments by several different persons who are in quasi-managerial positions above them. Employees are then unclear about their work priorities, about who is accountable for their work and what person to go to when they need help.

2.   There is a lack of clear accountability for the results of the work and the working behavior of first line employees.

When many different roles are given partial accountability for the oversight of first line workers, it becomes difficult to hold any given individual accountable for results of their work other than the employees themselves. In this situation first line employees are held accountable for results that are outside their control and get unfairly blamed for things that go wrong.

3.   There are no clearly specified managerial practices for first line managers to carry out in working with their subordinates.

When there is no clearly specified Stratum II first line manager, or where there are a variety of people supervising the first line, some managerial practices such as planning, task assignment, coaching and appraisal are done by different individuals, if indeed they are done at all. The result is a lack of clarity. No single immediate manager is accountable for equipment, maintenance and improvements. There is no single manager who can be held accountable for the results.

Addressing These Problems Requisitely

With the use of requisite organization principles and practices, organizations can significantly improve the operation of their first line units. The first steps to address the problems described above are to:

- establish Stratum II first line manager roles
- institute requisite management practices to be carried out by this manager

Establish Stratum II First Line Manager Roles

First line manager (FLM) roles need to be established at Stratum II. These roles should carry accountability and authority for the results of the work and working behavior of their Stratum I first line subordinates, for all the financial and physical resources and for process improvements. The FLM may have one or more assistants in Stratum I roles if required by the work, but these are not managerial roles.

Institute Requisite Managerial Leadership Practices

Managers at all levels throughout the organization, including first line managers, need to carry out the requisite managerial leadership practices described in this book.

The First Line Manager Role

Some of the reasons given by organizations as to why supervisors or assistant managers are needed rather than a full scale, fully accountable manager are:

- there are a large number of people to be 'supervised'
- some of the work may need to be done outside the manager's normal working hours
- continuing training is required
- the work must be done in geographically dispersed areas
- facilities, machines and equipment have to be continuously maintained

In many organizations, the response to these issues is to provide assistance to first line manager roles by a more experienced worker of Stratum I capability. Sometimes one or even two quasi-managerial roles are established above the first line employee. In such instances employees do not know whose directions they should follow when they get conflicting instructions.

For example, in one organization there were 105 first line workers below a first line manager. This unit was divided into five smaller groups, each headed by an 'associate' manager. Below each 'associate' manager were work coordinators, each handling five to eight first line workers. Situations such as this often exist because the response to the growth of a first line unit is to add layers below the first line manager. The requisite approach in dealing with span of control issues is to divide up the unit by adding one or more additional first line managers.

Stratum I first line employees usually have a good sense of who their real manager is even when there are intervening roles such as supervisor, lead, assistant manager and work coordinator. They know to whom they should go to get their problems resolved.

If, as is sometimes the case, the first full managerial role is not found until a role at Stratum III, this person is not readily accessible to the first line worker. In these instances, there is also too large a gap in capability between that of the first line worker and this manager. To be fully effective in their work, first line workers need a Stratum II first line manager.

Examine the Current Situation

It can be helpful to get a picture of the situation as it currently exists in an organization. There are a number of ways to do this.

One way to determine whether there is a Stratum II first line manager is to ask first line workers who their manager is. Often there will be two or three different answers within one work group. One organization was surprised when several employees said that they *did not know* who their manager was.

If there appears to be several roles managing first line employees, find out which role carries out appraisals and which decides merit increases. Sometimes employees are told, apologetically, that the work coordinator does the appraisals because it would be too onerous for the manager to do so since there are so many first line workers, but that the merit increase is determined by the first line manager.

As was mentioned above, consider the titles. Myriad titles such as supervisor, assistant manager, associate manager and work coordinator are often found. When these titles are used, it usually indicates that the role is not one that carries full managerial accountability and authority. This is even more evident if more than one role with these titles exists.

Multiple Layers between the Manager and the First Line Worker

When questioned as to why extra layers exist between the manager and the first line, a number of answers are often provided. One reason given is that career paths are needed to motivate first line workers. Another reason is that to move an individual up a grade to increase their compensation another role needed to be created, such as assistant or associate manager. Another reason is to aid in retention—that it seemed necessary to provide a role for someone who had grown in capability or who had been in a role for a long time to retain them for the organization. A common reason given is that the first line unit has grown too large to be handled by the manager alone.

Another reason, frequently found but rarely discussed, is that the manager shown on the organization chart is not capable of managing the unit and needs one or more 'assistant' managers to shore him or her up in an attempt to get the work done.

In an organization that is requisitely structured there will not be managerial and subordinate roles within the same stratum. Where there is such a 'jam-up' of roles within a stratum, called role compression, resentment and frustration build up and resources are ineffectively used.

Clarifying the First Line Manager Role

The starting place for clarifying a first line unit is to establish an FLM unit and role. This role carries the same accountability and authority as any other managerial role in the organization. It is a full managerial role, not that of a 'supervisor'.

The level of work of the first line manager role is in Stratum II, with the longest task(s) assigned to the role needing to be completed at somewhere from three months to one year. The type of complexity of information processing required by the individual in the role will be cumulative, that is the individual will be able to diagnose problems and in this way, add value to his/her subordinates by helping solve their problems and by providing context for their work.

By contrast, the longest tasks assigned to Stratum I roles need to be completed somewhere between one day and three months. The type of complexity required by individuals in these roles is the ability to follow a clearly prescribed pathway to the end goal. There is usually a hands-on component to the work.

Span of Control

How many first line employees an FLM can manage is a function of the work that needs to get done. An FLM may be able to manage from as few as five or so to perhaps as many as 60 or 70 subordinates, depending on the circumstances.

Variables that need to be considered in determining how many subordinates an FLM can reasonably manage include:

- whether or not shifts are involved
- physical location of subordinates
- diversity and complexity of the work
- how much direct output work the manager personally must do
- how many meetings are required
- whether or not assistant roles can be assigned

A major consideration here is the number of subordinates for whom the FLM can fully carry out requisite managerial leadership practices. In particular, this means that FLMs must know all their subordinates well enough to be able to judge their individual personal effectiveness and coach and provide them with individual development as appropriate.

For example, the FLM might be able to handle a group of first line subordinates toward the larger end of the range when all work takes place during normal working hours in one area, few meetings are needed, all workers do similar work in relatively unvarying conditions and the manager has an assistant to handle the administrative work.

Providing Assistance to the First Line Manager

The first line manager may need one or more assistants. These may be full time assistants called First Line Manager Assistants (FLMA) or they may be part-time specialist subordinates who have specific support roles. How many of these roles are required and what these roles are assigned to do is a function of the work that needs to get done.

First Line Manager Assistants

The FLMs may need one or more first line manager assistants (FLMAs) to help them. These are Stratum I employees who are assigned administrative, technical, scheduling or training work depending upon what is required. These are generally full time roles filled by individuals who have experience working in the unit.

The FLMA role is established to assist the FLM meet his/her accountabilities in some of the following ways:

- assigning tasks within guidelines provided by the FLM
- doing special training of colleague-subordinates as assigned by the FLM
- maintaining an environment of cooperative working to accomplish all the assigned work of the team
- carrying out specifically assigned tasks regarding administrative, maintenance, scheduling and technical outputs as direct output support to the FLM
- monitoring working behavior and adherence to safety procedures
- taking immediate action to deal with serious infractions of policies or regulations

FLMAs are not managers, and the role carries no accountability for carrying out management practices. FLMAs may or may not make recommendations to the FLM on the effectiveness of their colleagues depending on the situation and how the role needs to be established.

Specialist Operators in Part-time Support Roles

The first line manager may need only part-time specialist support from designated operators to help with administrative, technical, scheduling and training issues. When employees have a problem, they can seek help from the relevant specialist whose role is given this accountability and authority. This person would stop what he or she is doing to deal with the issue. (These specialist roles can only be created when the work of the role can be interrupted to provide the needed assistance.) When not engaged in their specialist work, individuals in these roles carry out their regularly assigned first line work.

Problems requiring assistance might include equipment that is not working correctly, resources that are missing, not understanding the process, confusion as to priorities and so on. For example, one production facility has regular turnover because of its undesirable location and difficult physical working conditions. A skilled operative who enjoys training others has been appointed training specialist. There are new employees almost every week. Whenever a newly hired person needs reinforcement or clarification of the basic training they received before starting their job, a training specialist is there on the floor to help them.

Involvement of Stratum III Managers

The Stratum III manager has the accountability and authority to provide the first line units for whose output s/he is accountable with a satisfactory working environment, including the physical and technological resources needed to achieve the assigned tasks. S/he also provides the human resources required, authorizing the necessary roles and determining where those roles are placed in Stratum I. This may be at high, mid or low within the stratum depending on the level of work required. This manager analyzes what support is needed by the FLM in training, scheduling and technical areas and establishes any Stratum I first line manager assistant or specialist roles that may be required.

The Stratum III manager also determines if Stratum II specialist roles are needed for the entire Stratum III unit. For example, a Stratum II administrator or a deputy for Stratum III manager may be needed to handle emergency situations on shifts where the first line manager is not present.

Stratum III managers review their FLMs' managerial leadership work carrying out managerial leadership practices, ensuring evenness and fairness of treatment of the FLMs' subordinates. The Stratum III manager also provides mentoring and individual development discussions to first line employees outside their present role. The Stratum III manager is accountable for ensuring that the FLMs work together in a manner that contributes to the successful achievement of the assigned output of the Stratum III unit.

The Stratum III Mutual Recognition Unit

This Stratum III manager oversees a Mutual Recognition Unit (MRU) in which s/he can recognize all the Stratum I and Stratum II employees. As mentioned earlier, MRUs are most effective if they are no larger than 250 to 300 people. This number appears to be the outside limit where it is possible for everyone in the group to recognize each other and that a Stratum III manager can effectively handle.

Involvement of the Stratum IV General or Functional Manager

The Stratum IV general or functional manager (GM) is held accountable by the Stratum V business unit CEO for ensuring that the site or department has effective, well-led MRUs that can produce the required output and continuously improve the way that output is achieved. S/he is accountable for translating the business unit goals into a direction that guides the operation in the site or department and for communicating that direction to everyone within it. From time to time the GM will hold three-level meetings to communicate directly with an entire group as needed.

GMs will not know first line employees personally but will shape the culture in which they work by the systems and practices they put in place and by their own actions and example. GMs are accountable for the processes used and for integrating the output of their mutual recognition units.

GMs provide leadership in significant site-wide or department-wide changes that influence the working environment at the FLM level. They lead the annual or semi-annual review of the human resources in the division to ensure the timeliness of judgments and the adequacy of talent pool development and succession management activities. As their Managers-once-Removed, GMs have specific accountability for mentoring and the individual development of the FLMs and other employees in Stratum II roles.

The number of first line units that are needed and can be resourced in an MRU is the decision of the GM. The GM will also be involved in preparing any slate of candidates provided to the MRU manager from which to select FLMs. The MRU manager will make the actual selection and is not to be required to take anyone whom s/he does not believe capable of doing the work in the role.

In one organization, the first line work that needed to be done at Stratum I was reviewed. The two layers between the FLM and his/her subordinates were removed and their roles were replaced by FLMAs and support specialists. When the number of people involved was reviewed by the GM, it became evident that an additional Stratum III MRU was needed.

Selecting First Line Managers

In selecting individuals for the first line manager role there are three major considerations:

- Do they have the necessary complexity of information processing at Stratum II to do the work of the role?
- Do they value the role? Do they want to manage other people?
- Do they have or can they acquire the necessary skilled knowledge to successfully carry out the role? (New FLMs should be trained for the role before they undertake it.)

All too often individuals who have superior technical knowledge and skills are put into FLM roles without considering their complexity of information processing and/or their commitment to being a manager.

Special Circumstances in First Line Units

Managing first line work may involve the special situations of unions and the need for shifts.

Unions

There is a tendency to regard subordinates at Stratum I who are union members as different, to feel that they can't become members of the company, that they have to be treated with kid gloves, and that there cannot be effective managerial leadership of people who are union members. This is a critical misconception.

It is extremely important that the unit manager make clear to first line managers that the union agreements and arrangements are matters between the union and higher management and that subordinates are subordinates. They are operators for whose work and working behavior their managers are accountable. Their managers should meet with them, pull them together into an effective working team, and ensure that they are getting effective collaborative working relationships.

Where a site or a department is union organized, the FLM must understand and work within negotiated agreements. What can and often happens is that the union members develop local customs and practices that they treat as though they were union agreements. They may implement practices that their union would like to negotiate, or embrace ideologies, political programs or values associated with their union membership, producing inflexible or restrictive practices that, once established, are difficult to eradicate. The FLM must work to prevent such practices or to eliminate them if they occur.

Multiple Shifts

Shifts may be necessary to handle the work flow. Issues involved when shifts are needed are addressed in the sections that follow.

First Line Shifts

There are two important findings from requisite consultative research that improve work on shifts in addition to having a clearly accountable Stratum II manager for each employee on each shift. These are:

1. One first line manager should be accountable for all shifts in a geographical area or a specific function
2. First line employees are often able to organize their own work and can be relied on to carry it forward without the need for direct supervision throughout every shift

These two findings apply whether there are three shifts covering 24/7 or just extended working hours with one and a half or two shifts in a 24-hour period.

One First Line Manager Accountable for all Shifts in an Area

First line units should be established with one Stratum II first line manager in charge of one clearly defined geographical/physical area or a specific function for all shifts in a 24-hour period. The FLM is accountable for using the physical and human resources to obtain optimum results from his/her area 24 hours a day. In this way, the best possible results are obtained.

With one person accountable for a specified area, for example, the usual maintenance and equipment difficulties are no longer a problem. A malfunctioning machine will be attended to and not left for the next shift. The first line manager in charge of that area sees to it that things are taken care of since accountability is clear.

One company that has 250 people per shift decided to establish eight first line manager roles, replacing 25 team leaders. They divided the geographical territory for the full 24 hours of three shifts among the eight first line managers. Once they determined what would be most workable, territories were established by making demarcations on the floor. By doing this they achieved clarity of managerial accountability and cut manpower costs substantially. A significant increase in productivity resulted within a few weeks along with a reduction in turnover.

Managing Multiple Shifts

To manage multiple shifts, FLMs need to arrange their schedules so that they come in half an hour early to be present for the end of one shift and then work briefly into the second shift. In this way, they are there for the work hand-over and are in touch on a daily basis with all three shifts. Where only two shifts are necessary the manager stays briefly for the hand-over. When the manager cannot be on hand for the shift hand-over someone acting on his or her behalf, such as a scheduling specialist operator, arranges the hand-over and schedules new tasks.

FLMs also need to arrange to work several hours into the evening and come in a few hours early for the night shift several times a month. From time to time FLMs also need to work part or all the weekend shifts, particularly if there are individuals who only work on weekends. This gives employees who work those shifts the opportunity to have sufficient access to their manager and gives the manager the opportunity to keep in contact with all his/her subordinates.

This varied scheduling is also necessary so that FLMs can stay in close touch with all their subordinates in order to judge their effectiveness from continuing first-hand knowledge and to coach them as appropriate. The FLM evaluates employees' effectiveness individually by accumulating information over periods of days and weeks without having to watch them continuously as they work during each shift.

FLMs will want to arrange to get all their subordinates together for meetings on a regular basis, possibly for an hour every two or three weeks. In many instances this will require paying overtime. These full group meetings are a necessary part of providing context to the group as a whole about goals and results and are the way the manager binds the group together as a cohesive unit.

Subordinates Can Often Direct Their Own Work on Shifts

One of the reasons that additional layers of management have been added between the real manager and first line employees is the mistaken belief that there needs to be a full-scale manager on hand for each shift if the operators are to do the work. In fact, employees on shift can be expected to work together under the ordinary conditions of collateral (cooperative) relationships between work colleagues. Such an arrangement does, however, require that clearly organized tasks can be assigned and that operating conditions are likely to be reliable for the whole shift.

Shifts other than the day shift often do not have many of the technical, scheduling and training support activities and services ordinarily available during the day. Individuals in specialist roles who have the knowledge and experience to know what to do, may have to be available to provide any assistance required in these areas. Having such individuals on hand allows evening, night and weekend shifts to operate effectively without their FLM on site.

Directing their own work when the circumstances are suitable allows employees the opportunity to use their full capability.

Handling Serious Problems on Shifts

In circumstances where Stratum I employees on shifts can do their own work without a FLM on hand throughout the whole shift, provision needs to be made for handling serious problems that may arise and all employees need to know what to do in case of emergency. Emergencies can include such things as serious illness or accidents, fighting, drunkenness or drug use, serious mechanical breakdowns and so on.

There are many possible ways to plan ahead for handling such situations. One of the easiest solutions is for the FLM to be available by phone or for a number of FLMs whose work is related to take turns being on call. In instances where there are several first line managers in a related area, one FLM can be scheduled to be available on each shift.

Another way of handling the problem is for the Stratum III or Stratum IV manager to have a full-time deputy on each shift to cover that manager's whole area. A deputy role is of great importance when there are serious risks of danger, as, for example, in mining operations or chemical plants. The deputy role is usually a role one stratum below that of the manager. The role does not carry managerial accountability and authority and does not provide input into personal effectiveness appraisals.

The deputy is authorized to act for his/her manager, with the manager's authority. In the manager's absence, the deputy can issue instructions to deal with the types of situations described above.

For example, in an organization with a number of small night shifts located in widely separated locations, the MoR determined that the shifts could manage their own work if two conditions were met: their FLMs had to be there for the hand-over, and a deputy to the MoR had to be available to respond to and, if necessary to, travel to any area that was having a problem.

Self-Managed Teams are not Appropriate

There is an important difference between a shift where employees direct their own work and self-managed teams. In the former situation, there is a first line manager accountable for the output of each first line worker. In self-managed teams the idea is that the group of employees is supposed to be accountable as a team.

Setting up self-managed teams undercuts the authority of the manager. Can the first line manager hold the team accountable for its work? How do you hold a group accountable? Do they get evaluated as a group or deselected as a group? What happens if the manager involved does not believe the work is going on satisfactorily? What happens if there is a disagreement between manager and the team or a team's spokesperson? Where does the accountability lie? Where does the authority lie?

Establishing self-managed teams is often a response to a situation where there is lack of effective managerial leadership or where there is no belief in the possibility of effective management. While there is sometimes a short term 'honeymoon' effect after setting up self-directing teams on the shop floor, such teams are not a medium-term or a long-term answer to the need for clear accountability and managerial leadership. Self-managing teams run into real trouble because it is impossible to determine who has accountability for what. They are usually discarded after a relatively short period of time.

The correct approach is to set up the conditions for effective managerial leadership throughout the whole system, from top to bottom, and to hold managers accountable for getting the required work done. In a requisite organization, fully authorized and accountable first line managerial roles are established at Stratum II, where the Stratum III unit managers hold those first line managers accountable for effective leadership of their first line personnel. **In Requisite work there are no self-managed teams.**

Determining the Requisite Structure for Shifts

Reorganizing first line units generally requires analysis of the work that is to be done. The units need to be designed so that the FLM can develop effective face-to-face relationships with individual subordinates. Where there are shifts, how geographical territories might best be structured needs to be thought through.

When a full Stratum II FLM role is established, it does not necessarily mean that the work that was formerly being done by the quasi-managerial roles goes away, although often a substantial amount of duplication can be eliminated. The work required needs to be carefully considered and sufficient roles need to be in place to get it done.

The basic question is always "what is the work we need to get done and how can that best happen?" In some cases the answer to this may involve establishing one or more additional first line units, while in other instances there may need to be a first line manager assistant or specialist roles or both.

Some of the questions that FLM managers working with their Stratum III MRU manager will want to consider include:

- How can the work best be divided up geographically so that a discrete area is under one FLM for all shifts in a 24-hour period?
- Does the structure of related units need to be reorganized?
- What is the amount of work on the different shifts? For example, the night shift may be relatively quiet, the weekend shift may also be quite slow or it may be the busiest shift of all. Does the structure of related units need to be reorganized?
- If the employees on shift are in separate locations, how can this best be handled?
- How many employees are needed on each shift? This number may vary widely based on the work flow.
- What kind of assistance is needed on shifts when the FLM is not on site? What kind of problems need to be solved? When the FLM is on site? Administration? Training? Technical? Work Coordination? Does this work have to be full time or can the person filling the role do first line work and provide specialist advice on a part-time, as-needed basis? Can the role combine administrative and training work? Technical expertise and training? How do these needs differ on different shifts?
- What kind of safety and/or maintenance expertise is needed?
- Can the administrative work be done largely on the day shift or is it necessary to some extent on all shifts?
- What types of problems that need attention typically arise on shifts? Can one FLM be deputized by the Stratum III manager to handle several first line units on the 2nd or 3rd shifts? Should a deputy for the Stratum III or Stratum IV manager be on hand because of the potential severity of the problems?

Benefits of Establishing Requisite First Line Units

Establishing requisite first line managers at Stratum II and organizing shifts requisitely require substantial analysis of the work and the situation. The implementation of requisite conditions of accountability, authority, management practices and organization design are the best guarantee that first line employees can and will take their place as reliable, involved employees with high morale. They will not be alienated, disappointed people criticized for results they cannot control, but will feel part of an organization that manages them appropriately and where they get satisfaction from using their full capability.

SUMMARY

Dr. Jaques studied managerial hierarchies in Chinese, Assyrian and Roman history and found certain general principles to exist over the centuries. This historical perspective, as well as his consulting research in successful contemporary organizations, has shown that there appears to be a universal pattern of organizational structure based on the nature of people and the nature of tasks as described in this book. These findings show that managerial hierarchies need to be organized vertically by functional specialties as described in this chapter. It is also critically important to have an idea not only of these functions and how they should be aligned, but also of the managerial layers within the functions required by the complexity of the work (introduced in Chapter One) and how the work flow and processes can most effectively take place horizontally across functions (described in Chapter Three).

Chapter 5

MANAGERIAL LEADERSHIP PRACTICES

"If you want to achieve effective and creative leadership in managerial systems you do so by changing the managerial system and not by trying to change the people."

Dr. Elliott Jaques

The requisite principles presented in this book underlie the managerial leadership practices described in this chapter. This includes both senior management practices with regard to creating the organization's vision, values and culture and the practices of all managers in relation to their immediate subordinates. Requisite managerial leadership practices can be clearly described and can be taught, which enables these practices to be established and managers to be held accountable for carrying them out.

As mentioned earlier the Manager-Subordinate relationship is a two-way working relationship. The manager is accountable for the work and working behavior of subordinates because the manager controls the resources available and decides priorities. It is the manager, not the subordinate, who controls the conditions under which the subordinate seeks to achieve the tasks assigned. The subordinate is accountable for using his/her best endeavors to achieve all output as assigned and for keeping the manager informed when problems arise. **Organizations achieve their results through managerial leadership.**

ORGANIZATIONAL LEADERSHIP PRACTICES

The head of an organization is accountable to provide and communicate the vision for the organization and to oversee the organization's values and culture. This leader establishes a sense of common purpose throughout the organization and sets the overarching conditions within which the employees can understand how to move together in the same direction.

Communicating the Vision

Communicating the vision of what is to be accomplished is an essential task of the leader of any organization whether it is a corporation consisting of multiple business units, an individual business unit, a factory or a department. Anyone who heads a unit must have in mind and must communicate the vision for that unit on a continuing basis. This vision must be communicated to all members of the unit at one time, whether 80, 8,000 or 80,000 people are involved. This is now easily possible using technology. The vision is not communicated to immediate subordinates who then communicate it further down to their subordinates. This practice leads to inaccuracy and distortion of the message.

In a Stratum VII organization the CEO provides a vision for the corporation in a 20 year or even longer time frame, outlining where s/he, in conjunction with the Board of Directors, sees the organization heading. In a Stratum V company or business unit the vision will be developed and presented in a five- to seven-year outlook and in a smaller Stratum IV organization the outreach of the vision will be somewhere between two to five years.

Corporate Culture

In his early work with organizations, Dr. Jaques identified and named the concept of 'corporate culture' in his 1951 book, *The Changing Culture of a Factory*. Corporate culture consists of a company's values, its rules and regulations, policies and procedures, customs and practices, its traditions, beliefs and assumptions and its common language. Corporate culture can be thought of as 'the way we do things around here'.

Corporate culture can be described, can be dealt with and can be changed. Organizational leaders can and must have the ability to modify aspects of corporate culture as part of the process of achieving the organization's goals.

For example, corporate cultures change when new technology is introduced. A new technology usually involves establishing new policies and changing procedures. The process often adds to the common corporate language. Just how the introduction of a given technology will change the culture needs to be considered and managed by the organization's leaders.

Corporate Values

The principles of Requisite Organization deal with such corporate values as justice and equity, the opportunity for appeal, fair pay, and equal opportunity to use one's full capability. Corporate values exist whether they are articulated or not. They are expressed in the organization's policies and demonstrated in its practices. The values a corporation espouses and demonstrates require the attention of the organization's leader. S/he must continually review how the organization is doing things to ensure that it is in line with the overall values of the company.

The behavior of the organization's leader also should be consistent with the corporate values. Trust and confidence are built when corporate systems are congruent with the stated values of the company and the leader's behavior and practices are consistently in line with these systems.

Contradiction is sensed by everyone and is a very substantial source of mistrust. For example, a leader may say that he wants all employees to have a balanced life with adequate time for family, friends and outside activities, but in reality, people know that they will need to put in 10 to 12 hour days on a regular basis if they wish to be successful.

Society's Values

The organization's leader must understand the values of the society or societies in which the company is operating and, within reason, the company has to work within those values. Values in Japan and Saudi Arabia are quite different from those in the United States, for example. The challenge is to understand the differences and, insofar as possible, to operate effectively in different societies while keeping values consistent with the overall company values and philosophy—no small challenge for the leaders of global corporations.

Requisite Values

Honesty, Respect, Fairness, Integrity, Opportunity and Trust are fundamental values embedded in Requisite Organization. Mutual trust is achieved in this system through openness and clarity. **Trust is defined as the ability to rely on others to do as they say and to follow established rules, procedures, customs and practice.**

Private Values

An individual's private values are his or her own business. It is not for the organization to dictate to individuals what their values should be. However, as part of the employment contract, employees must behave in line with the corporate values by adhering to the requirements of corporate policies and procedures

MANAGERIAL LEADERSHIP

All managerial roles in all functions at all levels in a requisite organization carry direct leadership accountability and authority regarding subordinates. For this reason, the term managerial leadership is used throughout in Requisite work.

Requisite structure provides the basis for managerial leadership by selecting managers who are one level of capability higher than their subordinates. This gives the organization managers who can work with a wider view of situations than their subordinates and who can set necessary and sufficient context for them, delegate tasks appropriately and make good judgments of personal effectiveness.

The essence of managerial leadership accountability is to enable subordinates to work together in such a way that each person can get on with his or her own work, knowing where the whole group is heading. In this way, everyone moves along together and the desired outcomes are achieved.

Managerial Accountability and Authority

Managerial accountability and authority were described in Chapter One. These concepts are reviewed here because they form the basis for requisite Managerial Leadership Practices. Without this minimum accountability and authority managers cannot be held accountable for the work and working behavior of their subordinates.

Minimum Managerial Accountability

Managers are held accountable, by their managers, for:

- the work and working behavior of their subordinates and for the overall unit/department results
- exercising managerial leadership by carrying out the required Managerial Leadership Practices
- building and sustaining their group of subordinates as an effective team
- their own personal effectiveness

Minimum Managerial Authority

To be held accountable for the work of their subordinates, managers need certain minimum authority with regard to immediate subordinates. This includes the authority to:

- veto the selection of a candidate they deem unsuitable for a subordinate role
- decide the assignment of tasks to their subordinates
- conduct personal effectiveness appraisals and decide merit increases within policy parameters
- initiate removal from role of a subordinate whom they deem unable to do the work of a role

MANAGERIAL LEADERSHIP PRACTICES

There are a number of simple, straightforward Managerial Leadership Practices for which all managers are accountable. Experienced managers for the most part are familiar with these practices and know that they are necessary. For a variety of reasons many organizations do not hold managers accountable for carrying out all of these practices. One of the major reasons is that they do not have the requisite policies and procedures in place to enable them to do so.

In a requisite organization managerial leadership practices are taught and required to be carried out. They are foundational to establishing **clarity and trust** and achieving increased effectiveness and productivity. These managerial leadership practices include:

1. **Managerial Planning** - Determining how to achieve the goals of the unit
2. **Context Setting** - Regular updating of the background within which the work must be carried out
3. **Task Assignment** - Assigning tasks specifying quality, quantity, target completion time and resources available
4. **Managerial Meetings** - Regular meetings with all immediate subordinates
5. **Managerial Coaching** - Helping individual subordinates to be able to carry out the full range of work in their role
6. **Personal Effectiveness Appraisal** - Judging how well each subordinate is working and discussing it with him/her on a regular basis
7. **Merit Review** - Annual evaluation of applied capability with a decision on compensation adjustment within policy
8. **Selection** - Practices for filling roles and choosing new subordinates

9. **Induction** - Introducing an employee to a new role and to the unit
10. **Deselection and Dismissal** – Processes for removing an employee from role
11. **Continual Improvement** – Seeking to improve processes that the manager controls

The Managerial Leadership Practices of planning and setting context were covered in Chapter Three and assigning tasks was covered in depth in Chapter One. These three practices will be briefly reviewed here and the remaining eight described in detail. These practices demonstrate why managers need to be one level more capable in complexity of information processing than their subordinates so that they are able to see the larger world in which the work of the unit takes place and then to plan, set context for subordinates and assign tasks appropriately. Managers integrate the output of their subordinates to achieve the assignments given to their unit.

MANAGERIAL PLANNING

Managers plan how to get the work of their unit done, who will do what and by when these task assignments need to be completed. Subordinates may assist in this planning but it is the manager who makes the decision.

CONTEXT SETTING

Managers set context for their subordinates in individual and in group meetings, letting them know why they are doing what they are given to do and the background in which they are operating.

TASK ASSIGNMENT

A **task** is an assignment to produce an output with a specified quality and quantity within a target completion time with allocated resources and within prescribed limits (policies, procedures, rules and regulations).

Assignments: Tasks and General Responsibilities

In addition to specific tasks, assignments may include actions that are to be taken when a triggering event occurs. This type of assignment is referred to as a **General Responsibility.** For example the safety manager has to communicate changes in the law when they are enacted and to update the safety manuals. These general responsibilities usually have specific tasks embedded in them as well as time parameters such as, in the above example, updating the manuals within a week and having a communication meeting within three days of notification of the change in the law.

Changes in Circumstances

When there are unforeseen changes in circumstances and assignments cannot not be completed as agreed, the subordinate is to inform the manager in time for adaptive action to take place. The subordinate can suggest some possible actions, but it is the manager who decides what is to be done and any changes to the assignment and priorities. This way of working results in all assignments being completed to QQTR and no surprises.

MANAGERIAL MEETINGS

All of a manager's immediate subordinates form the manager's team through which s/he gets the work of the unit done. One of the fundamental managerial accountabilities as mentioned above is to build and sustain a team of immediate subordinates capable of working together effectively with the manager and with each other. As part of doing this, managers at every level in the organization need to have regular meetings with their immediate subordinates. Managers meet with their subordinate team to review plans, priorities and changing conditions and to address problems and consider ideas for solutions. These two-way discussions are essential for clear, continuing communication and context setting.

When decisions are required as part of a managerial meeting, it is the manager who makes the decision. These decisions are informed by the knowledge, expertise and perspective of subordinates, but consensus, while useful, is not required. **Decision making is not a group activity.**

The manager meets on a regular basis with his/her full team of immediate subordinates. It is often useful for the manager to include all SoRs as well. Sometimes it is appropriate to meet with just one or more immediate subordinate managers and all of their subordinates, depending upon the issues. How frequently these various meetings are necessary depends upon circumstances. Many managers meet with their subordinate teams weekly and hold three-level meetings, including SoRs, quarterly or twice a year. One organization that was handling a critical turnaround held an audio conferencing meeting every morning involving all managers at Stratum IV and above in many locations. In rapidly changing fields such as the stock market, daily meetings are quite common.

There are two major types of managerial meetings. The first is information sharing, the second is idea generation.

Information Sharing Meetings

In information sharing meetings the manager provides context for the work of the unit by talking about the issues at hand and why certain kinds of tasks have been assigned. Problems are dealt with that affect the unit, the manager and his/her subordinates in their collaborative work. The information sharing portions of meetings provide an opportunity for the team of subordinates to see the big picture and also to discuss issues with the manager and with each other. Managers use the information gained to make decisions in these meetings or at a later time.

Idea Generation Meetings

Managers work on idea generation in meetings with subordinates when they want to deal with a problem or problems they may not know how to approach or where they would like to consider a variety of ideas. When doing this, managers work together with some or all of their subordinates and encourage them to bring forward ideas in an open discussion, usually with no decision made at the time. A method sometimes used is called 'brain-storming' where ideas are set forth without critical analysis to encourage a wide range of thinking and creativity. Idea generation meetings are important because they provide a setting in which the group has an opportunity to work together, to test each other's ideas, and to learn about each other on a continuing basis

Managerial Decision Making

Managers may make decisions in these meetings as a result of information that has come forward or s/he may make decisions at a later time. It is, of course, important to communicate these decisions.

Managerial Meetings

All managers meet regularly with their team of immediate subordinates and individually with subordinates

Managers seek input from their subordinates

Managers make decisions using information obtained in these meetings

Managers are not seeking to achieve consensus but rather to make a sound decision that the subordinates agree they can implement

Managers prepare the agenda for the meeting, keep the meeting focused, and ensure that follow-up tasks are assigned

COACHING

Coaching is the process by which a manager helps subordinates to understand the full range of their individual roles, what they need to do to perform the work of that role effectively, and what they need to do in order to develop in that role. The coaching of subordinates is a regular part of every manager's activities and an essential part of a manager's continuing review of each subordinate's personal effectiveness.

In order to guide the development of a subordinate in his/her current role, the manager generally has a sense of the rate of growth of that person's future potential. With this in mind, the manager seeks to provide work experiences that are consistent with that growth, providing any coaching, teaching and training necessary. The outcome from regular and appropriate coaching is continual improvement in the effectiveness of employees in their roles and the release of each employee's full capability. Managers are accountable to be proactive coaches.

Teaching and training are part of the coaching process. In order to clarify terminology that has multiple meanings, the term **teaching** is used in Requisite Organization to describe the imparting of knowledge to individuals by lectures, reading, e-learning and discussions. The term **training** is used to describe the process of helping individuals to develop or enhance their skills through practice, either on the job or through learning simulations. Skill that has been developed through training enables individuals to use their knowledge in problem-solving activities without having to reconstruct many of the routine decisions involved, thus freeing up the use of their judgment for other problem-solving activities.

Purposes of Coaching

The purposes of coaching are to help subordinates to:

- understand the full range of opportunities in their individual roles and what they need to do to take advantage of those opportunities
- add to their knowledge and skills
- share the manager's knowledge, skills and experience
- more fully understand, and hence be able to bring their behavior more in line with, corporate values and corporate philosophy
- be aware of any behavior that may become dysfunctional at work if it continues

Coaching does not involve trying to change a subordinate's values or personality, since that is neither a concern of the manager nor of the organization. If there are major behavioral problems, the manager must make it clear to the subordinate that continuation of the problem behavior is unacceptable. If the situation warrants it, the manager should make time available for a subordinate to seek off-site professional counseling, if s/he wishes to do so.

In coaching subordinates, a manager is concerned with their capability to perform the full range of work within their current roles. The manager is seeking to get work done by his/her subordinates in an effective and productive way and to enable subordinates to use their ability fully in doing their work.

Counseling

Counseling by the manager is done when someone asks for advice with a personal problem. Managers can give counsel in general terms. For example, "What someone else I know did with such a problem was this..." or, "You might think about the possibility of...". If this type of assistance is not adequate, subordinates should be referred for professional help if the situation is sufficiently serious.

Coaching Triggers

Managers will find that the need for coaching occurs as a normal by-product of work assignments, periodic reviews of progress and the ongoing personal effectiveness appraisal process.

There are five major reasons for coaching:

- person new to the role
- progress toward achieving assigned tasks
- the need to strengthen existing skills and knowledge
- readiness for development within the current role
- specific difficulties identified by the manager or subordinate

Person New to the Role

In addition to induction activities and orientation to their role, new employees or employees in a new role usually need coaching, in order to understand what is expected.

Progress Toward Achieving Assigned Tasks

A subordinate's work toward achieving his or her assigned tasks may be slower or faster than required by the manager. In either event, this situation needs to be monitored, adjustments made to work plans, and help given to the subordinate as needed.

The Need to Strengthen Existing Skills and Knowledge

Managers, both in the appraisal process and normal activities such as task assignment and meetings, will often identify areas of subordinates' skills and knowledge that need strengthening or improving.

Readiness for Development within Current Role

When a manager observes that a subordinate is ready for development within his or her current role, the manager discusses this with the individual and arranges the necessary activities to enable that development. Subordinates may also request developmental opportunities. In this event the manager determines, in discussion with the employee, whether or not the person is ready for that step and whether or not it is appropriate for the organization.

Specific Difficulties

Managerial coaching should take place whenever subordinates are experiencing difficulties in their role. This type of coaching must not be delayed until a performance review. Managers should also ask subordinates to identify areas where they may be having problems.

Problems may be related to the manager's task formulation and assignment process. For example, the goals may be too complex for the level of the subordinate's capability. There may also be difficulties regarding methods, resources, procedures or limits. These are matters to be sorted out in discussions between the manager and the subordinate. Problems may be associated with the nature of ongoing working relationships. Often these types of problems stem from the need to adjust the cross-functional accountabilities and authorities of the subordinate's role in relation to other roles.

A subordinate's temperament may cause problems. Managers need to handle such situations judiciously. As mentioned earlier, it is not the business of the manager to try to change the personality of any subordinate. It is appropriate, however, for the manager to point out the need for behavioral changes in areas where the person's temperament interferes with his/her ability to get work done. Employees should be referred for counseling if necessary.

Effective Managerial Coaching

Coaching consists of discussing with subordinates where the manager believes them to be working at the present time in terms of capability, their potential in their current role, and the things they are not able to achieve at the moment. This clarity enables the manager to provide teaching and training to ensure that subordinates enhance their skilled knowledge so that they can increase their applied capability and work more effectively.

As the manager identifies opportunities for growth in a subordinate's current role or deficiencies in the subordinate's performance, s/he should set aside sufficient time to discuss these issues with the subordinate as part of the ongoing coaching process. The manager indicates what the subordinate needs to learn in terms of knowledge or greater skill to improve his/her work performance, to overcome weaknesses or to solve problems.

Arising out of such a discussion, or as part of it, the manager might teach or train the individual, or arrange for teaching or training by others. As part of coaching, managers share with subordinates knowledge and skills gained from their own work experiences.

The subordinate must value this teaching, training and/or experience sharing if it is to be effective. If the subordinate does not value certain kinds of new knowledge and skills and does not benefit from the coaching, this must be taken into account when discussing his/her progress in the current role.

Coaching is one of the ways in which managers add value to their subordinates' work. It can be a time-consuming process, but it is central to building subordinate confidence, loyalty and sense of teamwork and getting the work of the group done. If a subordinate is not performing satisfactorily it is not only a problem for the person involved but for the manager as well, since it is part of the manager's accountability to provide sufficient coaching to enable subordinates to be successful in their roles.

The Role of the Manager-once-Removed in the Coaching Process

The full performance of the coaching process cannot be left to managerial choice and goodwill. Managers-once-Removed must see to it that their subordinates who are managers actually do coach on a continuing basis. To that end, MoRs must themselves act as appropriate role models by fully and effectively discharging their coaching accountabilities with their own subordinates. MoRs must also judge their immediate subordinates' effectiveness in coaching their subordinates.

Managerial Coaching

Coaching is an interactive process by which a manager helps each subordinate to understand:

- The full range of his or her role

- What she or he needs to do to perform effectively in that role

- What she or he needs to do to develop in that role

- The goals of coaching are:

  - Continual improvement of the employee's effectiveness in his/her role

  - The release of the full capability of each employee

PERSONAL EFFECTIVENESS APPRAISAL

Managers are accountable for judging the effectiveness of their subordinates in doing their work. No performance can be totally quantified. Appraisal of performance is based on the manager's judgment of how well subordinates handle the available resources and the impact of unexpected events. These judgments are some of the most important decisions managers make in terms of managerial leadership in relationship to their subordinates.

Performance Appraisal and Personal Effectiveness

Confusion exists in the field of management because of what is commonly called performance appraisal. The use of the word 'performance' with regard to appraisal creates problems. Managers would generally prefer to have performance appraisal systems based on objective indicators of output. In reality, people cannot be employed merely to produce designated outputs, since they cannot control the resources they are given or changing external circumstances.

People are employed to use their capability to do their best in producing the outputs that they are assigned. They should be paid for the level of capability they use in working to achieve the output. For this reason the requisite process is called **personal effectiveness appraisal** rather than performance appraisal.

In an organization that is requisite Manager A holds Subordinate Manager B accountable for the results of the work and results of the working behavior of Subordinate C. C works to produce the output that B assigns in terms of quantity, quality and time within resources and policy. C is employed to use his/her applied capability in working to produce the outputs that B assigns. Manager A appraises the personal effectiveness of Manager B and Manager B appraises the personal effectiveness of C.

Purposes of the Personal Effectiveness Appraisal System

The purposes of personal effectiveness appraisals are to:

- let subordinates know how their manager judges their personal effectiveness
- provide an opportunity for subordinates to express their views and have a discussion with their manager about their personal effectiveness
- provide an opportunity for managers to coach their subordinates and develop action plans with them for improved performance
- provide input into compensation decisions

Applied Capability

Applied capability in doing work in order to produce outputs was discussed in Chapter Two. An understanding of applied capability is important in judging personal effectiveness. Applied Capability is a function of a person's current potential capability, of his/her valuing the work, the degree of knowledge a person has that can be used in a skilled way and an absence of disruptive negative temperament. Negative temperament (-T) refers to the characteristics that inhibit someone's ability to carry out assigned work. Hence, -T can affect someone's applied capability.

The less interested individuals are in what they are doing, the less commitment they have to using their full capability. In order for someone to apply his/her capability as fully as possible, it is necessary for a person to value the role s/he is occupying.

Employees may choose to work below their level of capability for any number of reasons. For example, a corporate librarian in a Stratum III role, who would be capable of working at Stratum V, instead uses her full capability in running a successful community theater in her free time.

In determining a subordinate's personal effectiveness, managers are given a system that allows them to state their judgments in terms of the level at which that person is working. They judge how much applied capability each subordinate is bringing to bear in doing his or her work, with 'work' defined as what one does toward achieving a task or goal, not the actual output.

Appraisal as a Continuing Process

Personal effectiveness appraisal is not a once-a-year event. Managers and subordinates should have a continuing dialog in this regard throughout the year. In particular it is important for the manager to give the subordinate feedback whenever s/he has completed an important assignment. As part of this process, managers coach subordinates on a regular basis to help them become more effective in their roles.

The annual personal effectiveness appraisal acts as a summary of the coaching and personal effectiveness discussions held throughout the year. As part of this process targets for development in the subordinate's current role may be discussed and established for the coming year. This annual appraisal also provides input into the manager's decision about merit compensation for the subordinate.

Employees' Personal Effectiveness Accountabilities

Employees are accountable for using their skills, knowledge and experience in creative ways to work toward attainment of their assigned tasks. They are expected to use their full capability in working on the tasks they are given. Employees are accountable for clarifying their assignments with their manager, if necessary, and to let their manager know when they encounter problems that prevent them from achieving their goals.

The personal effectiveness appraisal system involves honest self-assessment on the part of the subordinate. This means identifying personal strengths as well as areas for improvement. Employees are expected to spend time and energy to take advantage of opportunities afforded by the company to develop the skills and knowledge necessary to grow in their present role.

Equilibration, the MoR's Role in Appraisal

As was mentioned in Chapter Three, in order for the personal effectiveness appraisal process to work properly, achieving consistency, fairness and balance, the MoR must review all of his/her subordinate managers' judgments of the level of effectiveness of their subordinates. This process is called **equilibration**. It ensures that one manager is not placing everybody up at the top all the time while another tends to give subordinates lower judgments of effectiveness and smaller salary increases. The quality of managers' judgments does vary and it is the MoR's accountability to see that employees are treated in a reasonably even manner.

It is the accountability of Managers-once-Removed to do an equilibration review, at least annually, in which s/he looks at the patterns in the appraisal process in each subordinate manager's group to ensure that they are all applying reasonably common standards.

MERIT REVIEW

In a requisite organization each employee is paid in accord with his/her level of applied capability as judged by his/her manager and is paid within a work band that is established based on the value of the role to the organization. Requisite compensation is dealt with in depth in Chapter Six.

Because a manager's complexity of information processing and the manager's role is one stratum higher than his/her subordinates, the essential conditions exist that enable a manager in a requisite organization to accurately judge personal effectiveness and to fine-tune individual pay.

The annual compensation review for an individual subordinate is part of the close working relationship between manager and subordinate in which the subordinate understands the discretion that the manager has with respect to judgments of his/her personal effectiveness.

If a manager is not coaching and providing regular feedback as to effectiveness, the subordinate can ask to have this done. If the manager is not fully carrying out these requisite Managerial Leadership Practices, the employee needs to ensure that his/her personal effectiveness is under review with the manager *during* the year and not a procedure that happens just once a year, causing the salary review to take place without a continuous and systematic background.

All too often organizations experience a period of several days devoted to rushed appraisals with no one getting any other work done. Then the process is forgotten for the next 12 months. Managers know they should talk with the immediate subordinates about their performance throughout the year, but in many organizations this does not happen. Requisite coaching and appraisal procedures require that personal effectiveness appraisal and coaching happen as a continuing, ongoing process.

Personal Effectiveness Appraisal

Personal effectiveness is the extent to which employees use their best efforts to complete assigned tasks, handling the unpredictable circumstances that may arise.

Evaluating personal effectiveness is a matter of managerial judgment, not just a quantitative statement of outputs.

This judgment provides the basis of the **manager's** decision on any merit increase.

SELECTION

Selection of someone to fill a vacant role occurs by having the Manager-once-Removed create a slate of candidates from which the immediate manager of the role chooses a preferred candidate. This screening procedure helps ensure the long-term stability, as well as the continuing development, of the organization's pool of talent.

The immediate manager is not authorized to appoint someone to the vacant role if that individual does not fit the requirements of the role as established by the MoR. MoRs are not to try to get someone placed in a role whom the immediate manager feels cannot do the work of the role. Immediate managers do not have to take any candidate whom they deem unacceptable because they do not believe they can do the work of the role. This is one of the minimum authorities of all managers. It ensures that managers have as subordinates only those individuals whom they judge capable of completing their assignments.

The Selection Process

When a vacancy occurs, or a new role is established, the following procedure provides a process that ensures fairness and justice and enables the manager of the vacant role to select a competent new subordinate.

Specifying the Role

The first step in the selection process is to describe the requirements of the vacant role on a role specification form that includes:

- the level of work of the role which indicates the level of complexity of information processing required
- the type of role which gives an indication of the values needed for full commitment
- the major tasks in the role
- the skilled knowledge and any professional qualifications that are needed

Human Resources Recommends a Full Slate to the MoR

The second step is for Human Resources to prepare for the MoR a slate listing in alphabetical order all current employees with the currently judged potential to work at the level of the role. These lists are blind with respect to gender, color, ethnicity, age and other biases. This list, for example, would include everyone judged to have mid-III potential for a mid-III role. This list should be prepared in three sections:

- Those currently in roles one stratum or more below their current potential capability who are being considered for a possible promotion.
- Any individuals who have been over-promoted to roles above their potential and who would be in line for a role appropriate to their potential.
- Employees with potential at the level of work of the role, who are in line for lateral transfers for career development.

Internal and External Candidates

An important policy with regard to fair treatment of current employees is that they are made aware of vacancies through the posting of roles as determined by policy. Vacancy notices should be circulated so that employees know about the openings and have the opportunity to apply to be considered for the slate being developed for the vacant role.

The organization has information on internal candidates with regard to judged potential capability, commitment and skilled knowledge. There is background information on their personal effectiveness from appraisals that are on file. The MoR knows many of the possible candidates from personal experience and the regular talent pool meetings. This information is helpful in developing a slate of possible candidates from employees who are interested in, and capable of, the open position.

If external candidates are deemed necessary, these individuals can be initially screened by Human Resources and/or the MoR. The list of the best qualified internal and, if desired, external candidates is reduced to consist of those with the best qualifications.

MoR Develops Short List

Once this list is created as described, the MoR develops a short list of individuals whom s/he judges able to fill the role requirements. In reducing the initial slate to a short list, the MoR will prepare an annotated list for discussion with the manager of the role.

The Immediate Manager Chooses from Short List

The immediate manager makes his/her selection from the short list. If the manager vetoes all the individuals on the short list, another short list needs to be prepared by the MoR. The hiring manager may exercise a veto only in terms of his/her judgment that an individual does not appear to have the applied capability to do the work required.

Selection

Managers select people for a role by deciding, in their judgment, if the person:

- Has the complexity of information processing (CIP) to do the work of the role; the mental capability needed

- Has the necessary skill, knowledge and experience to do the work of the role

- Values the work of the role

- Does not have issues of temperament that interfere with his/her ability to do the work of the role

INDUCTION

Induction is the process a manager uses to provide subordinates new to a role with the information necessary to do the work of that role. This process is sometimes called orientation or on-boarding. It is the immediate manager's accountability to let all new employees, or current employees who have been moved to a new role, know what is expected of them. Induction includes:

- a description of the role and the tasks assigned to it
- cross-functional accountability and authority
- current problems and priorities
- relevant policies and procedures
- reporting methods
- any other information that will help the employee gain a well-rounded knowledge of the role.

When an employee is new to the organization as well as the role, the manager can assign an experienced subordinate to introduce the newcomer to colleagues and significant people in other sections and help the newcomer learn about the organization. This person can tell the employee what it is like to work in the location, how to get around, how to get needed services and provide information about the customs, practices and conditions of employment.

Induction needs to take place in the first few weeks. Managers are to see that employees at every level are fully introduced to their role. Sound induction helps someone new to the role to begin productive work quickly. It also gives the new subordinate a reassuring sense of being in a reliable and trustworthy situation.

One organization that was implementing all requisite Managerial Leadership Practices found that by providing complete induction, mid-level managers became fully productive within two months of assuming a new role, whereas formerly it took up to six months for this to happen.

Managers Provide Induction for New Employees

Clearly describe the key assignments of the role

Describe working relationships and reporting methods

Explain how the role relates to other areas and departments

Provide all relevant policies and procedures

Discuss any current problems and priorities

Explain necessary safety practices

Provide specific learning/training opportunities

DESELECTION AND DISMISSAL WITH CAUSE

There are circumstances when the manager has to initiate the removal of a subordinate from his/her role. For example, the manager may have made a bad selection or the role may be changing in such a way that the person cannot reasonably be expected to keep up. When a manager judges that a subordinate is not able to carry out the work that is required, s/he has the authority to request this person's removal from a role, but not removal from the employment by the company. Dismissal for cause is a very different matter. The need for dismissal for cause arises when someone grossly and blatantly breaks laws, rules and regulations or when dangerous situations occur because of an employee's negligence. Both deselection and dismissal actions need to be documented in accord with company policy and legal requirements.

Deselection

There is a requisite process for deselection when it is necessary because the person cannot do the work of the role. The first step is for the manager to discuss the situation with the subordinate. If it is a case of not being able to keep up, the manager will point out where s/he judges that person's capability is unacceptable or describe to the person whatever non-performance the manager is experiencing. The subordinate in question has a chance to discuss the problem with the manager from his/her perspective. With this information in mind, the manager coaches the person and tries to help him/her improve.

If the unacceptable performance continues, the manager gives a warning and continues coaching in an effort to help the person perform successfully in the role. Throughout this process, the manager lets his/her own manager know about the situation. If there is still not sufficient improvement, the manager gives a second warning and provides continuing coaching. If the person feels unfairly treated s/he will have the opportunity to discuss it with the MoR. In this case the three people involved (the subordinate, the immediate manager and the MoR) meet together to talk about the situation.

If the person continues to perform unacceptably after the discussions, the coaching and the warnings, the manager will request that the MoR, with the help of Human Resources, attempt to find alternative employment, often referred to as **redeployment**, for this employee in the company. Sufficient time needs to be allowed for this to happen. If another place in the organization cannot be found, then the person will be released by HR on behalf of the company, with the same entitlements as someone let go as a result of downsizing. This is not a punitive situation.

Dismissal with Cause

Dismissal with cause occurs when an employee breaks the law, behaves outside generally acceptable norms or commits a major infraction of the policies and guidelines of the company such as theft, fighting on-site or dealing in drugs. The specifics for dismissal with cause are set by corporate policy. The immediate manager refers this type of dismissal to the MoR. Human Resources is involved to ensure adherence to local and federal policies.

CONTINUAL IMPROVEMENT

Continual improvement activities are essential to every organization. However, setting up a separate total quality (TQM) system with committees, councils, and quality circles undermines the work of the managerial system. Improvement activities should be in the hands of managers. Continual improvement is built into the managerial process. It is not a stand-alone undertaking. Committees, councils and teams cannot do the work that a manager can do and they cannot be held accountable as a group.

People are hired as individuals and can only be held accountable as individuals. It is managers who must be accountable for the improvement of the processes and systems that they are providing subordinates.

Managers hold their subordinate managers accountable to achieve improvement of the processes provided by that manager to his/her subordinates. Managers cannot hold subordinates accountable for the improvement of the processes that they have been given to work with because this is the manager's accountability.

If subordinates see ways of improving processes, they are accountable to inform the manager. Managers also discuss possibilities with subordinates for getting the work done better. This two-way working enhances everyone's effectiveness and satisfaction.

Subordinates' personal growth, or their individual continual improvement, is their own personal concern. A manager can set up conditions for subordinates within which they can achieve personal growth, but the manager cannot hold any individual personally accountable for that growth. If a person chooses not to improve his/her ability to carry out a role, when s/he has the current potential capability to do so, the manager discusses the consequences of this choice with the individual.

Steps in Continual Improvement

The steps necessary to get a solid continual improvement effort in an organization are to:

- hold managers accountable for the process
- maintain an ongoing analysis
- review and prioritize improvement projects
- provide assistance from staff specialists

Hold Managers Accountable for Continual Improvement

A continual improvement program cannot be set up as such. Continual improvement is not a program. What must be instilled throughout the managerial system is the idea that subordinates who are managers are held accountable by their managers not only for getting output through their subordinates, but also for continuously improving the processes that they control. These activities are an ordinary, ongoing part of their managerial leadership work and an important part of managerial accountability.

Maintain an Ongoing Analysis

Managers must maintain an ongoing analysis of the processes that they assign to their subordinates. This applies to work being done in all functions, all departments and at all levels. Managers need to ensure that their subordinates who are managers are paying attention to possibilities for overcoming problems where quality is suffering and not under good control.

Managers need also to ensure that, where possible, systematic, statistical methods of analysis are used. Every manager is held accountable for improving the systems within which s/he has subordinates working, since that is what the manager has control over.

Continual Improvement Priority List

Managers provide their subordinate managers with a list of items that they believe ought to be their priorities for projects oriented toward overcoming the most important blockages and shortcomings in the work processes. This list is kept under discussion and reviewed on a regular basis. As the managerial subordinates get the opportunity, they establish projects that allow them to tackle the topics that are of the highest priority. Managers hold their managerial subordinates accountable for always having at least one improvement project going on.

Staff Specialists Provide Assistance

Part of the regular work of staff specialists is to provide information and assistance to managers to enable continual improvement. For example, the HR specialists may inform managers about new legal requirements and help them revise procedures to conform to changes in the law.

Continual Improvement Project Teams

Setting up a special project team is one of the best methods for undertaking a particular improvement that a manager wants to get under way. Improvement projects should be established in the same way that a manager would establish any ordinary task, that is, the manager gives a subordinate manager a QQTR in assigning the project. The managerial subordinate is to produce a particular result, i.e., an improvement in the process being worked on by the team, to a specified quality and completion time with given resources. The managerial subordinate can either manage the quality project team directly or designate a team leader.

Continual Improvement on the Shop Floor

The people who are engaged in doing the work are in a good position to understand the work process, to know where the difficulties are, and to come up with suggestions as to what ought to be done. On the shop floor this means getting the cooperation and collaboration of operators. It is not necessary to set up self-directed teams to do this. It is essential to establish clear and effective managerial accountability, where every operator has a real, first line manager and there is no one between the operators and their first line managers.

These first line managers are held accountable for maintaining a relationship with each one of their subordinates and for operating as fully accountable managers with regular meetings with subordinates and all other managerial duties.

In a union shop first line managers are accountable for understanding the company's agreements with the trade unions and for ensuring that they work explicitly and consistently within those agreements. These are binding agreements, and the company is accountable for ensuring that they are carried out. They constitute limits or parameters within which everyone works. With these requisite conditions in place, first line managers can be held accountable for continual improvement by their managers, ensuring that work is being done effectively and, if there are problems, determining where improvement efforts should be directed.

Continuous Systems Improvement

In Japan in the late 1940s, Dr. W. Edwards Deming brought into focus both the statistical methods for achieving continuous reduction in process variance and the importance of attaining that reduction. Process variance reduction can be brought about by improving the methods themselves, by changing resources and by many other techniques. The aim is to move from a situation in which the control limits for processes are wide and to get those limits narrowed, so that these processes are controlled in such a way that the extent of variance is reduced. Japanese companies became excellent at continuing reduction of process variance, not just in manufacturing, but in all functions. This is the critical aim of the approach initiated and developed by Dr. Deming.

Dr. Deming taught the Japanese to introduce continuous improvement into the systems as they existed, that is, through the managerial system. He did this to ensure that first line managers were always working within quality limits, maintaining quality standards and producing their outputs just-in-time.

America took note of Dr. Deming's work in the late 1970s. It was erroneously perceived in the U.S. that the success of Japan's continuous improvement efforts was the result of quality circles, committees and teams. However, it has always been in and through requisite managerial work that continuous improvement has been achieved in Japan. The quality circle team processes were introduced into Japanese industry in the early 1960s, a decade or more after the great changes in Japanese quality and just-in-time working had been attained.

A major contribution of Dr. Deming's work was the application of statistical methods to systematic process variance analysis. These methods have great advantage when used by managers. All managers should understand systematic, analytical approaches based on statistical analysis. Managers need to understand variance in the processes that they are controlling, ways of analyzing to find where priorities lie, where maximum gains can be achieved by getting those processes under increasingly effective control and getting variance operating within narrower and narrower limits. This understanding leads to substantial savings in direct cost, in the speed at which work can be done and in quality.

Continual Improvement at Every Level

Continual improvement is necessary throughout the organization. The corporate CEO at Stratum VII looks for continual improvement on major issues that affect the whole corporation. The Stratum V business unit president has improvement projects underway that apply to the processes governing work throughout the unit, and s/he considers and communicates where improvement priorities need to be placed throughout all of the functions. In order for improvement to go on throughout the corporation, senior managers must carry out their own accountabilities for ensuring that continual improvement work goes on in their areas and that this accountability then cascades through the organization.

Continual Improvement

Managers continually improve processes.

Continual Improvement is integrated into a **manager's** role. It is not a separate function or committee.

Managers:

- Ask subordinates for suggestions

- Create an environment where employees openly offer suggestions for improvement

- Maintain a list of improvement projects

- Assign process improvement projects to subordinates as part of key accountabilities

The MoR determines the priority of these projects.

SUMMARY

The systematic application of managerial leadership practices constitutes requisite managerial leadership. All MoRs have the accountability to ensure that their subordinate managers are regularly exercising these requisite managerial leadership practices. As is evident from the activities described in this chapter many of them involve corporate policy and procedures such as selection, de-selection and dismissal. For this reason, Human Resources area is actively involved in establishing fully Requisite managerial leadership practices within an organization.

Chapter 6

REQUISITE COMPENSATION

"Paying employees fairly at all levels releases their full capability and results in continuing organizational success in a socially healthy workplace."

Dr. Elliott Jaques

The issue of compensation is a difficult and controversial one. How does an organization know how much to pay someone? How is the work of one person valued as against that of another? What is a fair amount of pay for a CEO to earn relative to the wages and salaries of others in the organization and with respect to the owners of the firm?

In Requisite Organization there are two basic underlying propositions about people at work and their compensation. The first proposition is that people seek to work at a level in which they can use their capabilities to the full. The second is that people seek fair differential remuneration for that work. Just what fair differential pay is and how to establish it in organizations is the topic of this chapter.

The terms compensation and pay are used interchangeably in this chapter to refer to the ***total*** monetary and non-monetary rewards people receive for their work. This includes such things as base pay, bonuses and incentive pay, deferred compensation, long term incentive pay and stock awards and options. The value of items such as cars is included if they are only granted to specific roles. Benefits such as insurance that are provided to all employees are generally not included.

THE QUESTION OF RELATIVE PAY

A major difficulty in determining what constitutes fair relative pay is the question "What is it that organizations ought to be paying for?" For example, how much should sales people receive as compared with individuals working in the accounting department, and how is this decision to be made?

The question of relativity, of differentials, of what one role receives as compared to another or of who gets how much as compared to whom, has always been a difficult problem. Dr. Jaques' findings about human capability, levels of complexity and requisite organization structure provide sound methods and procedures for understanding what an organization is actually paying for or ought to be paying for.

Requisite Organization principles and practices enable organizations to develop a compensation system that pays fairly for the level of work in every role in terms of the complexity of the work in that role and for each individual's personal effectiveness in carrying out his or her role. When employees receive fair relative pay, they feel fairly treated which has a positive impact on their choice to release their full creativity and capability.

The Requisite system is the first truly non-discriminatory one that provides a measurable means of determining **equal pay for comparable work**. In this system pay levels are in no way related to education, longevity, gender, race or any other discriminatory considerations. From the chief executive officer to first line workers, all employees have compensation related to the complexity of the work in the role they occupy. There are also no differences for occupations or professions. Engineers, accountants, scientists, administrators, managers, lawyers are paid for the level of complexity of the work in their role. The Requisite system enables all employees working in a managerial hierarchy to be treated consistently and equitably.

It is critical to understand, however, that **the Requisite system of compensation will only fully work in organizations that are requisitely structured where people are working at levels of work consistent with their current applied capability and that are using Requisite managerial leadership practices.**

In a Requisite structure managers are one Stratum of capability higher than their immediate subordinates, not merely a higher level in the same Stratum. As an example, first line workers are to be managed by a true first line manager, not by a more experienced first line employee who is often called a supervisor.

Establishing a Requisite structure requires clarity about two important concepts, current applied capability and work. As was described in earlier chapters, **Current Applied Capability** (CAC) is the ability individuals are using at present in doing a certain kind of work at a specific level within a stratum. This capability is a function of individuals' complexity of information processing, how much they value the work of the role and their skilled use of knowledge they apply to carrying out the tasks in their role. **Work** is defined as the exercise of judgment and discretion in making decisions in carrying out goal-directed activities.

In a Requisite Organization all comparable roles are placed within the same band in the same Stratum based on the complexity of the work in the role. This complexity can be accurately measured by the target completion time of the longest tasks required of a role. Individuals who have the necessary applied capability are paid within Work Bands for the role they occupy. There are three Work Bands within each Stratum and there are six Pay Steps within each Work Band. As part of the appraisal process managers place employees within a Pay Step based on their judgment of how effectively the individual is using his/her current applied capability. There is a consistent relationship between compensation in all Strata and there is no overlap between Pay Steps, Work Bands or Strata.

Work Bands and Pay Steps

Each Work Band has Six Pay Steps

FELT FAIR PAY

The principles underlying pay that is felt to be fair by the individuals working in an organization were uncovered by Dr. Jaques in his early work in the U. K. at Glacier Metal Company in the 1950's. The employees with whom he was working at Glacier told Dr. Jaques that they wanted to be paid in relation to the differences in the weight of responsibility that they felt in the work in their roles. Their idea was that individuals working at the same level of work complexity should be given the same pay. They asked Dr. Jaques if he could help them develop a way to measure level of work, the size of accountability and the complexity of different types of work. They believed that it should not be a matter of labor supply and demand, but that there should be fair pay for their work—where fairness would be the same total compensation for comparable work.

The request from this group led Dr. Jaques to the discovery of time span as a method of measuring work. He discovered that with increasing levels of work as measured by time span, individuals state pay levels they feel to be fair that increase with the increase in the time span of the role.

The concept of time span was introduced in Chapter One. The time span of a role is measured in terms of the task or tasks that have the longest target completion time that the immediate manager of the role actually assigns to the role. The time span of a role is determined by asking the manager of a role about the longest tasks s/he is assigning to a given role. Time span provides a simple, objective measure that enables roles to be compared against each other with regard to their complexity.

Continuing research has confirmed the existence of a consistent pattern in pay felt to be fair that is based on the differing levels of complexity of work in roles. Consulting research data over decades show that the same differential pattern of compensation is considered fair by the people working in organizations worldwide.

SETTING UP A REQUISITE COMPENSATION SYSTEM

There are five steps to setting up a Requisite compensation system once a Requisite structure has been established in the organization:

1. Determine the Requisite Level of Work of every role in the organization (both Stratum and Work Band within the Stratum)
2. Establish equitable differential values in the community or communities in which the organization operates
3. Decide how the company will pay relative to these values
4. Select the value of X. X is the boundary point between the highest compensation paid at Stratum II and lowest at Stratum III
5. Establish dollar (or other currency) values on the boundaries of Strata and Work Bands and Steps within the Strata based on felt fair pay multipliers

The five steps are:

1. Establish the Requisite Level of Work of Each Role

In order to have effective managerial leadership, a Requisite structure of layering (Strata) has to be set up with the first line employees in roles with time spans between one day and three months. The next higher Stratum, that of first line managers and some specialists and analyst roles, falls between three months and a year. The next layer of roles, typically that of department manager, has time spans between one and two years. Managers of functions are in roles having time spans between two and five years, and business unit presidents are in roles with time spans between five and ten years. In more complex organizations there are corporate vice presidents with time spans that fall between ten and twenty years and a corporate chief executive role with a time span somewhere between twenty and fifty years.

Stratum and Time-Span

Stratum	Time	Role
VII		Corporate CEO
	20 Years	
VI		Executive Vice President
	10 Years	
V		Business Unit President / General Manager
	5 Years	
IV		Functional Manger
	2 Years	
III		Unit Manager / Middle Manager
	1 Year	
II		First Line Manager / Specialist, Analyst
	3 Months	
I		First Line Employee / Clerical, Office, Factory
	1 Day	

Establishing Work Bands within Strata

Within each Strata three Work Bands are established, designated as High, Mid and Low. These bands provide a further basis for role classification. Having three bands in each Stratum gives Work Bands about 25% to 33% wide. This spread provides individuals with a realistic pay progression as they as they develop the current applied capability to move through the band. Narrower bands appear to feel constricting.

There are several ways to determine the Work Band in a Stratum where a role is to be placed:

- Determine the time span of the role

- Manager-once-Removed places the role in a Stratum and Work Band
- Select representative roles and compare roles against one another in the organization

Measuring Time Span

Time-span measurement is used to determine objectively the level of work of a role and the Work Band in which it falls. For example, if the time span of a role is 14 months, the role would be placed in the low band of Stratum III. If the time span is 17 months the role would be placed in the mid band of Stratum III and if the time span is 21 months in the high band.

It is the manager of a role who describes the longest task s/he is assigning to the role in a one-on-one interview. These tasks must be real tasks actually given to the role: they cannot be hypothetical.

MoR Judges the Placement of the Role

As well as using time-span measurement, the Manager-once-Removed, working with the immediate manager of the role, can intuitively consider what Work Band within a Strata to place a role. S/he judges if the role is the kind that needs someone with the capability to work toward the top of the Stratum or is the kind of role that can be filled by someone who has just been promoted from the Stratum below, or by someone with current applied capability somewhere in the middle. Managers (both the immediate manager of the role and the MoR) generally can make judgments of whether a role should be in the low, mid or high band of a Stratum based on their knowledge of the work needed in the role. The MoR selects the lowest band where s/he and the immediate manager of the role believe the required work can be accomplished.

Comparing Roles across the Organization

MoRs also may use representative roles where time spans have been done and compare roles with each other in terms of the complexity of work needed in the role.

Once roles have been placed in Bands within Strata based on the level of work of the role, the MoR meets with all of his/her immediate managers to compare the role placements to ensure that comparable roles are all in the same Band and Stratum.

Work Bands

	High	
IV	Mid	Functional Manager
	Low	
	High	
III	Mid	Department Manager
	Low	
	High	
II	Mid	First Line Manager
	Low	Specialists
	High	
I	Mid	Operator/ Clerical
	Low	

The MoR Decides

Whatever methods or combination of methods are used, the Manager-once-Removed is the person who makes the final decision regarding the Work Band within a Stratum in which a role is positioned. This is done in consultation with the immediate manager of that role, but it is the MoR's decision because the issue relates not only to the level of work required by the role, but has an impact on the allocation of resources in the unit.

Pay Grades and Titles

Work Bands can provide the basis for grades if they are desired. For example, Stratum I Low, Mid and High can be designated as grades IL, IM and IH or 11, 12 and 13. In Stratum II, bands can be designated as grades IIL, IIM, IIH or 21, 22 and 23 and so on.

Titles too can be established to coordinate with Strata and Work Bands. For example, the Vice President title can apply only to roles at Stratum IV, Director only to roles at Stratum III, First Line Manager to roles at Stratum II where the individual manages others and a descriptive title used for a Stratum II specialist role. For example, Senior Engineer can be used for a II High role and Engineer for a II Mid role. (It is strongly recommended that the title of manager not be used unless the role actually manages subordinate roles.)

All too often in organizations that are not requisitely structured, grades and titles drive the compensation system and pay increases reflect longevity in the company rather than the value of the work of the role to the organization. The lack of a clear understanding of what work is and of the differing complexity of work leads to the situation where organizations become structured not for getting work done but for providing grades, pay levels and career progression.

2. Determine Local Differential

The amount of compensation that is felt to be fair differs from community to community, from country to country and by type of organization and industry. To understand local conditions it is necessary to conduct a study of, where possible, about 20 or more roles in several similar local organizations. Whenever possible, it is useful to gain information about roles that have time span of days and weeks, roles with three-, six- and nine-month spans, still other roles with two-, three- and five-year time spans. These spans represent the Low, Mid and High bands of Strata I, II and III. If possible it is also helpful to have bands of five-, seven- and ten- year time spans (Stratum IV). It is especially important to identify to compensation of roles at the top of the High Band of Stratum II and the bottom of the Low Band of Stratum III. This is the time span of one year and determines the X factor in compensation relativity, as described in detail in this chapter.

When the time span of work at these levels has been ascertained, individuals in the roles being studied are asked the following confidential question, "Regardless of what you are actually being paid (and regardless of the work you would like to be doing if the work you are doing is not of total satisfaction to you) what do you think would constitute fair total compensation for the work that you are being given to do?"

If the findings are similar to those of Dr. Jaques and his colleagues in 15 different countries over 55 years, a consistent pattern will be found with individuals in a community who are working at the same time span naming the same felt fair total compensation, plus or minus about 5%. In this way, what constitutes felt fair pay norms can be found for the communities where the organization has employees. This provides a beginning sense of the values to be considered for a Requisite pay structure.

When someone with a one-year time-span role indicates that X dollars is felt to be fair for his or her level of work, those with a two-year time span describe about 2X as fair, 4X at five-year time span, 8X at ten years and 16X at 20 years. At a three-month time span, statements of felt fair pay are about 55% of X and at one-day time span 31% of X will be considered as fair.

There are a number of additional sources to get a sense of pay that is felt to be fair in a given type of organization and the communities in which it is located. These include collecting information from job applicants, recruiters, exit interviews, surveys and compensation consultants. Bear in mind, however, that it is difficult to match the level of work of roles (Band and Strata) when using data gained from these sources.

Equitable Differential Pay Example

Stratum	Time Span	Multiplier	Annual Compensation
	20 Years	16X	$1,920,000
VI			
	10 Years	8X	$960, 000
V			
	5 Years	4X	$480,000
IV			
	2 Years	2X	$240,000
III			
	1 Year	X	$120,000
II			
	3 Months	55% X	$66,000
I			
	1 Day	31% X	$37,000

2017 US$

Compression in Government and Public Service

In the public service area, pay levels are more or less equivalent to those in industry at Stratum I, II and sometimes in III but in Stratum III and IV there often begins to be a pay compression phenomenon, so that at the higher level public positions tend to fall farther and farther behind equity. In not-for-profit organizations also, compensation at the higher levels is often substantially lower than the pay levels in the profit-earning sector. Nonetheless, senior public servants have the same sense of fair pay differentials that are found in industry.

In government positions in the U.S., a congressional cap exists at the top which results in a compression in pay levels at the higher grades. In the military, the three-star and four-star generals have pay levels that are way below their counterparts in industry, and they are well aware of this. In some eras, individuals in public and social services accepted pay compression because of issues of security, retirement benefits and the gratification and satisfaction that they get out of their work. At other times conditions have resulted in government employees being better compensated than those doing the same level of work in private industry. However, even then the senior managers in these government organizations still had substantially compressed compensation, giving them a sense that society failed to recognize and compensate them for the true value of their work.

Pay Enhancement

There is an opposite aspect of pay compression and that is pay enhancement. Sometimes the pay of people working in an organization is compared to compensation received by professional athletes and stars in the entertainment industry. This is not a useful comparison because these individuals are not employees and there is no managerial hierarchy. They are not receiving an employment salary: they have private entrepreneurial contracts. People talk about the *manager* of a football team, but the professional players are not the subordinates of the team manager. Sports teams are a totally different system from that of a managerial hierarchy.

Similarly traders and brokers are also somewhat different from employees in a managerial hierarchy. Generally they do not receive a wage or a salary—they earn what they earn. Individuals in these high-commission roles are not employees in the true sense. Their work does not fit into the ordinary manager-subordinate relationship. The same is true for partnerships. Partners take a draw out of the till and if at the end of a given period of time there is money in the till they take more, if there is not they return the money to pay the bills. The partners are the owners of the organization: nobody else is arranging the financing to keep their salaries on an even basis. None of the compensation issues being discussed in this paper are relevant to entrepreneurial situations or to partnerships.

In recent years there has been a serious issue of compensation inflation for the CEOs of certain organizations. This topic is dealt with at the end of this chapter.

3. Decide Company Policy with Regard to Equity

After felt fair pay is determined for the communities of interest to the organization, the next decision is how the organization is going to pay in terms of local circumstances (similar to, above or below) and in relation to equity: full equity, some kind of compression, or whatever explicit policy the organization chooses to establish.

For example, a specialty chemical company decided to pay at roughly 15% above local equity in order to attract especially well qualified employees. A small insurance company in the same area chose to pay at about 10% below local equity.

As was mentioned earlier, often not-for-profit and government organizations pay relatively Requisite compensation for roles in Stratum I and II but compress pay ranges in Stratum III and above. Conscious decisions need to be made about how much compression and at what Strata this will occur. Requisite compensation structure provides a rational basis for considering these critical decisions.

4. Determine the Value of X for an Organization

Once the policy with regard to local equity is made, the boundary between Stratum II and Stratum III is established. This number represents the value of X.

5. Establish Values for Each Stratum and Work Band Boundary

With X decided upon, values can be established for each Stratum boundary. Values are put on one-day, three-month, one-year, two-year, five-year and ten-year boundaries between Strata. **In Requisite compensation there are no overlaps between Strata or between Work Bands within a Strata.**

Strata and Work Band Example

Stratum	Time Span	Annual Compensation	Multiplier
VII	50 Years	3,840,000	32X
VI	20 Years	1,920.000	16X
V	10 Years	960,000	8X
IV	5 Years	480,000	4X
III	2 Years	240,000	2X
II	1 Year	120,000	X
I	3 Months	66,000	55%X
	1 Day	37,000	31%X

2017 US$

For example: If local equitable pay for a one-year time span, the Stratum II/III boundary, is $120,000 per year, this represents X. The entry pay for Stratum I at one day would be 31% of X or about $37,000 and pay at the I/II boundary would be $66,000 (55% of X). Compensation at the III/IV boundary for roles with a two-year time span would be 2X and $240,000 and at the IV/V boundary 4X or $480,000. It would be 8X at the top of Stratum V or $960,000.

An Excel based calculator for establishing these boundaries is available by emailing nmrlee@aol.com.

Broadbanding

Dr. Jaques' concept of establishing compensation ranges based on level of work, at the top and bottom of Strata with no overlap, gave rise to the idea of broadbanding salaries. The problem with using a broadbanding system in organizations that are not organized requisitely is that there is no rationale for layers in the organization, and the bands do not have the clear measurement afforded by time span. Furthermore the bands are often more or less a full Stratum wide, making the spread too large for managers to handle effectively.

Merit Increases

The amount of money available for increases is decided as a matter of corporate policy. Generally a pool of money is allocated that will be used for merit increases or sometimes a decision is made that no increases will be given in a specific year. If funds are available, at the time of the personal effectiveness appraisal, the immediate manager determines which step within a band the employee is working and what merit increase each subordinate is to receive. Decisions about merit increases are based on the manager's judgment of how effectively each subordinate is using his/her applied capability. There are six Pay Steps within each Work Band. Dollar values are placed on the boundaries of each step. This enables about a 4% to 6% spread within each step. There is no overlap on the boundaries of these steps.

For someone who is performing at a level which, if continued, would be unacceptable in this role, that person receives no increase. (That situation, of course, would be in the process of being addressed through coaching and other means and both the MoR and Human Resources will have been made aware the problem.)

For the subordinate who has in some respect fallen short of fully expressed effectiveness but who is working with his or her immediate manager on improving, the manager may want to consider a merit increase of 2% or 3%. An increase of less than 2% is generally considered too small to have meaning.

Special consideration needs to be given when the subordinate occupying a role does not have the full complexity of information processing (CIP) necessary for the role because of a conscious compromise the manager had to make in filling the role. This person does not receive the same merit increases as someone who has the CIP needed to do the role. It is important not to have such individuals become overpaid since at some point they will probably be moved to a role suitable to their capability which will be in a lower Work Band.

When a subordinate has demonstrated enthusiasm and initiative and has generally fulfilled expectations, the manager may want to consider giving that person a 4% or 5% increase. This amount moves the subordinate at a steady pace through the steps in his or her role and feels like solid recognition for effective work during the year.

When an employee provides a special service to a company, a spot bonus can be given, if desired. This provides valuable recognition for the employee but does not affect the overall compensation structure.

Where a manager judges a subordinate's effectiveness to be significantly above what is expected, the situation is referred to the MoR. Separately from the manager's personal effectiveness appraisal, the MoR will consider whether a promotion to a role in a higher band is called for should an appropriate position be available. When a promotion occurs, a 10% to 25% pay increase may be needed in order to bring the SoR's compensation into line with the level of work of the new role and the employee's complexity of information processing.

Where there is no suitable role for an individual who is judged capable of a higher level role, s/he will eventually hit the top of the range in the band. Changes in the whole pay structure will move such people up in compensation over time. Only rarely should the range be exceeded with a special rate for that person if retention is a serious issue. The compensation range of Work Bands is based on the value of the complexity of the work to the organization, not on time in role or whether someone has more capability than that required by the role.

Merit pay is based upon the Pay Step within the Work Band where the manager judges an individual has been working during the past year. All individuals who are judged to be working with the same step in the same band are paid within that step. An employee gets a merit increase generally to the extent that his or her level of current applied capability is judged to have increased, again assuming corporate policy has made funds available.

Work Bands and Pay Steps
Stratum III Example

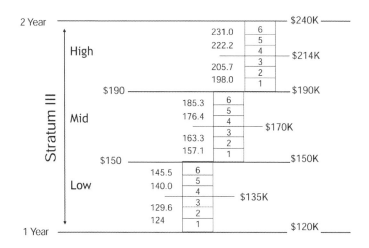

As part of the annual merit increase process managers judge employees' effectiveness in carrying out their current role. Managers judge each immediate subordinate as to whether s/he is exercising a level of current applied capability consistent with the role requirements. If the answer is yes, the manager then considers if the employee is performing like someone in the top half or the bottom half of the band of the role. If in the top half (or in the bottom half) the manager then judges if the employee is performing at the top of this half, like someone who is just able to do this level of work or like someone in the middle. Each immediate subordinate is placed in that step and the manager selects an amount falling within that step for the merit increase. The manager enters the judgment for each subordinate on a form that is submitted to the manager's manager (the MoR of those being rated) for comparison for fairness, referred to as **equilibration**.

Where an employee is judged to be using capability below the level required for the role, this situation is already being dealt with by the manager and the employee and has been brought to the attention of the MoR and Human Resources.

Manager-once-Removed Equilibration

MoRs equilibrate the judgments of their immediate managers with regard to personal effectiveness appraisals and in merit increases for Subordinates-once-Removed. Where necessary the MoR discusses with a manager any pattern of appraisal ratings or increases that the MoR considers overly lenient or overly strict. MoRs then have a meeting with all of their immediate managers together to review the appraisals and merit increases of all SoRs.

MoR's Equilibration Judgments

MoR: <u>Chan</u>   Department/division: <u>Marketing</u>   Date: <u>12/5/xx</u>

Manager's Name: Arbour	Manager's Name: Lewis
Working Above Stratum:	Working Above Stratum: Domingo

18	James		18	White	
				Nizar	
	Khan				
17	Davis		17	Kendall	
	Kenyon			Kolwalski	
16	Chou		16	Birk	
				Benson	
	Black			Brown	

ADJUSTING COMPENSATION TO
ECONOMIC CIRCUMSTANCES

With a Requisite compensation structure in place as described, the compensation system can be adjusted in relation to movements in economic circumstances, locally, country-wide or within a given industry. This is done by varying (increasing or, quite rarely, decreasing) the pay structure for changes in the National Earnings Index. It is possible to determine the way in which earnings levels have been moving in any given region or industry nationally by examining federal or local labor statistics.

When the earnings index for an industry in a region moves 2% to 3%, an organization should consider moving the whole differential pay structure by the same amount. This brings the pay structure in line with the general movement and is a separate activity from the merit increase that individuals receive.

Individuals tend to have intense feelings about pay that are related to how they are doing relatively compared with others in similar circumstances (which shows up in the Earnings Index), rather than with the cost of living which affects everyone. This is the reason that the entire compensation system needs to be adjusted on the basis of changes in the Earnings Index rather than in the Consumer Price Index (CPI).

The belief that pay has to be kept in line with movements in the CPI is seriously flawed. An employment system cannot guarantee to maintain employees' standard of living. Whether that nation can maintain a given standard of living for its citizens is an issue for the country as a whole. No organization can guarantee to maintain the standard of living of its employees because it has no control over external prices and the CPI. What an employer needs to do to ensure fairness in pay is to see that its compensation structure is consistent with the movement in the Earnings Index, ensuring that there will be general changes in the pay structure in line with norms in its industry and its community. It is up to those who work in the organization to select the standard of living that they can buy with their earnings.

COMPENSATION IN LARGE ORGANIZATIONS

An organization may choose to set up the same kind of compensation structure throughout a given country or it may want to vary compensation according to local differentials. There may be different decisions about the value of X for different subsidiaries of a corporation. These are typical complications in large scale organizations.

With a common measurement in level of work, regardless of locality, regardless of local, national or international differences, Requisite principles provide a baseline against which to develop sound policies— policies that are made explicit and policies that people can understand and accept.

Having time-span measurements provides the ability to compare equitable pay for comparable levels of work, with work levels measured exactly the same way in Omaha, London, Dallas and Singapore. This is not to say the compensation will be the same in each of those cities, although in global organizations it is sometimes quite similar.

SKILL SHORTAGES AND SPECIAL CIRCUMSTANCES

Organizations do have to pay for scarcity in certain professional areas for limited periods of time. An example is the premium pay that most information technology specialists received for many years. There simply were not enough individuals to fill the roles available and additional pay was demanded by those with the required expertise. As technology has evolved some specialties are in oversupply, while others remain in very short supply.

Companies need to do whatever is required to staff as needed, but the compensation system should not be skewed to accommodate this problem. The issue is handled by adding whatever premium is required to hire the people with the needed skills. Employees receiving premium pay should be aware of how much this premium is above the normal compensation for the level of work of the role and that the premium pay for this role may be temporary.

When the scarcity no longer exists adjustments occur over time to bring the compensation in line with the system in the company. Assuming the role is still needed by the organization, the current employee usually does not get a salary decrease but also does not get merit or earnings index increases until the pay is back in line.

In some instances it is necessary to provide compensation above the pay structure to attract employees to a certain geographic region or other special circumstance. These situations are also dealt with separately and the premium pay is given the employee as necessary. These amounts are sometimes referred to as 'red circled' rates.

FAIRNESS IN COMPENSATION

The research findings of Dr. Jaques with regard to differential compensation does not put a value judgment on the fact that, for example, someone who has the capability to manage a five-year time span feels that s/he will be fairly paid when receiving four times the compensation of someone who is capable of work at a one-year time span. These are research findings that appear to be norms of fairness that exist in society. These norms have been obscured by the underlying assumptions that people are commodities or that people are out to get the most they can and that they do not have feelings of what is fair pay.

The evidence is to the contrary and it shows that norms do exist as to a differential sense of equity in compensation for work at different levels of complexity of work. Requisite Organization provides a yardstick in the concept of time span that enables managers to know precisely what is going on with regard to the amount of accountability carried in different roles and to compare roles with each other.

Time Span and Felt Fair Pay

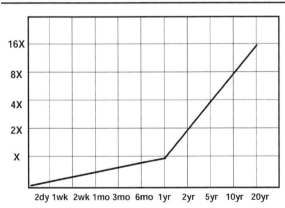

This allows global organizations to manage compensation fairly. Stratum III work in Hong Kong is the same as Stratum III in Denver, and is the same as Stratum III in Lagos. Having that knowledge, it then becomes possible to set not <u>uniform</u> standards throughout, but <u>differential</u> standards related to local conditions, all operating in terms of the same underlying structure.

Having a measuring instrument for level of work and a systematic structure within which to use those measuring instruments provides the foundation for an effective universal payment structure throughout an organization. What is needed are the underlying Requisite conditions that make fair compensation practices possible.

COMPENSATION AND GLOBAL ORGANIZATIONS

Research and experience show that Requisite compensation principles apply throughout the world. There is the same relationship to X world-wide. By determining level of work of a role and establishing X within a given country it is possible to establish felt fair pay regardless of the differing components of compensation in various countries.

Depending on the country, compensation components may include such things as a 13th month, a mandatory year-end bonus, various pension and social welfare benefits, perquisites ranging from meal tickets to cars. It is, of course, necessary to apply labor laws in any country where an organization has employees regardless of the number of employees working there. An interesting, but not surprising, finding is that for many roles in developed countries, total compensation, when converted into U.S. dollars, is more or less the same for comparable work.

There are situations when the ability to attract an employee to work in certain locations requires that the individual receive compensation similar to that in the home country. In these situations it is recommended that the employee receive the local felt fair pay with any additional amount deposited in an account in his/her home country. The employee can use these funds where and when s/he wishes.

WHAT DO EMPLOYMENT ORGANIZATIONS PAY FOR?

A major proposition in Requisite Organization is that **all employees, including those who are managers, are paid for continually doing their**

best in carrying out their assignments. Employees are accountable for using their best judgment to make decisions to overcome everyday problems that inevitably arise because conditions change.

Changing conditions include such things as extremes in weather, lack of needed materials or staff, changes in market conditions, political situations, unexpected actions by competitors and so on. The ability to adapt to prevailing conditions is the reason that human beings are employed by organizations. Where conditions are totally predictable, machines, robots or computers can often carry out the processes.

For example, in an organization whose product is delivered automatically in much the same way as natural gas, manufacturing is done near the coast of the Gulf of Mexico. When a major storm disrupted production for a substantial period of time, people had to make continuing decisions as to which customers would receive how much product during the emergency. The need was to keep the customers operative and as satisfied as possible under the very difficult circumstances. Computers provided data but did not make the critical decisions in a situation with unclear and continually changing aspects.

Managers are Accountable for the Results of the Work and the Working Behavior of Their Subordinates

An important proposition in Requisite Organization is that while all employees are held accountable for using their best efforts, they cannot be held accountable for the results of their work. Employees do not control the resources available, the quantity and quality designated, the due date or the prevailing circumstances. When employees are doing their best there is nothing further they can do.

It is the manager who must adjust timing, resources and prioritization where there is a problem in the initial task assignment or as a result of changing conditions. In a Requisite Organization, the manager is accountable for the results of the work and the working behavior of subordinates. When this practice is followed, the result is heightened morale and a minimizing of politics and game playing.

INCENTIVE AND RESULTS-BASED PAY

There are certain roles that are customarily paid by a combination of base salary and incentive pay. Many of these roles are sales related or in the customer service area. When incentive pay is part of the compensation for employees whose decisions do not directly affect the bottom line, (for example, the pricing of the product being sold) there are negative results both for the company and for the individuals involved.

Incentive Systems Lead to Manipulation

Results-based incentive compensation systems lead to manipulation. There are many games that can be played in any incentive system to achieve the maximum pay in a given year. Some examples are:

- Selling products/services that achieve the commission numbers rather than selling products suited to the customer
- Selling things to a customer that are not needed at all (This sometimes happens in financial advisory positions.)
- Loading up a tame customer at the end of the year and then taking returns the following year

Game playing such as in these examples goes on all the time where incentives are involved and everyone realizes it. Astute sales people quickly figure out how to maximize the incentive system for their own benefit rather than acting on what is best for their customers and for the organization in which they work. The focus gets misplaced from the perspective of the organization and the customer to the employee's personal financial success. The incentive system drives this type of behavior.

Sometimes individuals who are in incentivized roles are of a higher level than the role requires. They use the incentive system to gain compensation more in line with their actual level of capability. This enables them to earn more than the role is worth to the organization: it often enables them to earn more than their managers as well. (When this is the situation, consideration should be given to employing sales people as independent agents rather than skewing the compensation system.)

The fact that individuals understand what is fair pay for their level of work results in their being aware if they are overpaid and feeling a certain amount of guilt about the situation. People who are underpaid are also aware of this and are usually resentful.

Incentive systems frequently get out of line both for the level of work of the role and the complexity of information processing of the incumbent. In one organization a lead sales person received more compensation than most of the senior vice presidents because of how the incentive system was constructed. This is a situation that could not continue and eventually the person lost her job. There were hard feelings all around and the real problem was in the incentive system.

Problems with Incentives

Relationships and cooperation among employees are casualties of the competition for rewards. Many of the conditions that result in a bonus are beyond the control of the employee. Individuals know when they receive a reward they did not deserve or have compensation withheld through no fault of their own. Employees often focus on doing what earns them a bonus rather than on accomplishing assigned tasks and doing the needed work. Incentive systems tend to create a workplace in which people feel controlled, not an environment that is conducive to trust.

Incentive systems are usually annually based. Higher level selling may require longer-term vision of two, three or five years to establish certain key customers. This part of a salesperson's work will often not get the attention required because of the short-term focus of their compensation system, even where they possess the time horizon necessary to do the work. To overcome this problem one organization pays full, fair pay for sales people in this type of work and these 'big game hunters', as they are sometimes referred to, work over many years to land important clients.

Incentive schemes are expensive to construct and administer. They do not foster the behavior that is truly needed or wanted over the longer term. For example, the cost to devise and administer incentive pay to branch people in many banks is far higher that any benefits derived for the company from additional sales. Furthermore, the system in this case is often an attempt to incent people for the use of Stratum II diagnostic behavior in a role that is established at Stratum I and where the individuals' primary tasks require following clear-cut Stratum I pathways and not deviating from them.

In incentive systems there is usually no allowance for performance conditions that vary significantly from those that were predicted. When conditions change, it is often difficult to change an incentive system fast enough to fit the new circumstances. A classic example occurred when IBM lost control of the personal computer market because they assumed there would not be a major market for desktop computers or distributed computing. They continued to invest in their strategy of producing mainframes and provided their sales force with incentive plans designed to maintain dominance in the mainframe market. It took several years to reconstruct their incentive system after they realized the importance of personal computers. It took the company decades to recover.

Managers need to be able to set priorities and rapidly modify them when conditions change. In an incentive system the incentives set the priorities and reduce flexibility in changing circumstances. Incentives cause managers to appear manipulative and colleagues to appear as obstacles to each other's success. **Incentives undermine the managerial system and managerial accountability.**

Some questions to consider in the use of incentives:

- Is the prevailing thinking that sales people, or others who are incented, are paid proportionally for doing less than their best and that they will only do their best when they are working at the aspect of their roles where the incentive applies?
- Why is it felt that carrots need to be dangled in front of people in some roles to get them to do their best?

- What behavior are the sales people, or other incented employees, receiving incentives for? What of that behavior is not part of normal expectations?
- What if something needs to be done that does not fall into the present incentive system?
- Can the organization get its best sales people to work on the hard projects instead of picking up the easy sales?
- Is the incentive system undermining the organization's effort to make pay more fair and more equitable?

CHANGING TO FAIR COMPENSATION FROM AN INCENTIVE SYSTEM

Moving from incentive pay to a fair compensation system requires a number of steps.

- Establish a Requisite structure, placing work at the right level in the organization.

  Much selling work is done at one or more levels below the true complexity of the work. An example was given above of the bank teller who is asked to cross-sell bank products to customers, but who does not have the ability to diagnose the customers' issues in order to make useful recommendations. The bank teller role is generally in Stratum I and requires following prescribed processes. Stratum I work does not require the ability to analyze or diagnose.

- Staff roles with individuals who have the necessary complexity of information processing for the work of the role.

- Provide a value-adding manager for each role who plans the work appropriately in the needed time frames.

  Sales people often have as their manager someone whose role actually is that of a coordinator and who is of their same level of capability. The management of sales people often takes place through the incentive system. Incentives substitute for having a true value-adding manager who is one level of capability higher..

The most successful salespeople in incentive systems rarely want to become a sales manager or worse yet, do not want to take a role that combines both selling and managing. In these roles they cannot maximize their compensation. If they are forced into a sales manager role the company gets a poor manager and loses a good salesperson. Many organizations make this mistake over and over again.

- Use Requisite managerial leadership practices including having the manager establish tasks and their priority.
- Consistent, maximum results need to be determined by a manager and results are usually impacted by external conditions over which salespeople have little or no control.
- Pay people fairly for the level of work of their roles.
- Expect all employees to do their best every day.

The result is that the organization will achieve more sales with less cost and have more satisfied employees in the process.

COMPENSATION FOR CEOs AND SENIOR EXECUTIVES

Senior executives at Stratum V, VI and VII may have a portion of their compensation based on achieving performance targets where these individuals have an impact directly upon profitability. Boards and shareholders generally prefer paying high total compensation at these Strata if some portion of the compensation is merit award and brings risk into the situation. There may be a split payment with perhaps 50% to 75% in fixed compensation and 50% to 25% depending upon performance.

Over the past several decades CEO pay has become excessive for a number of reasons, including a lack of understanding of differing levels of complexity in organizations, the differing level of work in the CEO role and the differing capability of the CEOs themselves. The lack of a conceptual framework with which to establish differential remuneration causes salary surveys to be seriously flawed. For example, a Stratum V CEO role may be erroneously compared to a Stratum VI CEO role causing substantial inflation in the compensation of the Stratum V CEO.

These problems have led to an inappropriate upward spiral of CEO compensation. This spiral has been further compounded by captive boards, a short-term focus on market valuation and a lack of clarity of the actual amount of total compensation. Following a number of extreme and destructive examples of problems in large corporations, legislation has been enacted in the U.S. that requires more transparency in the area of senior executive compensation. Investors and boards of directors are taking a closer look at the reasonableness of the total compensation received by CEOs and other senior executives. Yet, most boards and most compensation consultants would not be able to answer straightforward questions such as:

- How many management layers does the organization need?
- How do we know?
- What is fair compensation for the CEO?
- Compared to what and to whom?
- Does the CEO demonstrate full capability to fill the role?

It is critical for boards of directors, HR professionals, compensation consultants and the CEOs themselves to have an objective way to answer these questions and measure these differences. Requisite Organization principles provide the answers to these questions.

SUMMARY

Employees at all levels in organizations value their own work and their own capability and they value it as compared to the capability of others. In employment situations people do place differential value on work that is more complex, as against work that is less complex. This understanding and these values actually exist in society. Requisite compensation principles enable organizations to handle pay differences in a fair and just way.

Differential work as measured by time span provides for differential pay. Each true differential level of work has been identified consistently to be worth two times more in total compensation than the Stratum directly below. The current applied capability of the person in the role is taken into consideration in decisions on merit increases. Removing incentives and paying compensation related to the complexity of the work of the role results in increased openness, trust and cooperation between managers and subordinates. Paying employees fairly at all levels releases their full capability and results in continuing organizational success in a socially healthy workplace.

Chapter 7

REQUISITE SUCCESSION MANAGMENT AND TALENT POOL DEVELOPMENT

"Individuals seek their deepest satisfaction in the opportunity for levels of work and future levels that match their maturation of potential capability."

Dr. Elliott Jaques

In this chapter the requisite procedure is described in detail that is used for establishing and maintaining an organization's essential pool of talent and for enabling the continuing review of all employees. Understanding the current and future capability of employees in the organization provides the basis for succession planning and for managing succession in the roles critical to the organization. In Requisite work, the term Talent Pool Development (TPD) is used to embrace the review of all employees on a regular basis as well as planning for succession and developing employees to fill roles when needed in the future.

Every organization needs to ensure that it has employees available to do the current work and those who will be able to fill anticipated future staffing needs. At the same time the organization needs to provide an environment in which each person can be assured of proper consideration of his or her potential capability in the context of possibilities.

In order to use Requisite practices and procedures effectively for a talent pool system, Requisite structure and Requisite staffing need to be in place. Having a Requisite structure ensures that levels of work have real meaning and that everyone has the same understanding of the level of complexity of work at each Stratum and in any given role. Requisite staffing provides employees with work they are capable of doing and a value-adding manager.

All Managers-once-Removed (MoRs) from the CEO on down are accountable for overseeing the talent pool process in their area. This accountability for maintaining the best possible talent pool to meet the immediate and future needs of the organization is among the most important accountabilities of every MoR. In this work they are assisted by their immediate subordinates. The TPD process is carried out with two levels of management reviewing the individuals at the next two levels lower in the organization. MoRs are generally assisted by a specialist or team in Human Resources who assist in facilitating the talent pool meetings and in capturing the relevant information for future use. A Requisite consultant is often involved in the initial stages of establishing the Requisite Talent Pool Process.

In a large organization made up of several departments or business units, this process will take place within each unit and for the corporation as a whole. Even in the largest corporations the talent pool can be dealt with by seeing to it that the business unit talent pool procedures are in place and operating, and that this information is feeding into the corporate talent pool. All of the talent pool information can then be integrated and examined in a systematic and continuing way.

MoRs and managers are the ones who make judgments of their subordinates' and SoRs' Complexity to Information Processing, with the help of the Requisite consultant in eliciting these judgments initially, often assisted by an HR specialist in Requisite Talent Pool who captures the information. Initial judgments of all employees are made. For subsequent judgment recording it is only necessary for the HR specialist to collect information about those employees where their manager and

MoR believe there has been an observable change in Complexity of Information Processing. Reviewing all employees including first line workers provides fairness in the succession planning.

For example, in a Stratum VII corporation Stratum V Presidents and their Stratum IV immediate subordinates will consider the persons in their unit at Stratum III and Stratum II as well as anyone working in Stratum I roles who is judged capable of working at a higher level. They will also seek to identify anyone working at Stratum I who is judged capable of work at Stratum II.

In a very large organization there will also be talent pool meetings within each Stratum IV unit where functional managers work with their Stratum III subordinates to review persons in Strata II and I. This provides an understanding of the talent pool available in each area so that succession planning can take place within that unit.

With this work completed the Stratum VII CEO, in a meeting with their Stratum VI Executive Vice Presidents, consider individuals in Stratum V and Stratum IV roles and anyone in a Stratum III role judged currently capable of working at Stratum IV. The CEO meeting provides an overall look at the organization and enables planning to move key persons from one area of the organization to another, as desired.

Example of Two Pools of Talent

Stratum		
VII	CEO	
VI	EVPs	
V		BU Presidents
IV		Directors
III		(Managers)

Stratum		
VI	EVPs	
V	BU Presidents	
IV		Directors
III		Managers
II		(First Line Managers)

TALENT POOL OBJECTIVES

The major objectives of the corporate talent pool development process are to:

- understand key roles that need filling now and in the future and identify possible candidates to do so
- provide equal opportunity for everyone to achieve a level of work consistent with his or her current capability as possible within the organization's needs
- ensure continuity of leadership from within through regular talent pool review
- establish a system enabling the Manager-once-Removed to mentor each Subordinate-once-Removed and plan individual development activities
- aid in retention of valued employees
- review the total talent pool to ensure that there are sufficient employees to fill the future needs of the organization

THE REQUISITE TALENT POOL DEVELOPMENT PROCEDURE

The steps in the Talent Pool Development procedure are as follows:

- Judge the Complexity of Information Processing, both the Current and Future Potential, of each employee in the organization
- Identify key roles currently needing to be filled and those roles critical to the organization for which succession planning is desired
- Identify specific employees who could fill key roles
- Identify other employees who have future potential but where no specific future role is currently apparent
- Mentor each Subordinate-once-Removed by the MoR
- Create individual development plans as relevant
- Review the total talent pool

Key Concepts Used in Judging and Discussing Individuals

Tasks differ in degree of difficulty and people differ in their ability to do tasks of varying complexity. The Requisite concepts of Complexity of Information Processing (CIP), Current and Future Potential Capability (CPC and FPC) and Current Applied Capability (CAC) provide concepts and common language to express these concepts when discussing differences in employees' suitability for any specific role. These precise definitions provide a common language to explore and discuss critical issues in talent pool management both for the present and the future needs of the organization. These concepts will be reviewed in detail before examining the steps in the talent pool development process.

Complexity of Information Processing

As was introduced in Chapter Two, a person's complexity of information processing (CIP) is the complexity of mental activity a person uses in carrying out work. CIP determines the maximum level at which that individual could work at any given time in his or her maturation, if s/he valued the work and had the necessary skilled knowledge. Complexity of information processing can be thought of as mental capability. It provides the ability to do a given level of work. CIP has to do with such things as:

- The number of factors that can be dealt with
- The rate of change of these factors that can be handled
- The ability to identify, pattern, order, categorize, synthesize and generalize information
- The ambiguity of factors that can be managed
- The ability to foresee problems and avoid or manage them
- How far in the future an individual can conceptualize

CIP provides the ability to do a given level of work based on its complexity which is reflected in employees' judgment and decision-making capability. **Time span** is the measurement of the longest tasks that must be assigned to a role. This determines the complexity of the role. An individual's **time horizon** is the longest time into the future that he or she is able to conceptualize. The goal in filling roles is to match an employee's time horizon with the time span of a role. Time span, time horizon and role complexity are dealt with in detail in *Requisite Organization* by Dr. Elliott Jaques as well as in earlier chapters of this book.

Managers can judge the complexity of information processing of their subordinates and SoR's as:

- at or above the manager's own level
- just right to be an immediate subordinate
- two or more levels below their own

The judgment of two or more levels below their own provides the sense that there is a need for one or more managers in between that subordinate and the manager making the judgment. If the managers doing the judging do not have the required capability for their role, they are not able to judge appropriately. Hence, roles need to be Requisitely structured and individuals of the right level of complexity need to be filling those roles in order for the Requisite Talent Pool Development to take place effectively.

Managers make these judgments based on experience working with their subordinates, delegating assignments and evaluating the results. It is part of every manager's role to make these judgments and, in fact, managers cannot stop themselves from doing so. This is partly how managers make decisions about assigning tasks. It usually takes about six months of experience with a new subordinate to feel fully comfortable with judging his/her CIP.

MoRs must make opportunities to get to know all of their Subordinates-once-Removed sufficiently well to make confident judgments of CIP. It is not the role of HR to make these judgments, but rather to facilitate the process.

When the judgments of the Manager and the MoR differ by a Stratum, it is necessary for them to discuss the reasons for their differing judgments and attempt to arrive at agreement. (An example would be an instance when a manager judges the individual capable of working at Stratum

III and the MoR's judgment is that the individual is only capable of a role at Stratum II.) If they cannot agree, the MoR's judgment prevails and a question mark placed by the judgment to indicate that both must observe the person more thoroughly and review the judgment again later to seek agreement.

MoRs and managers may experience anxiety in making these judgments because they are so key to each employee. For this reason it is important to recognize they are not value judgments about a person, but rather an attempt to evaluate an individual's ability to perform satisfactorily in a given role at a certain point in time. These judgments are in the best interest of both the individual and the organization.

Suitability for a Role

The ability to do the work in a specific role is based on four factors, each necessary but not sufficient by itself:

- complexity of information processing
- skilled knowledge
- values that provide the commitment to do the work of the role
- no behavior that interferes with the work getting done

To fill a role satisfactorily an individual must have at least the minimum CIP required. Skilled knowledge is an umbrella term that includes knowledge that is acquired, skills learned though practice, experience, aptitude and any required degrees, licenses or certifications. A candidate for a role must have the minimum skilled knowledge required or be able to acquire it in a timely fashion.

The work of a role must be valued. If someone is not interested in the work s/he is doing or does not want that level of accountability, it is difficult to be committed to the work and to apply one's full capability.

With regard to negative behavior, someone may be deemed unsuitable for a role if that person has significant negative temperament that gets in the way of accomplishing the work of the role. **Temperament is defined as the method of behaving or reacting that is characteristic of a person.** This is also referred to by Dr. Jaques in his later work as

required behavior and can also be thought of as considering **whether or not a person is willing and able to demonstrate the behavior required by the role.**

There is a caution here that the term 'required behavior' not be used as it may be seen as a rational to use the confusing concept of **competencies.** Over the years many organizations have sought to define a list of personality characteristics that appear to be needed for various types of roles. This list contains words that are ill defined and do not help determine whether or not someone has the Complexity of Information Processing for a role. Furthermore there does not seem to be any special set of traits that enable success in one role relative to another. Dr. Jaques compiled a list of more than 200 words sometimes considered essential for different roles and found that attempting to apply them to roles was a "fruitless and time consuming" undertaking and that not one or a collection of several was "necessary in any special degree for any particular occupation". What is necessary as mentioned earlier is that an individual has the Complexity of Information Processing and skilled knowledge for a specific role.

Where a behavioral issue is determined to exist, it is sometimes difficult for a manager or an MoR fully to judge an individual's CIP and potential. If there is evidence of negative temperament, the first thing to look for is any organizational issues that may be making it difficult for people to work together effectively. It is only when managers are confident that the organization's structure and practices are satisfactory (and requisite) that it is time to consider an individuals' behavior at work to determine if they have any characteristics that will negatively affect their ability to progress in the company. The concern in the workplace is whether an individual is sufficiently free of behavior that interferes with getting work done.

For example, the issue is not how sociable someone is, but whether that person is so abrasive that it is difficult for him or her to work with others.

In talent pool meetings all four aspects of suitability for a role are considered when discussing whether or not an individual might be appropriate for a specific role.

Suitability for a Specific Role

- Complexity of Information Processing

- Skills, Knowledge, Experience

- Commitment, Values Role

- No negative temperament issues that get in the way of getting the work done.

Current and Future Potential Capability

Potential Capability is the maximum level at which persons could work, given the opportunity to do so and provided they value the work and have the possibility to acquire the necessary skilled knowledge. It is the Complexity of Information Processing that they possess at any given point in time. This is the level of work that people aspire to and feel satisfaction when given the opportunity to do. Managers can and do judge each of their subordinates with regard to both their current and their future potential capability and it is one of their important accountabilities to do so.

Current Potential Capability (CPC) is the highest level at which someone could work **right now** if the above conditions with regard to skilled knowledge and commitment were met. In other words, CPC is his or her present level of Complexity of Information Processing.

Future Potential Capability (FPC) is the level at which someone would be capable of working **at some specified point in the future**, say five or ten years from now, if he or she gained the skilled knowledge and valued the work. Future Potential Capability is someone's Complexity of Information Processing at some specific point in the future. Managers are generally able to judge both current and future potential capability for their subordinates with reasonable accuracy when Requisite staffing, structure and practices exist.

Managers-once-Removed can make these judgments wherever they have sufficient familiarity with Subordinates-once-Removed. It is MoRs' accountability to know all of their SoRs well enough to make these judgments of their SoRs with confidence. A number of suggested ways of doing this are given later in this book.

Questions that are asked to assist managers and MoRs in judging future potential capability include:

> *Do you think this individual will be able to work at the next level in the organization at some point in the future?* If the answer is yes, ask about when the manager believes they might be able to do so.

> Then ask: *At what level in the organization might the person being discussed be able to work by the end of his or her career, if s/he were able to gain all the required skilled knowledge and wanted the role?*

Managers and MoRs are usually able to answer these questions without much difficulty. **Be sure in these discussions not to talk in terms of numbers, but speak about the roles by the titles used in the organization.** For example, ask when someone might be able to work at the Director level or the Vice President level, not by referring to the number attached to someone's judged level of CIP.

Mode

The trajectory that individuals follow in the maturation of their CIP (their potential) tends to follow patterns that Dr. Jaques identified as a result of decades of study of the development of tens of thousands of individuals in many organizations. These trajectories are referred to as a person's Mode. Mode is the highest CIP that a person could reasonably be expected to achieve. It can usually be identified by considering at what level a person might be able to work in their 60's and 70's, toward the end of their career. Managers generally have a good sense of this. Plotting the judgment of an individual's CIP on the Potential Progress chart will give an indication of the probable Mode of that person.

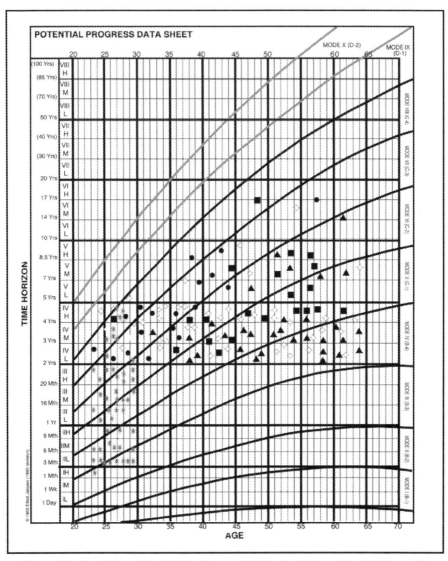

This Chart illustrates how a person's Complexity of Information Processing matures over time. The horizontal scale shows age and the vertical scale shows CIP. The curved band shows in broad terms the maturation of an individual's potential. The band as a whole indicates Mode or the ultimate potential an individual might be expected to reach.

Pads of these charts are available from www.casonhall.com. The chart is especially useful in examining an organization's talent pool in its totality both at present and also as it appears with persons listed progressed into the future, for example five years from now. Various symbols and colors can be used to indicate departments, gender, ethnicity, anticipated retirements and so on which enable issues and problems to be identified.

Current Applied Capability

As was described earlier, *Current Applied Capability* (CAC) is the ability someone is using in doing the work of the role s/he is occupying. Applied Capability is always related to the person's current role. The four aspects of applied capability are the same as in suitability for a specific role described above. In an organization, individuals are responsible for using their current CIP to the full, ensuring that they are sustaining the necessary skilled knowledge and valuing the work. In doing regular appraisals of personal effectiveness a manager judges how well each subordinate is doing in these areas. Judgments of CAC are used as part of Talent Pool discussions in helping determine who is to be considered in succession plans and for providing appropriate development plans.

There is an important difference between the Current Potential Capability that someone has at a given time and the amount of Applied Capability the person actually uses or applies in a given task or role. Current Potential Capability is often higher than the capability that someone is applying at the present time. A person's **full** potential capability for work is often not able to be used because there is something out of line—the skilled knowledge may not be complete or s/he may not value that particular task or role sufficiently. It is also possible that there may be personal problems or health issues involved.

Requisite Talent Pool Discussions

The discussions about suitability for role that take place in requisite talent pool activities use the concepts described above of Complexity of Information Processing (CIP), Current Potential Capability (CPC), Future Potential Capability (FPC), Mode, Current Applied Capability

(CAC) and Suitability for Role. Consequently, all persons participating in the discussions are using the same concepts in considering a given individual for a specific role. Requisite talent pool discussions proceed in a constructive way and, generally, little time or concern needs to be given to issues of personality or temperament. These meetings are often quite different from the experience one has had in succession planning discussions in non-requisite organizations which many times focus largely on personality issues.

STEPS IN TALENT POOL DEVELOPMENT

There seven steps in the Requisite process for Talent Pool Development and Succession Management as they are initially used in instituting this procedure are described in detail in the section of the chapter.

1. Judge each Employee and Compare the Judgments

Each employee is judged by his/her Manager-once-Removed (MoR) and immediate manager with regard to Complexity of Information Processing, considering both current potential and future potential capability. When making these judgments MoRs and managers do so by considering individual's' CIP relative to the complexity of his or her role, hence a Requisite organization structure needs to be in place. As mentioned earlier, the complexity of a role is measured by the longest task(s) that a manager assigns to that role, referred to as the time span of the role.

It is not possible to make good judgments of someone's capability if that person is not working for a manager who is one level higher in capability because that manager will not be assigning tasks of an appropriate level of complexity and with appropriate time spans.

MoRs also make preliminary judgments of their Subordinates-Twice-Removed where they know these individuals sufficiently well.

Immediate managers make judgments of their subordinates. These judgments are adjusted, if necessary, in discussions between the MoR and the employee's immediate manager. The judgments are then reviewed by the MoR and all of his or her immediate subordinate manager in discussions comparing all individuals at the next two levels down. These are called **Gearing** meetings. Judgments are adjusted as necessary as a result of these gearing discussions in which judgments are compared. In these Gearing meetings the MoR works with his/her subordinates to ensure that one manager is not judging subordinates and SoRs too highly and another too stringently. Managers sometimes use 'wishful thinking', that is, they may tend to judge that the role incumbents capable of their roles even when at some level they are aware that this is not fully the situation. In the group meetings judgments are adjusted as necessary.

The MoR has the final decision as to the CIP of SoRs because it is up to the MoR to make the determination of whether or not a person is able to work at the level immediately below the MoR and hence can be considered for a promotion. The regular review of judgments of each individual's CIP enables the organization to look at everyone's capability in equal opportunity terms, that is, to look at potential regardless of gender, race, age, or socio-economic background. The Gearing process, which is described in detail below, provides further checks and balances to ensure that all employees are fairly judged and fairly treated. The Requisite talent pool process results in each individual being considered regardless of any factors that might reflect bias or prejudice. It is a Requisite value in any employment organization to regularly consider all employees in terms of their potential and explore opportunities to use that potential.

Managers and MoRs prepare to discuss the future potential (FPC) of each individual in the talent pool and if and when they expect the person to be able to work at the next level higher. It is the MoR's responsibility to have a good sense of each SoRs current and future potential. As was mentioned earlier, it is not an immediate manager's accountability to select and prepare his or her successor.

The result of this work is a list of all employees indicating the MoR's judgment, the immediate manager's judgment, the agreed judgment and the person's Mode. By plotting the person on the Potential Progress Data Sheet described above, the Mode that is shown helps confirm the CIP judgment. Two key lists are usually maintained separately showing all persons judged to be Mode IV and above and hence possibly suitable at some point for senior management positions and those judged Mode III who could fill middle management positions.

Judgment Chart

Department/Unit: ....

Manager-once-Removed ....

Manager: ....

Date: ....

Name	Age	Birthdate	Job Title	Manager	MoR	Judgment date:		Judgment date:		Judgment date:	
						Mgr.	MoR	Mgr.	MoR	Mgr.	MoR

2. Identify Roles for which Succession Planning is Needed

In succession planning, it is necessary to determine key roles that will need to be filled now or at given point in the future. Both planned replacements and unanticipated openings are taken into account. MoRs, working with subordinate managers, determine which roles in their area need to have individuals prepared to fill them. They further identify approximately by when those roles are likely to open up due to circumstances such as retirements, promotions, and organizational change and growth.

If, for example, the Chief Financial Officer has announced she is retiring in a year, the company will want to ensure that individuals who might be suitable for that role have been identified as well as plans put in place for any development each person might require. This will enable one or more employees to be ready to be considered to fill the role when it comes open.

There are three aspects of role identification. One is to identify in the talent pool those individuals who may be able to fill roles currently open. The second is to look at roles where there is sufficient time to prepare one or more individuals to fill roles when they are expected to become vacant. The third is the need is to have a contingency plan in place in the event of an unplanned role opening. The use of the Requisite talent pool process on a continuing basis provides well-considered succession plans as well as up-to-date information in order to have contingency plans in place if a role that is especially critical should open up unexpectedly.

With regard to any role that becomes open, if it is filled by an internal person, then that person's role becomes open in turn. This cascading effect is important to bear in mind where there are aa series of roles that are critical to an organization.

The result of this talent pool work is a list by unit, or function, of key roles for which succession plans need to be in place.

3. Identify Specific Individuals to Who are Able Fill Key Roles

After initial judgments of CIP of all individuals have been made and geared, the key roles are considered one at a time. First, roles that are currently open are discussed. All persons who are judged to have the required CIP are considered with regard to their suitability for the role being discussed. As already described above, suitability for role involves the person:

- having at least the minimum required CIP
- the necessary skill and knowledge to do the role, or the ability to acquire it in a timely fashion
- valuing the role and having commitment to the work of the role
- no behavior that would interfere with doing the work of the role

This discussion takes place between the current manager of the individual, the manager of the open role and the MoR as well as any others in the meeting who have experience with the person in question. The discussion includes not only information on current and future potential but also with regard to current applied capability. (For this reason in organizations where appraisals are all done on the same cycle it is useful to schedule talent review meetings reasonably soon after the annual appraisal process is complete.) As in all requisite staffing, the MoR needs to agree to the acceptability of any candidate. The manager of the role then makes the final decision.

Once roles that currently need filling are determined, planning for key role succession in the future takes place in a similar manner described with regard to suitability for role. It is helpful, where possible, to identify two or three succession candidates for each role.

Succession management data is usually kept both by the MoR and by the person in HR who is the specialist in Talent and Succession Management.

Role Review and Succession Planning

Title of Role: ....   Date: ....

Department: ....   MoR: ....

Level of Role: ....

Possible Candidates			
Judged Capability			
Values Role			
Knowledge/Experience			
When Ready			

Notes/Actions: ....

Capability	Values Role		Knowledge/Experience		When Ready
Now	Y	Values Role	Q	Qualified	Now
or	M.	Maybe in future	M	Maybe with IDP	or
Number of years	N.	Does not value role	X	Unlikely match	Number of years

4. Identify other Employees with Future Potential

In the talent pool discussion, there are often persons with current and future potential who come to light but for whom there is no specific future role identified. These individuals are, of course, very valuable to the organization and are also to be considered for individual development plans. These plans would be of a more general nature. Once again this information is kept both by the MoR and the HR specialist.

Employee Review

Employee:		Date:
Title:		MoR:
Judged Current Capability:		Manager:

Role and Role Level			
Judged Capability:			
Values Role			
Knowledge/Experience			
When Ready			

Notes/Actions:

Capability	Values Role		Knowledge/Experience		When Ready
Now	Y	Values Role	Q	Qualified	Now
or	M.	Maybe in future	M	Maybe with IDP	or
Number of years	N.	Does not value role	X	Unlikely match	Number of years

5. MoRs Mentor each SoR

Mentoring is the process by which an MoR helps SoRs to understand how they are judged at present and how their potential might be applied to achieve full individual and career growth in the context of the needs of the organization and the opportunities that are available or may become available. It is essential that the Requisite mentoring process (described below in detail) be commenced and operational so that MoRs confirm their judgments of the Complexity of Information Processing with each of their SoRs. Judgments of each person's CIP are a matter between that person and his/her Manager-once-Removed. These judgments are regularly reviewed as part of the talent pool process and with the individual involved.

Should the judgment not be confirmed by the employee, it is considered questionable and is reviewed on a continuing basis until agreement is achieved. Sometimes specific tasks are assigned to determine if the judgment is correct. When an organization is requisitely structured and the discussions are held privately between the MoR and the SoR, such disagreements rarely happen.

Mentoring sessions take place more often with those employees who are more capable than the roles they occupy in an effort to retain them for the organization by providing continuing development. These sessions need to take place less often with employees in roles for which they are suited and who are not expected to move to higher level roles. The results of these meetings should to be communicated to the HR Talent Pool specialist in order to keep the files up-to-date.

6. Create Individual Development Plans

MoRs work with SoRs individually to determine developmental activities outside those required in their present role. There is generally one or more persons in the HR function who participate in this process and help to oversee the carrying out of the plans. These activities are discussed by the MoR with the individuals for their agreement and are also discussed with the individuals' immediate manager so that the manager is aware of and agrees with any necessary time commitment of the employee required by the plan. (Coaching and training for development within employees' current roles is carried out by their immediate manager.)

Often development plans focus largely on education outside the company. There are many other ways in which needed development can be carried out such as temporary assignments, lateral transfers and project team participation.

Individual development plans are kept by the MoR, the individual involved and the HR specialist. It is the individual's and the MoR's accountability to see that the plans are completed.

Individual Development Plan

Date prepared: ....   MoR: ....

Employee: ....   Date reviewed: ....

Manager: ....   Date reviewed: ....

Area of development	Objectives	Specific actions	By whom? By when?	Date completed
Education/Knowledge Courses, Training (off the job)				
Experience In present role, other roles, team assignment, etc. (on the job)				
General Need for coaching? Mentoring Other?				

Comments: ....

....

....

7. Review Total Talent Pool

To review the talent pool as a whole, individuals are plotted on a Potential Progress Data Sheet. Icons are used showing each person's judged CIP and position on the chart. These icons can be coded by shape and color to show such things as geographical area, function, department, gender, etc. The purpose of this charting is to identify gaps or oversupply of persons in age groups, at various work levels and in different functions. This chart enables the talent pool to be looked at as a whole to ensure that there is sufficient talent to provide future human resources for the organization. Current and emerging issues in this regard are readily identified through this process.

THE INITIAL ESTABLISHMENT OF THE TALENT POOL PROCESS

The first time the talent pool process is undertaken, it is fairly time consuming. Subsequent talent pool activities require much less time and meetings generally take place expeditiously. The initial steps focus on collecting the information on every employee so that there is an understanding of the total talent pool and to ensure fairness. This data collection is facilitated by the HR Talent Pool specialist. When this is done the initial succession planning work can be undertaken.

Steps in the Initial Talent Pool Process

1. MoRs make initial judgments of each SoR and any subordinates-twice-removed with whom they are familiar.
2. Managers make initial judgments of each subordinate and SoR.
3. MoRs hold individual meetings with each subordinate manager to review initial judgments.
4. MoRs meet with all subordinate managers to compare judgments in a Gearing Meeting.
5. MoRs hold mentoring meetings with Subordinates-once-Removed.
6. Talent pool information is entered on the Potential Progression Data Sheet and succession issues for the unit as a whole are reviewed.
7. Key roles are identified for which succession planning is desired.
8. The initial Talent Pool meeting is held discussing candidates for current and future role filling.
9. Total Talent Pool findings on the Potential Progress Data sheet are reviewed.
10. Individual development plans are created where relevant and MoRs meet with employees about their plans

These steps are described in detail below.

1. Initial MoR Judgments

MoRs judge the Complexity of Information Processing of all their SoRs and compare judgments against each other, making any desired adjustments. (It is helpful in working with managers who are making their initial judgments for the consultant to have the assistance of someone from HR who is being trained in the Requisite process.) In making these judgments the MoR considers at what Stratum individuals are capable of working now in terms of their CIP, without taking into consideration whether they have the needed skills and knowledge. This judgment of CIP is just that. The other aspects of suitability for role are reviewed when considering a person for a specific role. The MoR also makes judgments of the CIP of any Subordinates-twice-Removed whom they know sufficiently well.

In making a judgment of the Stratum in which someone is now capable of working, the MoR then considers whether the individual is:

- capable of working at the higher level of that Stratum
- more like someone at entry level
- or, somewhere in the middle

The designations of High, Mid, Low or H, M, L are used. The names are entered on a Gearing chart in pencil in the appropriate place. The MoR compares the placement of SoRs on this chart, adjusting these judgments as necessary (gearing) until s/he feels that individuals are at their proper level relative to others.

Gearing Chart

Date: _____   Manager: _____

	Boundary
Level	High
	Mid
——	Low
	Boundary
Level	High
	Mid
——	Low
	Boundary
Level	High
	Mid
——	Low
	Boundary
Level	High
	Mid
——	Low

It can also be helpful to consider when someone might be able to work at the next higher Stratum and when he or she might be able to do so, if it appears that s/he will mature there. It is useful to also make a judgment as to the highest level individuals might be able to work by the end of their career. With these judgments in mind, this information can be reviewed on the Potential Progress Data sheet to see if it roughly follows the maturation bands.

For example, in one organization two Stratum VI Vice Presidents judged a young man who was 27 to be currently able to work in a role at V Mid. This would indicate he was possibly Mode VIII or higher. On reflection and discussion with the Requisite specialist, they agreed that this did not seem correct and that they were probably over-judging this person's current CIP.

The Potential Progress Data sheet can also be used to compare individuals as to which maturation band current judgments of their CIP places them and comparing the Modes in which they fall. An example is an employee who is judged at a current level that would place him or her in a Mode VII, yet the MoR is reasonably sure that person would likely never be able to do that level of work. This information will cause the MoR to reconsider the current judgment of CIP and to hold further discussions with the individual's immediate manager and with the individual. Reviewing the Mode indicated on the Potential Progress sheet also helps a manager confirm the judgment of current potential because the Mode it indicates also seems correct.

It is essential to bear in mind that judgments of capability are approximations and that the process of making these judgments is dynamic. People are not judged once-and-for-all in a static way. People grow and change over time and at different rates. Furthermore, at any given point there may be circumstances that inhibit an individual from using his or her full capability for a period of time for reasons that are not always apparent. It is, therefore, necessary to reconsider judgments on a regular basis. This is done once a year at a minimum and in many organizations it is done twice a year. Rapidly growing organizations sometimes have quarterly talent pool reviews.

With regard to the judgments of a CEO's immediate subordinates, this is initially done by the CEO with the help of a Requisite consultant. The CEO's judgments of his/her subordinates are discussed by the CEO with the relevant individual for agreement but are not used in the CEO's talent pool meeting. Where the Board of Directors is involved with the organization, board members act as the MoR for the these individuals. Requisitely, it is the Board who will select the CEO's successor.

2. Immediate Managers make Judgments of their Subordinates' CIP

The specialist in requisite talent pool development meets with all managers involved in the talent pool to document their initial judgments of each subordinate's CIP.

3. MoRs discuss their Judgments with the Immediate Managers

The MoR meets with all his/her immediate subordinate managers one by one for an initial comparison of MoR's and the manager's judgments. If necessary, the MoR adjusts his/her judgments based on information that comes to light in this meeting. In the event of disagreement the MoR's judgment prevails, but the judgment is regularly reconsidered until agreement is achieved. It is particularly necessary to keep reviewing differences of opinion where the judgments are one or more Strata apart.

For example if the Stratum V MoR judges an SoR who is in a Stratum III role to be currently capable at 2 Mid and the immediate manager judges that individual to be able to work at 3 Low, continuing discussions are needed. It this example, not only are the judgments of the individual's capability in different Strata, but the MoR also does not believe the person is capable of the role in which he or she currently placed. This is a situation that the MoR and Manager need to address. Further information in a situation such as this will come to light as part of the MoR's mentoring meeting with the person.

It is useful to use Roman numerals to denote Strata and to use Arabic numerals when indicating judgments of a person's CIP. This way it is immediately apparent whether it is a judgment of complexity of a role or a person's CIP. Roman numerals can also be used to designate Mode. For example 3 M/IV is used to indicate someone judged with current CIP in Mid 3 who is Mode IV, that is, someone who is judged capable of working in a role at Stratum IV at some point in his/her career.

4. The Initial Gearing Meeting

When the above steps have been completed the initial Gearing meeting can take place. The judgments of the MoR and all immediate managers are consolidated on a chart for review. The HR specialist can do the actual work of plotting the individuals, compiling lists or entering the information into a computer program. This plotting of the judgments enables all the SoRs of each MoR and the SoRs of all of their immediate subordinate managers to be compared—two levels of management judging all individuals at the next two levels down. Individual contributor subordinates of the MoR who have experience with the next two levels down are also included in the Gearing meeting as they also can provide useful information in the Gearing discussions.

Each individual is compared with others who are judged to have the same level of CIP and adjustments are made as information comes to light. Once again consideration of the Mode indicated by a current level of CIP can assist in confirming a judgment. Gearing meetings ensure equal treatment of all employees and act as a safeguard against inaccurate judgments or over- or under-estimation by managers, contributing to the fairness of the process.

Where there are any unresolved disagreements between the MoR and the manager about the CIP of any individual, the discussion continues in an attempt to come to agreement. If agreement is not achieved the judgment is set aside and disagreement noted. This will be taken into special consideration when the MoR holds the first mentoring meeting with that individual.

An example is that of an employee in a Stratum II role whom the manager judged currently to be 4 Mid capable. He explained to his manager (the employee's MoR) that this particular person ran a small business on the side and used her employment to guarantee income to pay a child's college expenses. There is no requirement that people use their full capability at work if they choose to occupy a role below their CIP.

When all SoRs are reviewed, the MoR's Subordinates-twice-Removed are discussed and compared. This discussion also includes anyone from the next lower Stratum who is judged to have a CIP at the same level at the S2R's. These judgments are entered on a form that is used to track judgments over time.

5. The First Mentoring Meetings

After the initial Gearing Meeting has taken place MoRs begin the mentoring process with each of their SoRs. This initial mentoring should take place before the organization continues the talent pool process further. The completion of the judgment process occurs when the MoR has reviewed the judgment of CIP with each individual and he or she has agreed with it. Only in fully carrying through the MoR mentoring process can there be reasonable confidence in these judgments.

As well as confirming the MoR's judgment of the individual's CIP, the MoR discusses the SoR's relevant interests and values as well as seeking a detailed understanding of his/her knowledge and skills. This discussion takes place with regard to the person's current role and continues on to roles that the individual might be interested in filling in the future. These roles may include possible lateral moves in addition to possible upward steps. The MoR is seeking knowledge of each SoR's interests in relation to possible roles in the organization.

As was emphasized earlier, in these individual meetings, **judgments are discussed in terms of the roles in the organization, <u>not</u> by using numbers.** Numbers are used only for designating the level of complexity of roles in the organization and as a shorthand for discussing individuals in talent pool meetings.

In a mentoring meeting with an individual, the MoR will be discussing the aspects of suitability for specific roles including skilled knowledge, values in terms of what types of roles are interesting to the person and any possible issues of negative temperament. Where there are serious temperament issues the discussion can cover the behavior required by the organization and the consequences for continuing to demonstrate unacceptable behavior.

Complexity of Information Processing is discussed in terms of how suited persons are to their current role and when they might be capable of filling a role at the next level higher, if this appears to be the case. Discussing what types of roles an individual might be interested in later in his or her career can be useful and enlightening. These discussions can also reveal some indications of the individual's time horizon, which is the term given to the farthest in the future a person can conceptualize.

Mentoring discussions are generally held with each SoR once a year. However, for someone who is maturing rapidly with regard to CIP, more than once a year may be desirable. For employees who appear to be in the role for which they are currently suited and who are not expected to further mature in CIP, these discussions can be held every two or three years to let them know they are valued for their contribution to the organization.

The success of the talent pool process depends to a large extent upon the reliability of the MoRs' judgments. Creating confidence in these judgments results from using the following steps:

- reviewing judgments on a regular basis
- comparing them one against the other (gearing)
- discussing them with the individual's managers and with all of the MoR's immediate managers
- confirming them with each SoR

6. *Plotting the Talent Pool on the Potential Progress Data Sheet*

When an MoR has assembled judgments of the CIP of SoRs and Subordinates-twice-Removed that feel reasonably comfortable, and has confirmed them in mentoring meetings, these judgments are plotted on a Potential Progress Data Sheet. The plotting is usually done by a designated individual in the Human Resource department. These judgments of CIP are approximations: it is important not to try to be too precise in plotting. When plotting any person on the progression bands it is useful to use a circle about as wide as the size of the bands within a Stratum rather than using a small dot to indicate an individual.

The plotting of all individuals under consideration together on one Potential Progress Data Sheet provides a picture of the SoR's and the S2R's within a unit. It becomes readily apparent where there are gaps in the present talent pool that will need to be filled to achieve future plans. It is also equally apparent where there is an oversupply of people of a specific level of CIP. This enables planning about what to do in the area of oversupply where there are not expected to be positions available. In areas of undersupply steps need to be taken to employ individuals for openings where future gaps are anticipated to occur.

The icons on the chart can be progressed as a group to show what the pool can be expected to look like at a given point in the future, perhaps in five and ten years. The issues may be immediate observable and the HR specialist can also provide an analysis of the issues shown by the talent pool chart for review in MoR meetings. For example, in one organization where icons were coded for retirements, the group realized that within five years, as much as 25% of the work force would be eligible for retirement. This led to some serious discussions on how to fill those roles and also how to retain the organization knowledge that was going to be lost.

When the talent pool has been charted, the work of succession planning can begin.

7. Identify Roles for Which Succession Planning is Desired

These roles can be identified during the initial gearing meeting described in Step 4 above or the HR talent pool specialist can gather the information from the appropriate managers prior to the talent pool meeting. The MoR should review and approve the list

8. Hold the First Talent Pool and Succession Management Meeting

Once individuals' CIPs have been judged and the gearing and mentoring meetings have been held, the MoR and immediate subordinate managers hold the first talent pool and succession management meeting. Key open roles are first discussed and all employees with the necessary CIP are considered. As mentioned earlier, discussions center around each person's skilled knowledge and whether he or she would value the role. If necessary, any behavior is discussed with the focus on issues that would interfere with the person's ability to accomplish the work of the role.

The MoR approves any candidates deemed suitable for the open role and the manager of the role decides whom to select. This is the normal requisite process whereby an MoR determines the slate of candidates for a role and the immediate manager chooses who will fill the role from the list.

Once discussions of all open roles are completed, the roles needing succession planning are considered. All employees who have the required CIP or whose CIP is judged to mature to that level by when the role needs to be filled, are reviewed with regard to suitability for the role. The goal is to identify two or three possible succession candidates for each role wherever possible. It is sometimes necessary to hold more than one meeting to complete the initial talent pool work.

After all the identified roles have been discussed, any employees who are believed to be able to move to higher level roles at some future time, but who have not been identified for a specific role, are considered one by one. Possible future roles or types of roles for which they might be suitable are identified.

9. Review the Potential Progression Data Sheet

As part of the initial talent pool meeting the group, as a whole, reviews the total talent pool chart developed in Step 6 above. The issues apparent on the talent pool chart can be discussed with regard to possible solutions. This includes instances when there are insufficient individuals of a given age group and CIP to meet the organization's future needs and where there may be too many people in an age group or capability range.

10. Create Individual Development Plans

Working with the assistance of the HR talent pool specialist, the MoR creates an individual development plan for each employee being considered for future roles. This can be done subsequent to the talent pool meeting. These plans need to be coordinated with any plans the immediate manager may have for development within the current role. The MoR determines what organization resources are to be provided to employees as part of their development for the future. Employees determine how much of their personal time and energy they choose to put forth based on their ambition and aspirations.

The Comprehensive Organization Chart

A useful tool in talent pool meetings is a chart that contains detailed information about every employee. This chart, called a Comprehensive Organization Chart, can be developed once the first judgments are gathered. It can be used in the initial talent pool meeting and updated for each subsequent meeting.

On the Comprehensive Organization Chart each role is shown as a box on the chart in the appropriate stratum and band with the reporting relationship indicated. Included in each box is:

- The Title of the Role

- Name of the Role Incumbent (or 'Open' if the role is not currently filled)

  If there is a grade in addition to the band within a Stratum that grade is included in the box. When an organization uses SAP or an HRIS, it is also useful to include any number given to the role and any number given to the individual.

- Total Compensation for the Past Year

  There generally are two versions of the Comprehensive Organization Chart. One shows the total compensation, the other does not. In the first instance this version of the chart is for the manager and his/her manager to review for compensation equity. The second version without the compensation is used in talent pool meetings. Using the chart showing compensation in the talent pool meetings leads to discussion outside the topic of role filling and succession.

- The Most Recent Judgment of CIP and possible Mode that it indicates

  As part of the requisite process this judgment has been discussed between the manager and the MoR. It also has been discussed between the MoR and SoR and that person's agreement gained. The person's Mode is also indicated.

- An Arrow Up or Down where Relevant

  An arrow is placed next to individuals' names to indicate when they have CIP judged one stratum higher or lower than their current role.

Where there are a number of individuals in the same role the names, compensation, judgment, mode and arrow can be in a list below the box containing the role title. A double line is used around the box if the role manages subordinates.

For talent pool meetings it is useful to blow up these charts on a plotter and post them in the front of the room so that everyone participating has all of this information.

Comprehensive Organization Charts have many uses outside of the talent pool process. They provide a holistic view of the organization levels, reporting relationships, role compression and gaps, span, diversity, and compensation equity. Color and other coding methods can be used to indicate such things as location, department, gender, anticipated retirement and so on. These charts and their use is described in greater detail in an article in the Appendix.

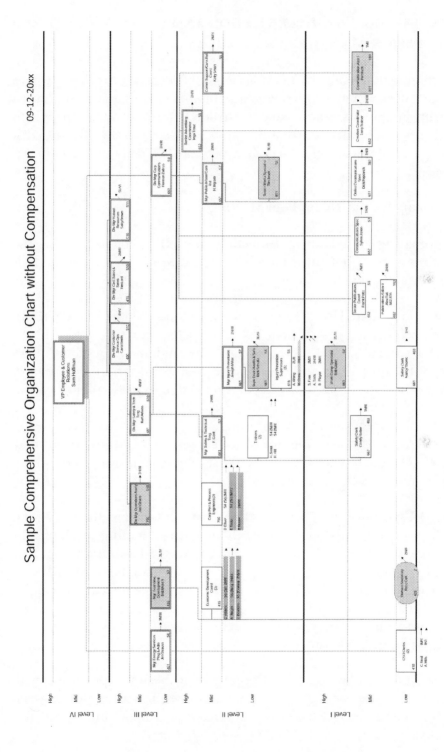

Sample Comprehensive Organization Chart without Compensation   09-12-20xx

CONTINUING THE TALENT POOL AND SUCCESSION MANAGEMENT PROCESS

In subsequent talent pool meetings it is only necessary to take up where the last meeting left off, to review and modify current plans, to change existing judgments as necessary and to add new roles and new people to the list. Much of this information can be collected by the HR specialist prior to these meetings which then take far less time than the initial meeting.

Preparing for the Talent Pool Meeting

In preparing for talent pool meetings the HR specialist reviews the existing talent pool information with the MoRs and each of their subordinate managers covering:

- An updated list of individuals and an updated list of judged CIP

The HR specialist reviews with managers their judgments of subordinates and SoRs, recording any changes in their thinking in this regard. Additions or deletions to the list are made due to personnel changes.

- Key open roles needing filling
- Any additional roles for which succession needs to be planned
- The current succession plan list, identifying those roles which might need to be revisited

The HR specialist then prepares these lists and reviews them with the MoR prior to finalizing them for the meeting. Meetings are typically held once or twice a year, but in rapidly growing organizations they may occur quarterly. This succession planning information is also useful for any role filling that needs to take place outside the formal meetings.

Develop a List of Persons who are at Risk of Leaving the Organization

A useful list to develop as the organization becomes proficient with the talent and succession management process is a list of persons who may be considering leaving the organization, called an 'at risk' list.

Employees are often at risk of leaving because they are under-employed, that is, in a role that does not use their full capability. This sometimes occurs when there is not a role open in the company that is at the right level for the person. As part of the talent pool process persons believed to be at risk can be discussed with regard to the reason they may be at risk. Ideas can be generated as to what might be done to enrich their current role and/or development activities they might be given in an effort to retain them until an appropriate role opens up.

MENTORING AND INDIVIDUAL DEVELOPMENT

In Requisite work, mentoring is the process by which a Manager-once-Removed helps Subordinates-once-Removed to:

1. understand their potential and how the full use of that potential might be developed to achieve career growth within the organization
2. achieve full use of their capabilities as they themselves seek and as opportunities in the organization allow

Mentoring is so essential to individual and organization development that it must not be a haphazard effort done by volunteers or something provided by HR or outside consultants. It is among the most important accountabilities of MoRs at all levels.

As mentioned earlier, it is up to MoRs to make the final decision as to the judgment of employees' potential capability, both current and future. It is MoRs who are accountable for knowing who of their subordinates-once-removed are possible successors to their immediate subordinates or are ready for other assignments or promotions elsewhere in the organization. The MoR determines what might be possible for each SoR from a larger organizational perspective. MoRs also decide what developmental resources are to be committed to any given SoR within organizational policy. SoRs decide what they want to do and how much personal time and energy they wish to invest.

Why the Manager-once-Removed?

Why is mentoring the accountability of MoRs? Historically, many organizations have expected managers to choose and develop one or more successors for their role. There are obvious reasons why this is an unwise practice. The foremost reason is that someone selected to move up will then be working at the same level as that of the manager. It is therefore the manager's manager who is in the best position to make a judgment as to when employees have, or are likely to have, the capability to move up to the next level.

In the Requisite process, it is MoRs who are held accountable for understanding the talent pool strengths and weaknesses of the organization two levels down, because that is the pool from which successors emerge for filling vacancies among the positions at the level immediately subordinate to them. The MoR has a wider view of the organization and is in a position to judge where any given SoR's CIP, skilled knowledge and values/commitment might be most appropriately used.

There are other reasons, as well why the immediate manager is not the best person to determine when an individual is ready to move up. These include the situation where the manager does not wish to lose the individual from the unit or where the manager and subordinate do not get along well so that the manager may not wish personally to see this individual promoted. The gearing process helps achieve fairness in these situations. A number of organizations use a practice of 'give one, get one' to help with the former issue, that is, if a prized employee is needed elsewhere in an organization then that manager, when s/he has an opening, is among the first considered to select a valued employee from another area in the organization..

A major purpose of mentoring is to let employees know that they are recognized for who and what they are as individuals, and that this recognition involves more than their present performance in their current role. Mentoring establishes a relationship that allows each employee's capability and contribution to be recognized, not just by the immediate manager, but by the organization as a whole. The mentoring process is equally appropriate and necessary for SoRs who have future growth potential and for those who appear to have matured into the highest level of CIP that they will use for the rest of their working career. The meetings with individuals with growth potential take place more frequently.

Mentoring is a process that includes:

- helping SoRs understand their potential and how the full use of that potential might be developed
- providing an opportunity for SoRs to consider their interests, values and aspirations in the context of the longer term needs of the organization
- discussing specifically what SoRs should be doing to develop themselves, with a larger perspective than just that of their current role
- exploring possible opportunities for lateral transfer experiences and project assignments when appropriate
- reviewing possible upward moves that may be available now or are anticipated in the near future
- helping to keep SoRs challenged in their existing roles if they are unlikely to change roles in the foreseeable future
- helping SoRs to achieve as full a use of their capabilities as the opportunities in the organization allow and as they themselves seek

Mentoring requires no special counseling skills on the part of MoRs. In these discussions when held one-on-one, people are generally realistic about themselves and desire to be so. They are eager to have discussions about their future and to know that they are valued by the MoR and the organization. The CEO is the one to lead the process of systematic mentoring and then see that it is carried out at each level. It then becomes embedded in the organization resulting in an atmosphere of strong mutual trust, grounded in reality.

Timing of the Mentoring Process

The mentoring process should take place formally every one or two years, depending upon the expected rate of growth of the company and the maturation of the individuals concerned. During a period of rapid expansion mentoring may need to happen more often than once a year for some employees. An SoR may also request a mentoring session outside the normal schedule when s/he feels such a meeting would be helpful.

Judging Potential

The MoR is the person accountable for judging each SoR because the MoR is further removed from the SoR in terms of Complexity of Information Processing than is that person's immediate manager. Therefore, the MoR is better able to judge that person's future potential in the organization. Furthermore, only someone working at the MoR level can requisitely give an SoR a promotion to the next stratum.

MoRs must keep in mind that judgments of potential are subject to change and must always be checked against the SoR's own assessment and that of the immediate manager. However, the MoR is ultimately accountable for making the assessment that will be used. It must also be remembered that assessments are constantly under review and are a reflection of what the MoR believes at a given point in time. These judgments are kept track of over time to see the pattern that results. This is done by entering the data on a Judgment Chart along with recording who made the judgment and the date when it was made.

There is often an erroneous assumption associated with assessments of potential. This assumption is the incorrect belief that everyone aspires to move upward in the organization regardless of their capability. Individuals are generally aware of and realistic about their own potential. Unless inappropriately goaded by parent or partner, they do not seek to overextend themselves by progressing above the capability that they truly feel they have at any given time. Rather, people seek work that is consistent with their current potential and they seek progression to match their future potential as it develops. Publicly individuals may overrate their current potential in order to bolster their self-esteem. In private, most individuals are realistic about their current and future potential. This is particularly evident in one-on-one mentoring meetings between an employee and his/her MoR.

Having the MoR share and discuss all judgments of potential with the SoR before firmly committing to one that is recorded is an important safeguard in achieving sound evaluation of an SoR's potential. This enables the SoR to understand the MoR's judgment and to have the opportunity to put forward his or her side of the issue. If the SoR is not happy with the judgment, the MoR should leave it open until s/he has had a chance to investigate it more thoroughly. In situations of this kind, over time MoRs may uncover additional information that would cause them to confirm or revise their assessments. At the very least, the MoR should formally note that the SoR does not agree with the assessment.

Decisions with regard to the development of individuals outside of their current role are made by the MoR in consultation with the immediate manager and with the SoR involved. Human resources staff can assist in the developmental activities of individuals as requested by MoRs, but they are not to make judgments of current and future potential of individuals or decisions about developmental needs and opportunities.

Mentoring SoRs

Mentoring ensures that every individual is treated with care and concern and has the opportunity for continued equality of treatment. The process has four aspects:

1. preparing some preliminary ideas about each SoR, reviewing the CIP judgment and other relevant information with the immediate manager
2. having the SoR consider interests, values and goals
3. holding the mentoring meeting to discuss the CIP judgment and the SoR's future objectives and to create developmental plans with the SoR where relevant
4. gaining the SoR's agreement and planning follow-up as needed

The mentoring process has the following specific steps:

1. Get to know SoRs
2. Gather Preliminary Ideas
3. Hold the Mentoring Meeting

4. Gain Subordinate's Agreement and Plan Follow-up

Step One: Get to Know SoRs

MoRs need to make the opportunity to get to know each SoR well enough to be able to judge current and future potential and to provide meaningful mentoring. MoRs must make opportunities to have a number of serious talks with their SoRs to gain additional knowledge about them.

An important source of MoRs' information about SoRs occurs in meetings with the immediate managers of SoRs with regard to the formal annual personal effectiveness appraisal. MoRs will also want to discuss with the SoR's immediate manager the continuing coaching work that has been going on with the subordinate during the year and any development activities that are underway with the regard to the SoR's current role. MoRs hold meetings with their immediate subordinate managers for the express purpose of gathering information about their SoRs.

MoRs also take into account the views of other appropriate persons who have knowledge of their SoRs. When using second-hand sources of information, MoRs should check these sources for accuracy and lack of bias. The MoR must be confident that this information is sound and also ensure that s/he has adequate first hand experiences with individual SoRs.

MoRs need to plan work-related experiences and personal contact with their SoRs, without interfering with the immediate manager's day-to-day working relationships with them. For example, MoRs can, with the agreement of the immediate manager concerned, seek to provide occasional opportunities for their SoRs to work for them in a direct output support role or on a project team the MoR is leading. The opportunity to work directly with the SoR enables the MoR to observe the SoR's current approach to work. These assignments are also developmental for the SoR because s/he can become acquainted with some of the issues and problems at this higher level in the organization.

It is useful for MoRs to hold three-level meetings in particular for setting high level context for the work of the unit but also as an opportunity to observe SoRs. From time to time MoRs attend meetings that their subordinate managers are holding with their subordinates, who are of course their SoRs, to make additional observations.

Observing the SoR in his or her current role and in project work helps the MoR evaluate whether or not the SoR is capable of work at the next higher level in the organization.

Step Two: Gather Preliminary Ideas

The MoR and the SoR need to take time to consider both the SoR's potential and what can be done to work toward fully using that potential. Prior to a mentoring session the SoR will need to take adequate time to consider his or her own future in the light of personal values, interests and goals. MoRs will need to consider questions such as:

- Is the SoR capable of the level of work complexity in his/her present role or is the present role beyond the capability of the SoR at this time?
- Is the SoR at ease with the difficult tasks in this role?
- Is the SoR under-utilized at this time?
- If the SoR is under-utilized or not capable of his/her current role, what might be a better use of this person's ability in roles that are at a higher or lower level in the organization? Specifically, what might those roles be?
- Are the SoR's interactions with others appropriate and does s/he demonstrate the required behavior?
- Does the SoR approach his/her work with enthusiasm and apply his/her full capability?
- What level in the organization does the SoR now have the potential to work? (his/her present level? one level above? the MoR's level?)

> about a year from now?
> three years from now?
> five years from now?
> by the end of his/her career?

In each of these instances, what roles might that person fill?

Prior to the mentoring meeting, the MoR has made a tentative judgment with regard to the SoR and reviewed it with that person's immediate manager. It is important for the MoR to keep an open mind because evidence may come forward in the interview to change the tentative judgments. The MoR compares his/her current judgment of the SoR with judgments of all his/her SoRs and reviews information from gearing meetings.

The MoR should have in mind some individual development activities for the SoR. Developmental activities may include such things as on-the-job training, formal courses, committee and project team assignments or temporary role assignments. Human resources can often provide help in planning developmental activities. Such activities are also valuable for employees who are in an appropriate role and where there are no present plans for a role change. Development for employees in this situation might include identifying work experiences that give them an opportunity to expand their repertoire of knowledge and skills in new areas within their current role. This may include training in a new technology or being assigned new tasks. There is frequently the opportunity for continuous improvement projects in which such persons can participate.

MoRs, as mentioned earlier, discuss their plans for individual development with each SoR's immediate manager, since the developmental activities need to be coordinated with the person's work schedule. Such scheduling is for the immediate manager and the SoR to work out.

MoRs seek to ensure that SoRs are not denied upward mobility because of current work demands. Immediate managers must be willing to approve positive transfers and/or promotions appropriate for the development of the individual and that are required to meet the current and future needs of the organization for well trained, capable people. Immediate managers participate in planning such transfers and promotions. These moves should not come as a surprise to them.

The MoR works closely with the SoR's immediate manager in situations where there is no planned role change. These SoRs may not require mentoring each year, but they need to be recognized for their contribution, reassured of their continued value to the organization, and be helped to understand that their aspirations and the needs of the company may change at some future date.

Step Three: The Mentoring Meeting

The focus of the mentoring meeting is on the individual's potential, both present and future, his or her interests/values, any behavioral issues that may be hindering progress, and skills and knowledge needed in line with developing potential. More than one meeting may be required, depending on the circumstances. The first meeting typically takes about an hour or more, subsequent meetings may take less time.

The initial meeting may cause some anxiety on the part of the SoRs. Most organizations have not used this requisite practice and have not had the MoR regularly meet with SoRs to discuss how they are viewed by the organization and their future aspirations. After the first meeting employees generally look forward to these discussions which are such an important part of their individual development.

The desired outcome of the meeting(s) will be agreement between the MoR and the SoR as to that person's current and future potential and as to developmental activities that will help the SoR work toward achieving his or her potential both now and in the future.

The MoR initiates the mentoring discussion by obtaining the SoR's view of significant events in his/her career as well as information on that person's interests and aspirations. The MoR can then relate these views to his/her judgments of SoRs' potential.

As discussed earlier, the MoR should not commit to a final judgment that is recorded until after the mentoring meeting. If there is disagreement and the SoR believes that his/her potential has been underestimated or overestimated, this disagreement must be resolved by the MoR and SoR in a follow-up meeting or meetings prior to the individual development discussion. When the SoR's interests/values, skilled knowledge and any behavioral issues are carefully separated from his or her potential, it is rare that there is disagreement around the SoR's potential. Should disagreement continue, the MoR can report the lack of agreement, both parties can work with Human Resources on the issue or, if necessary, the matter can be referred higher.

Once an individual's potential assessment has been completed and agreed upon, the discussion should turn to his or her career interests and aspirations and then to developmental needs. These needs are discussed both in terms of general objectives and of specific development that is desirable. In some instances it may be possible to identify specific means of achieving developmental objectives, including details as to how and by when. In other situations it may not be possible to specify actions in this meeting since the developmental activities may involve other people, such as training by the immediate manager, transfer to another area and so on.

After relevant people have been contacted and when the outline of the developmental activities has been agreed upon, further work may still be required to confirm the details with regard to specific actions, resources and accountability.

Following are two brief examples of a mentoring discussion.

MoR: "Julie, I'm glad we have this time together to discuss your current work and to think about any future roles in the organization that might interest you. In our talent pool meeting there was general agreement that you are doing a fine job in your managerial role and that you have the potential to move to a role at the next Stratum when there is an appropriate position open. How do you feel about that?"

Julie: "Yes, I feel that way too and I've been thinking about what I might like to do."

MoR: "Let's consider what roles you feel you might be suited for and discuss what additional experience you might need."

In a mentoring discussion with a person not yet fully filling their role, the dialog might be similar to this:

MoR: "Larry, in our talent pool discussion it was generally agreed that you need additional experience in your present role before being considered for a move. What do you think about that?"

Larry: "Well, I've been working as hard as I can to do all the things my manager assigns, but I do find some of them difficult. I just don't understand some of the work as well as I would like to. My manager is helpful whenever she can be. We discuss the problems and she gives me some coaching but I'm still having difficulties keeping up. Having these tight deadlines is a lot different than college assignments. I think it will take me some time until I master this work. Even so, I do aspire to be a programmer analyst and one day even an information architect."

MoR: "Let's review this again in six months or so, unless you'd like to talk sooner, and we'll see how things are going. We can begin then to look at what additional experience might be useful to help you prepare to be a programmer analyst."

Step Four: Gain Subordinate's Agreement and Plan Follow-up

The subordinate will need to agree with the assessment and the developmental plan. If there is no agreement further meetings are held until there is a mutually agreed-upon judgment and plan for development. The immediate manager, working in conjunction with the subordinate, coordinates the subordinate's schedule of work and developmental activities. The MoR and the SoR will usually arrange meetings to review progress and make future plans. The Talent Pool specialist acts as facilitator in this process.

Mentoring is Essential to the Organization and to Each Individual

Mentoring is not an accountability that can be taken lightly or viewed as something that takes place only if and when an MoR finds time. MoRs must make the time to mentor their SoRs. MoRs set an example for all of their SoRs who are MoRs now, or who will be in the future, by fully carrying out this process. Mentoring skills are an essential component of the accountabilities of MoRs.

SUMMARY

Managers are required, as part of their work, to regularly assess the potential of the employees in the organization. Judging the future potential of their SoRs is the responsibility of Managers-once-Removed. This accountability is among the most important duties of MoRs at all levels because it is the source of the organization's future growth, as well as a source of guidance to individuals with regard to their growth possibilities within the organization. It is also a vital step in the retention of employees.

Talent Pool meetings between the MoR and his/her subordinate managers to review all employees the next two levels down from the managers is a continuing process. As was mentioned earlier this should be done at least once or twice a year and even more often in a rapidly growing organization.

In discussions with Dr. Jaques he roughly estimated that about 35 to 40% of the population have the CIP to work in Stratum I roles, another 35 to 40% have the CIP for Stratum II roles, about 10% for Stratum III, perhaps 5% for Stratum IV and very small percentages in descending amounts are able to work at Stratum V roles and above. Hence it is probable that there are not many individuals who have the Complexity of Information Processing to fill management roles at mid-level and above. Organizations need to be aware of and carefully nurture those who are able to do so.

Requisite Talent Pool and Succession Management provides a deep understanding of the human resources available in the organization from which ensure that there are internal candidates prepared to fill roles that become open and to make critical individual staffing decisions.

Chapter 8

THE NOVUS STORY

In 1991 Mitsui & Co. Ltd. and Nippon Soda, Ltd. jointly acquired the Feed Ingredients Business from Monsanto Company. Dr. W. Joseph Privott, who was then running this business, was asked to become president of the new company. The new owners gave Dr. Privott the freedom to organize this new entity as he saw fit.

One of his early activities was to seek out ways of creating a work environment that would result in both business success and treatment of employees in a socially responsible way—providing a great place to work. As part of that effort, Dr. Privott attended a week-long seminar at the Levinson Institute. Dr. Elliott Jaques presented part of the seminar.

The ideas Dr. Jaques set forth appealed to Joe and he believed they would help him achieve his objectives for the new company. In particular, the logic and internal consistency of Requisite Organization concepts interested Joe Privott because they provided an approach to management as a science rather than an 'ad hoc' art. (Joe is a Ph.D. scientist as were many of the senior managers at Novus at that time.)

Joe Privott found in Elliott Jaques' ideas a practical approach that would help him not only enable Novus to achieve its mission and be financially successful but also to provide a healthy place to work. Joe asked Elliott who he would suggest to come to St. Louis to help implement the system, and Elliott suggested Nancy Lee, who had been working with his ideas for a number of years. Joe asked Nancy for a commitment of two weeks a month until the implementation of requisite concepts was well underway.

Thus began an almost ideal requisite project. Here was a newly formed company where the private owners gave the president the freedom to establish the philosophy and practices that he felt were most appropriate. One year from its founding of Novus work started toward establishing a requisite organization.

Background on Monsanto and Novus

In the 1950's Monsanto, a St. Louis-based company, began applying chemistry to and developing businesses in three areas related to feeding the world: plant production, animal production and food production. It was soon recognized at Monsanto that the most significant payoff was in the area of herbicides for more efficient plant production. Monsanto, therefore, focused most of its resources in the plant area but maintained small businesses in animal and food production.

In the mid-1970's, Monsanto scientists made a major discovery that led to a new lower cost in the production of methionine, a nutritional animal feed additive. In the early 80's Monsanto built the world's largest methionine plant and began to grow market share. Joe Privott was brought in as the plant was being built to develop and execute the marketing plan.

By 1990 Monsanto again decided its strategy would be to focus most of its efforts on crop chemicals with an emphasis on biotechnology. The company also decided to divest the Feed Ingredients business which had methionine as its major product.

During the new company's formation it acquired a name which, under the circumstances, was very appropriate. One of the employees suggested that the company be named Novus, a Latin word which roughly translates as 'new beginning', and this name was adopted.

In the early years, Novus' mission was 'help meet the growing worldwide demand for high quality, affordable food'. There were 160 employees and gross sales were about $250 million dollars.

A New Beginning using Requisite Principles and Practices

Early steps in the introduction of requisite organization included:

- educating the senior management team of nine individuals
- analyzing the present organization
- getting preliminary judgments of the complexity of information processing of each person in the top three levels.

Educating Senior Management

The senior management team was introduced to requisite concepts as part of their regular weekly management meetings. These meetings were extended to allow a one hour presentation on a particular aspect of RO followed by a question and answer period. These presentations by Joe and Nancy were intended to both educate these managers and gain their agreement as to the reasonableness and usefulness of these concepts. Nancy also prepared a brief written paper on each key concept for use in these meetings.

Novus was fortunate to have Sir Roderick Carnegie visit early in the project when he made a presentation on requisite concepts and his experience with them as CEO of CRA, an Australian mining company. His question and answer period helped the senior management explore their doubts about requisite procedures. Rod had worked for more than a decade with Elliott in the formation of many requisite concepts. Rod's visit brought a great deal of credibility to the Requisite Organization approach and also provided encouragement to senior management to spend the necessary time and energy to implement the system.

Analyzing the Extant Organization

Nancy undertook a review of the extant organization, that is the organization as it currently existed in terms of roles, reporting relationships, work being done and time span of key tasks in each role. She interviewed Joe first as to the work he was expecting of each the management team's units and key accountabilities he was giving to each subordinate manager.

Next she interviewed each member of the management team as to their understanding of the results that were expected from their units. She then explored how they divided this work up among subordinate roles. At the same time she sought data on some of the longest tasks for which they believed they were responsible, as well as information on the longer tasks they delegated to subordinate roles. Occasionally Joe's view and the understanding of a given manager were not fully aligned. When this was the case, Nancy worked to achieve full clarity and agreement.

This information yielded a picture of a Stratum VI organization comprised of five layers where virtually all the roles were Stratum II to Stratum VI. There were very few roles at Stratum I.

Stratum VI Organizations

At that point in time, the early 1990s, Elliott felt that a Stratum VI company was perhaps somewhat unstable and needed to grow to a Stratum VII or become a Stratum V organization. This had been his observation up until that time, although he was not able to articulate fully his reasons for the possible instability of Stratum VI companies. (Subsequently he came to believe that Stratum VI companies were viable as he experienced more and more of them, possibly occurring because they actually had only five layers, with most Stratum I work being handled by technology.)

In fact, Joe was interested in growing what had been a Stratum V business group within Monsanto, into a Stratum VII company that dealt with a wide variety of related products. He sought to have these products added largely through acquisition, but internal development and joint ventures were other possible avenues.

Initial Judgments of Employees' Complexity of Information Processing

Joe provided initial judgments of the Complexity of Information Processing (CIP) of each of his subordinates and Subordinates-once-Removed. (Joe's judgments over a number of years were recorded. Not surprisingly the changes in the judgments paralleled the expected growth in complexity of individuals as anticipated on the Potential Progress Chart developed by Dr. Jaques.)

The senior management team also judged the complexity of information processing of their subordinates and Subordinates-once-Removed. This gave a picture of the capability of the employees from Stratum VI to Stratum III.

Joe felt Elliott's approach to judging complexity of information processing clarified the issue of capability and separated it from values, knowledge and temperament. Requisite Organization provided concepts, a vocabulary and tools to consider these quite different issues and to talk about them.

Addressing Issues of Temperament

As the power of the use of requisite practices began to become evident at Novus, Joe turned his attention to issues of temperament. He wanted a method of understanding and discussing issues of behavior and a way to take temperament into consideration in staffing decisions. His goal was to find a way to assist individuals and groups to behave more effectively at work.

Nancy recommended Ken Wright, a specialist in this area, who also has a deep understanding of Requisite Organization. Ken used the Human Synergistics' instrument as an information gathering tool and catalyst both for individual discussions and to enhance understanding of interpersonal issues within groups and teams. Work in this area began along with the ongoing implementation of requisite practices.

Examining Cross-Functional Working Relationships

Another area that was addressed early in the project was that of the interface between units. An off-site meeting was held, to review areas where improving clarity in accountability and authority between roles reporting to different managers would likely produce increased effectiveness for Novus. The requisite descriptions of Task Initiating Role Relationships (TIRRs) were used as the means of addressing some of these issues and specifying what the roles involved needed to do. Joe was aware that this was often a source of interpersonal problems that were apt to lessen when the relationship between roles in different areas were clearly described.

In practice it was found that not all of the TIRRs were needed and a smaller subset was developed for ongoing work in this area. These relationships were renamed Cross Activity Relationships (CARs) to indicate that not all of the requisite concepts were included.

Developing Requisite Processes for Novus

Working with the Manager of Human Resources, Sabrena Hamilton, a document was developed to clearly state Key Accountabilities. This document coordinated with an appraisal document designed at the same time that was intended to be used both informally at mid-year and for the formal annual appraisal.

A manual was developed for all Novus managers that described the integrated process of identifying and communicating to each employee their key accountabilities, providing feedback and coaching when tasks were completed and judging overall personal effectiveness. These processes plus the other eight requisite managerial leadership practices were described in the manual. The full set of procedures, as well as the manual, was entitled The Novus Management System (NMS). Sabrena and Nancy also reviewed all Novus policy documents to modify any aspects of policy and procedures that were non-requisite.

Key Accountabilities Document (KAD)

This document was designed to include key tasks and general responsibilities, team assignments and critical cross-functional accountability and authority. A general statement was included to the effect that persons in managerial roles will also be judged with regard to their full use of the requisite managerial leadership practices. (Novus' document is similar in design to the Role Specification form recommended as Requisite.)

Personal Effectiveness Appraisal (PEA)

One of the areas of extensive discussion in designing the Personal Effectiveness Appraisal process and the document was whether or not to include 'exceeds expectations' as well as 'meets expectations', 'below expectations' and 'unacceptable'. The decision was made to follow Elliott's recommendation of not including an 'exceeds' rating, since meeting expectations is what is expected of all employees.

Joe Privott found that an important contribution made by requisite concepts was that accountabilities should be identified by the manager's intended time to completion. This might well be shorter or longer than the annual appraisal cycle. When it was necessary to judge tasks lasting more than a year for the annual review, managers were given the option of considering the setting of a milestone in the progress of that task.

Educating Employees about the Novus Management System

With the KAD and PEA and the Novus Management System (NMS) manual ready for use, each member of the senior management team set up an educational session for all of their subordinates. Nancy assisted in these programs which were held not only in St. Louis but around the world as part of regional meetings.

Novus has many Stratum II individual contributors and it quickly became apparent that a shorter version of the manual was needed to educate them from their perspective with regard to the Novus Management System and to communicate expectations of the accountability and authority of all Novus employees. This version of the NMS was prepared and also used as part of the educational program.

These programs were completed throughout the world over a period of about three months.

Other Requisite Practices

As the second year of requisite implementation began with the task assignment and appraisal processes in place and the initial education completed, attention turned to other requisite practices such as selection and orientation. Nancy and Sabrena wrote a manual to aid managers throughout the world in applying requisite principles in interviewing and selecting employees. An orientation program was designed and provided to newly hired employees.

Level of Work and Organization Structure

Issues of organization structure and the level of work in each role had been reviewed during the first year of the implementation. Principles used here were provided as part of the educational process. Some changes had been made where, for example, a role incumbent was found to be not of the level of complexity of information processing required by the work of the role. But it was not until this point that a decision could be made in determining how level of work was to be used in Novus.

It was decided by Joe to use two, rather than three bands, within Strata I, II and III and have only one band in the higher Strata. Novus roles were placed in these bands using a combination of time span measurement and executive judgment as to what would be required in the future. Roles were calibrated across the organization with all senior staff working together. Over time, the staff was gradually deployed requisitely, based on judgment of complexity of information processing and the other aspects of suitability for a role, which are values and skilled knowledge.

Compensation

After two years of work resulting in Novus being organized requisitely in terms of roles and role incumbents, it then became possible to turn attention to the compensation system. It is only when an organization is requisitely structured and staffed and requisite managerial leadership practices are in place, that it is possible to implement requisite compensation.

Sabrena Hamilton was a specialist in compensation and had many years of experience in traditional compensation, especially with regard to its application in a global company. She asked several compensation specialist organizations to assist her in using requisite compensation, but none were able to integrate requisite concepts into their existing methodologies.

> "So, I had a number of conversations with Thad Simons, corporate counsel, and Nancy on this topic and then shut myself in a room for two days to fully understand the implication of using 'X' and pay differential based on level of work of a role, as the basis of total compensation. I made some initial calculations as to what this would look like in some of the many countries around the world where we have employees.

> "It became apparent to Thad and me that since we had uniformly defined complexity of roles worldwide we could benchmark pay at each level and then adjust as needed to the realities of various labor markets. We separated pay increases from structure movements. Our calculations included all aspects of compensation such as benefits, which tend to vary widely between countries plus the annual and the long-term incentive plans. While we will never have a totally requisite compensation system since we have incentive pay for all employees, we were nonetheless able to apply most of the principles successfully. And we found that once you understand and apply the basics of requisite compensation, you don't need compensation specialists to keep the system going."

Talent Pool Development

In addition to being corporate counsel, Thad Simons was also the head of new business development and human resources. Working with Sabrena and Nancy, he set up a requisite talent pool process beginning in year two. The senior management team met several times a year to review all roles that needed to be filled in the next several years and all employees who had the CIP required by these roles.

Discussions focused on each employee with regard to their qualifications in terms of what they valued in the work environment; their education, experience and skilled knowledge. A major outcome was to share information as to each employee's CIP as agreed by their manager and MoR and get additional information on each person.

A form was developed that captured information in terms of who was considered:

- ready in the areas of CIP or when they might be ready
- whether they valued the role in question (or what steps should be taken to explore that further)
- whether or not they had the necessary skilled knowledge (or what needed to be taken to develop it and plans for that to happen)

Talent Pool meetings were regularly scheduled to repeat this process. In addition, all employees who were judged capable of working in middle management roles (Stratum III) or higher were reviewed by the group to calibrate judgments between the senior manager and Joe and to review and add to the pool of talent on a continuing basis.

The senior management team commented on how constructive this approach was compared to earlier experiences some of them had had where issues of personality were largely the focus of attention.

Embedding the Novus Management System

Also starting in the second year, Joe Privott instituted an annual review of the full Novus Management System at the annual meeting of employees in St. Louis. He conducted this review personally, sending a clear message of the importance of these practices and ensuring that all employees were familiar with the requisite practices contained in the NMS.

These annual education sessions consisted of three parts: one was Joe Privott's review of the NMS; the second was a review of Human Synergistics to continue to enhance personal understanding of behavior in the business setting and interpersonal cooperation; and the third was the presentation of a number of workshops on other management skills such as giving feedback, coaching, communicating clearly, making effective presentations and dealing with cross cultural issues. Much of the material was developed by Nancy and all of the material was consistent with requisite principles.

Joe also participated in all new employee orientation sessions giving the segment on the NMS, demonstrating his commitment to it. He also used each issue of the Novus newsletter to address some aspect of the NMS.

He ended these articles and the educational sessions by asking employees "to hold him accountable for following the System" and stating that he would "hold them accountable for doing so as well."

Thoughts about the Novus Project

Joe Privott retired from Novus in 1999 and subsequently became a consultant to corporate presidents, helping them understand and implement Requisite Organization. Following are some of his thoughts about his experience of bringing these concepts into Novus.

> "During the years of implementing requisite ideas we learned a lot that helped us. One of the things that appealed to me initially about Elliott's ideas is that it gave us tools to make clearer judgments about individuals. We all make those judgments but with requisite concepts and language, we had a sophisticated mental model of what we were doing which gave us more confidence in our judgments of individuals. There is a tendency to want to quantify performance but one needs to make a judgment about whether each person was operating at

full capability under the prevailing circumstances. This can't be measured; it has to be judged. Elliott's concepts gave us a frame of reference for making and reviewing these judgments of employees' effectiveness under prevailing circumstances."

"The concepts embodied in 'capability' and 'level of work of a role' were especially helpful in understanding situations where individuals, who had been capable of their roles, seemed no longer effective as the organization and the work grew in complexity. This problem is common in successful and growing organizations and is a very difficult one to deal with. Understanding its causes is a giant step toward deciding how to resolve the problem while valuing the worth and dignity of the individual involved."

"The talent pool process we developed using requisite concepts helped us to think about the organization we needed in the future in terms of roles and the level of work that would be involved. We had a common language to do an assessment of our current talent pool and analyze our current staff in terms of their complexity of information processing (CIP), their values and knowledge, skill and experience. We then had a sound basis to provide development plans for specific individuals that we wanted to prepare for future roles."

"Temperamental issues were handled by Ken Wright's work which helped key employees to see themselves with objectivity and how their behavior at work affects others. One of my key employees told me that he couldn't stop himself from having his first thoughts about ideas be negative ones, but he could control what he did with those thoughts. He said that once he realized the impact of this behavior on others, he learned to stop himself from making cynical, put-down remarks that cut off creative discussions."

"As one involved in Novus from its inception, I had a passion to drive the company forward successfully. Using requisite principles gave me additional courage and confidence to develop my vision for the company and implement it. Along the way there were some events that were particularly significant in our ability to use and embed requisite concepts. One was the opportunity to discuss issues directly with Elliott in addressing problems. He was always available to Nancy and me by telephone and visited us in St. Louis on several occasions. He is sorely missed."

"Another was the day Rod Carnegie, former CEO of CRA, spent with us. Bringing in someone who had fully experienced requisite implementation and who had personally wrestled with the issues that arise while doing so, was a very important event giving me confidence and courage to continue to push forward in getting buy-in from my senior team and in enabling us to continue to move ahead."

"The combination of an understanding of differences in the complexity of information processing (CIP), with an understanding of temperaments and resulting behavioral patterns, was a powerful thing for me. It gave me a 'scientific basis' for designing the organization, assigning staff to roles and diagnosing performance shortfalls. Ultimately it gave me a basis for deciding on appropriate corrective actions. These were usually making reassignments to get a requisite role/CIP relationship, but occasionally it was coaching to help an employee manage a potentially dysfunctional temperament so as not to exhibit dysfunctional behavior. What I also found was that employees are better able to manage their potentially dysfunctional temperaments when they are assigned to roles with a level of complexity that matches their level of mental processing capability."

Joe's comments on the results of implementing RO, in conjunction with a focus on temperament, are that:

"Excellent business results were achieved (in both growth and profitability) compared to competitors and a healthy, constructive place to work was established. What started as a small unit in Monsanto that had 3% share of the domestic market grew to have 35% share of a world market that was itself growing at 6% and 10% annually. Using requisite principles contributed substantially to our success over the years and enabled me to deal openly, fairly and honestly with my employees."

Novus in the 21st Century

With Thad Simons as president of Novus, the corporate vision has evolved and it is now to 'help feed the world affordable, wholesome food' and Novus' goal is to 'build a self-renewing multi-product company'. Novus does business in 83 countries.

Requisite practices, embodied in the Novus Management System, continue in place and are well embedded in the culture. Attention to setting clear goals and enhancing individual effectiveness, has enabled Novus in four years to improve efficiency from about $1.5 million in sales per full time employee to more than $2.5 million. The clarity, logic and consistency of requisite organization principles provide a substantial foundation for guiding and integrating the work of employees who are located in 24 countries. With sales approaching $500 million and a continuing strong growth rate of more than 10% per annum, Novus is an outstanding example of a successful global organization that has implemented requisite principles and practices.

Chapter 9

THE ROCHE CANADA STORY

By Charlotte Bygrave
Formerly Senior Vice President, Human Resources

Background

The pharmaceutical industry has long been one of the world's most complex. In the early 1990's that complexity began accelerating at a spectacular rate.

F. Hoffmann-La Roche, Ltd., one of the leading global, research-oriented health care companies, realized that this rapidly accelerating complexity meant 'business as usual was no longer an option'. The industry's critical issues were growing in intensity—patent expirations, price pressures, drug development challenges, and regulatory and political pressures.

'Roche' responded to these issues with mergers and acquisitions, improved manufacturing processes, licensing-in of new drugs, and strategic alliances. They articulated other new directions, including managers acting as coaches and mentors, not commanders and controllers, the elimination of 'turfs' and organization silos, and the building of a stronger goal and process orientation.

In 1995 the senior management of the Canadian affiliate of the company, Roche Canada, asked Elliott Jaques and Nancy Lee to help them build an organization that could meet the demands and expectations of their corporate parent and achieve success, short and long term, in this unprecedented business environment.

The following highlights the work the Canadian senior management began with Elliott and Nancy to:

- establish an optimal organization structure;
- clarify accountabilities and authorities and cross-functional working relationships;
- develop the talent and capability of employees;
- establish high performance project teams; and
- implement the best managerial leadership practices to strengthen organizational governance, performance and success.

Roche Canada Prepares for the 21st Century

Early in 1993 the president and CEO of Roche Canada, Donald B. Brown, and his management team held an off-site meeting to identify responses to company and industry issues that would provide the highest value 'payoffs' to move the Canadian operation forward.

We considered several of the latest and best management practices—re-engineering, total quality management, and leadership training and development. However, we eventually decided that while these approaches were sound, they would be fragmented, partial solutions to what we sensed were far more fundamental and systemic issues. We needed to find an approach that would help us better define our issues and provide long lasting solutions.

A few months after the meeting, I attended one of Elliott's workshops on the Requisite Organization principles and practices. He presented a science of organization and management, clearly defined concepts about the underlying structure of the organization—its parts and properties and the relations between them. He explained that many organizational issues, widely diverse in appearance, were often just dissimilar forms of the same thing or had the same root causes. Many of the problems of organization and management were problems with the systems we used and not actually problems with the people.

I began to think that perhaps this was an approach the Roche Canada management team would find useful. It could help address issues such as:

- retaining talent;
- creating a learning organization;
- eliminating 'turfs' and functional silos affecting individual and organizational performance;
- helping managers get better at managing people;
- realizing the anticipated benefits of mergers; and
- improving the execution of our plans.

I presented the Requisite Organization approach to Don Brown, and he quickly saw it as a set of comprehensive, logical and integrated principles and practices that could help us structure and manage the organization for success. After learning about the principles and how to apply them in a three-day intensive workshop led by Nancy Lee and Kathryn Cason, the senior management group unanimously agreed that these principles represented the way they wanted to manage the people and the business. Moving ahead to implement the principles was delayed, however, due to other business issues.

About six months later, after a major acquisition (Syntex Corporation) and under the direction of a new president and CEO, Vic Ackermann, the senior managers wanted to know 'what had happened with those principles' and felt we needed them more after the acquisition than we did before it. Perhaps the principles could help us better manage the challenges of integrating two organizations.

I was asked to take on the role of internal project manager and work with Elliott Jaques and Nancy Lee to develop a plan for optimizing the organization structure needed as a result of the acquisition. We expected that with the right or requisite structure we'd have a critical part of what was needed to achieve the anticipated benefits of the acquisition and long term success.

Organizing To Deliver Roche Strategy

Working with Elliott and Nancy, the management team learned exactly what organization structure was and why it was so essential to developing and executing strategy while providing a socially healthy organization.

Vertical Organization Alignment

First, Elliott's time span concept and definitions of levels of complexity of work were applied to help the management group answer that most vexing question of how many working levels or layers the new organization should have.

Elliott interviewed the president and CEO to discuss his mandate and what he hoped to achieve. Together they discovered the level of complexity of work in his role and the boundaries of the top organization level. Next they discussed what Vic expected from each of his vice presidents to determine the complexity of work and organizational level of these roles. Nancy Lee and I interviewed managers below the vice president level and measured the time span for all other roles throughout the organization.

The time span concept reflected Elliott's 50 years of research which showed that the more complex the work, the further out in time it extends, and the greater the capability required to do the work. It was the task in a role with the longest targeted completion time that determined the complexity of work in the role and the capability required to do the work.

With time span we determined just the right number of organization levels we needed, defined the unique complexity of work to be done at each level and placed each role at the right level.

We established how far into the future were the longest tasks that each manager assigned to each of the roles in the organization. There was a high correlation between this time span method and our job evaluation system in measuring role complexity, but time span proved to be more effective and efficient. We were now using a single clear concept for measuring work complexity, and it enabled us to place roles at just the right organization level. It was definitely value added to our job evaluation system.

Using time span we were able to delve deeper into the meaning of work complexity and descriptions of its nature at each organization level. We learned that work complexity changes state from level to level and that the type of information processing or 'mental horsepower' required to do the work at each level was different.

One of the most fundamental concepts of the Requisite Organization approach is that levels (called strata in requisite work) in an organization are a reflection of levels of human capability, and the alignment of that capability and the complexity of work would be a prerequisite for success in the challenging environment in which the company was operating. Unless we got this alignment right, sustainable organization growth and development would be greatly constrained.

The information that Elliott, Nancy and I gathered showed that Roche had the right number of organization levels. However, the challenge would be ensuring that the capability of employees filling each role was at least equal to the complexity of the work in the role.

Along with my Human Resource Directors, I became well versed in applying the time span method so that we could support the management team in establishing and maintaining the right number of vertical levels and the role complexity required to do the work of the new organization.

Functional Organization Alignment

The management team next examined the somewhat top heavy and fragmented, functional structure resulting from the recent merger.

We decided on the best grouping of core business functions or mainstream operational and support functions (Sales, Marketing, Regulatory Affairs, Clinical Research, etc.) to sustain focus on customers, markets, competitive shifts, and other significant changes in the external environment. We developed clear definitions of accountabilities and authorities within and across functions.

The changes in the organization's vertical and functional alignment set the foundation for carrying out the long term strategic, operational and tactical, as well as the day to day, work of the organization.

Establishing Better Cross-Functional Working Relationships

Elliott, Nancy and I held workshops with each function to identify cross-functional working relationships negatively impacting the quality and speed of work done across functions. Managers identified issues related to cross-functional accountabilities, authorities and role relationships. We assisted the accountable managers, the first manager that had accountability for all of the relevant functions, in resolving issues in a way that made good business sense, and improved individual and departmental working relationships.

For example, the Marketing, Regulatory Affairs, and Clinical Research functions were able to work more efficiently together after the president clarified the accountability and authority that he wanted the vice presidents of each function to have with respect to the development of marketing materials. He assigned to Regulatory Affairs, the group accountable for securing government approval to market drugs, monitoring and auditing authority for all materials with respect to their scientific and medical accuracy. The Clinical Research function had the accountability and authority to provide input/advice to Regulatory Affairs. The Marketing function retained accountability and authority for the final production of medically and scientifically accurate marketing materials.

Managers learned the importance of clarifying cross-functional accountabilities and authorities, establishing conflict resolution mechanisms and setting context for conflict resolution by their direct reports working across functions.

Organization silos and the lack of collaborative efforts thought to be due primarily to negative 'politics' and 'personality conflicts' were lessened due to greater clarity of accountabilities and authorities between roles and functions. These clear cross-functional accountabilities and authorities replaced the vague or ill-defined integration mechanisms often used by organizations such as 'matrix organizations', 'dotted-line relationships', 'liaison task forces', 'sponsors and champions' and committees.

Clarifying the cross-functional role relationships allowed people to get on with their work in a more effective way, reducing conflict and inefficiencies and releasing employee energy, initiative and creativity.

The HR team and I found ourselves busy helping managers prepare new role specifications to clarify and communicate cross-functional accountabilities and authorities that would facilitate more collaborative work among individuals and functions.

Establishing High-Performance Product Development and Launch Teams

With the optimal vertical and functional alignment of the organization established and clear accountabilities and authorities defined, we had a new framework for analyzing and resolving various problems, including those experienced by the product launch teams.

It had become apparent that the Canadian product development and launch teams were not functioning as well as anyone had expected.

Vic had established six or seven of these cross-functional teams and had assigned accountability and authority for the teams to the Executive Committee. He had experience working with these types of teams and knew their value to the timely launch of new products. A few weeks delay in launching a new product could cost the organization millions of dollars.

The teams were producing good outputs and results but they were 'leaping high hurdles' and 'running obstacle courses' to do so. The director of New Product Development and internal coach for the teams asked me for assistance in reviewing the teams' issues. She and I agreed to bring in an external consultant to help the teams identify their issues. With the help of this consultant the team identified their issues, but the team leaders decided that they were unable to find resolutions to their problems.

They needed the help of senior management and requested time on the agenda of an Executive Committee meeting to present their issues:

- They were quite pleased to be team leaders. However, several members of the committee were assigning tasks to them and this workload, along with that assigned by their 'home base' managers, was no longer bearable and soon it would be impossible for them to continue performing well. Frankly, they had too many 'bosses to please'. Could the Executive Committee help them resolve this problem?

- The 'home base' or functional managers still expected completion to standards of 100% of the 'regular' work they assigned to their direct reports who were on the teams. Who would decide the work priorities? Who would help the team members 'mend' the deteriorating work relationship with their 'real' or 'regular' managers?

- Team members had concerns with performance appraisals and compensation for the 'two jobs' they were performing. What effect should their team work have on their annual overall performance appraisal and compensation awards? Who would appraise their 'team work' and decide on rewards and recognition?

- Team leaders and members were having difficulty fielding questions from their peers regarding how one got chosen to be on a team and especially appointed team leader. Employees knew selection criteria had not been established and concluded the decisions were 'political'.

- There were other conflicts to be dealt with. Who would help resolve problems within the teams or between the teams and other functions and departments after team leaders had exhausted their best influencing and persuasive skills—to no avail? What accountability and authority did team leaders and members have anyway? How were team leaders and the team's consultant to solve problems such as members' non-attendance at important team meetings or a member's sub-optimal performance? Who could initiate the removal of a team member from the team when removal was warranted? How should the teams and the functional departments interact? Were the 'home base' or functional department managers in any way accountable for the teams' success and performance?

On hearing the complaints, the Executive Committee was somewhat shocked. They had no idea of the extent of the teams' problems. They considered a number of solutions, including giving the teams a 'break', controlling the flow of work to teams through one identified committee member, more 'technical' training for the teams, and, of course, granting much deserved rewards for the team members.

While these measure were somewhat helpful they did not address the root causes of the teams' issues, which we learned were organization structure issues such as lack of clear role relationships (accountabilities and authorities) between the teams and the functional departments (Marketing, Regulatory, Clinical Research); appointment of an accountable manager/executive for the teams; effective selection criteria for team members and leaders; and effective conflict resolution mechanisms.

How to structure and manage six or seven critical teams—the number growing due to several new products in the pipeline—was an organization design problem which even brought a 'furrowed brow' to Elliott's face. A small senior management task force was formed with Elliott as the external consultant and me as the internal advisor to review the issues. Elliott advised us that our product launches required two very different types of teams, project and coordinative teams. We would also need to know how to transition from project teams, needed to analyze and recommend a product's inclusion in the portfolio, to coordinative teams, which were needed to plan and execute the development and launch phases of the product launch process.

We analyzed and resolved the teams' issues using Requisite Organization design principles and practices. We developed:

- the accountabilities and authorities of team leaders and members for both project and coordinative teams;

- clearly defined role relationships between teams and the rest of the organization;
- selection criteria and processes for team leaders and members;
- processes for delegation of authorities; and
- guidelines for applying human resource management policies— personal effectiveness appraisals, rewards and recognition, training and development, and other types of team support.

Guidelines for establishing and maintaining the teams were reviewed, revised and documented. The new team design and infrastructure embedded in a well-designed larger organization reduced team frustration, increased morale and enabled the teams to get on with their work, including moving down the path to reducing launch times.

Celebrations were held and rewards and recognition granted. Elliott's principles were turning out to be useful and practical 'stuff'.

Assessing the Talent Pool and Communicating the Results

Roche, as with all organizations, had increasing concerns about talent retention. A well-designed organization structure would be meaningless if the company could not retain and develop good talent.

A talent pool assessment process was developed to determine the strength of the current and future talent pool and the requirements for training and development, recruitment, and succession planning.

The process cascaded from the top to the entry level of the organization. Elliott, Nancy and I held discussions with immediate managers and their managers about the capability of each of the individuals on their teams. It was a clean and efficient process. Unlike previous methods which asked managers to rate employees on several different skills, behaviors, traits and factors indicating capability, this process had one central question or focus—at which organization level did the individual have the capability to do work now, if they could get the necessary training and experience and if the role was one which the individual valued doing?

Elliott and Nancy prepared and previewed with me a 'wall-sized' progression chart showing all the data collected in our discussions, the organization level at which each individual could work today, his/her judged capability level, and predictions about how that capability would mature over time.

I led a meeting of the Executive Committee to review and discuss the talent pool information displayed on the progression chart. The entire talent pool was displayed and the committee could determine whether or not the organization had the current and future talent needed. The committee also reviewed the information for employee development and succession planning, and information to help managers and their managers develop and sustain an effective team of people. As the discussion progressed, changes were made to some assessments to achieve the highest levels of fairness and accuracy of assessments.

We decided on a pilot test to communicate the assessment results to 50 randomly selected employees (stratified sampling). The pilot test results showed that these employees felt that the new system produced simpler and fairer assessments: simpler, because employees and managers were using the same language and concepts about capability and considering one major factor; fairer, because of multiple inputs, including the employees' own input. They especially liked knowing assessments would be reviewed on an annual basis. The judgments were not 'once and for all' judgments, but could be changed as significant and additional information about an employee's capability was revealed through the completion of task assignments or other accomplishments.

The pilot results showed that 49 of the 50 employees agreed with the assessments and all 50 commented that they felt the process was an excellent one. Our policy was that disagreements about assessments were noted and marked for review and resolution at a later time when more information was available.

While the immediate manager provided input to the assessment of a direct report and helped him/her prepare for talent pool discussions, it was the immediate manager's manager, the Manager-once-Removed, who made the decision about an employee's capability and who was accountable for helping that employee understand how his/her capability could best be developed in the context of the company's business requirements.

Roche Canada could see that, long term, effective management of the new system would allow for more accurate forecasting and planning of human resources, better training and career development programs and more appropriate and respectful treatment for all employees.

Managerial Leadership Training

Creating and presenting managerial leadership training programs was another important part of the Requisite Organization approach at 'Roche'.

Having the required capability was a necessary but not sufficient condition for effective management—managers needed to be trained and held accountable for specific managerial practices. The training placed emphasis on management practices, not on 'management styles'. As long as a manager's behaviors were within the limits or bounds clearly articulated by the company, we learned to leave their personalities alone.

Nancy Lee, my staff and I provided all managers with opportunities to understand the managerial practices and the minimum authorities they needed to lead effectively and earn the trust of their direct reports.

Through roles plays and discussions each practiced:

- selecting new employees;
- training and coaching;
- conducting two-way planning meetings;
- setting context, direction and prescribed limits;
- defining tasks;
- appraising performance;
- conducting merit reviews; and
- initiating the removal of a direct report from a role.

Managers-once-Removed learned they were accountable for: setting context and direction for the work of the two levels below them;

integrating cross-functional work flows; human resource planning and development; and making sure that their immediate managers exercised effective managerial leadership practices and treated their direct reports equitably and with respect.

These practices became the backbone of the company's management training for all management levels. Our human resource management system and policies had been modified where necessary to be consistent with this training; that is, policies and procedures related to recruitment, interviewing and hiring, personal effectiveness appraisal, career planning and advancement, and reward and recognition.

The training and development of Roche managers would ensure that managers were using consistent management practices, in line with the organization's values, to secure the willing commitment and best endeavors of their direct reports. This would enable achievement of the organization's desired outcomes and results, better employee morale and improved governance. Even our senior managers said they enjoyed the training and found it beneficial.

Requisite Rewards and Recognition

There were changes to other important policies and practices at Roche. We took an approach to rewards and recognition that was far 'outside the box' and that eliminated predictive criteria-based bonus schemes.

The nature of work is complex, and employees must face and overcome unpredictable and unanticipated obstacles on their way to achieving a task/goal. This unpredictability, inherent especially in the complex work in the higher-level roles, renders predictive criteria-based pay systems somewhat ineffective. These systems make no allowance for actual performance conditions that vary significantly from the predicted conditions; rather, they focus and reward employees for achieving or coming close to achieving a certain level of results or outcomes, usually quantitative. This directs employees to focus on how to achieve the numbers, which could require behaviors not consistent with doing the right thing given the circumstances. Also, one employee might accomplish more complex and higher quality work under more difficult circumstances but with lower quantitative results and might therefore receive a lower bonus than another, whose less complex work under less difficult circumstances generated higher quantitative results and therefore a larger bonus—for example, the inevitable 'windfalls' in sales.

As a result, bonus programs sometimes caused poor morale, precipitated employee behaviors outside of acceptable standards, and created poor relationships between management and employees. Employees would often ask "what does the bonus, compared to base pay, reward or pay me for? Does it mean the company does not expect my full commitment and best performance for the base pay I receive?" These were difficult questions to answer.

Each of the three Roche Canada business divisions had the authority, however, to decide what they felt was best for their business—to retain or eliminate bonus pay schemes. They decided to roll incentive pay into base salary. Two divisions retained incentives as a small part of total compensation for the Sales and Marketing staff.

Special awards, reviewed by the appropriate manager and the human resources department to ensure consistency of treatment, could still be granted to any employee for exceptional performance. These cases were determined after the fact—that is, at the end of the performance period.

There was a great deal of work for the human resources department in reviewing the impact of this change on salary driven benefits programs and particularly on the defined benefit pension plan. It was a change affordable by the company.

The entire compensation program was reviewed to ensure pay ranges were linked to organization levels and levels of complexity of work. Clearly defined role accountabilities and alignment of work complexity with organization levels reduced concerns about lack of equity and fairness in performance assessment and increased consistency and reliability among managers in judging performance. Managers were able to make more accurate judgments about performance and recommend fair merit increases. We replaced the five performance appraisal categories, which ranged from 'outstanding performance to unacceptable performance', with six performance categories which would enable more accurate judgments of an individual's performance against the requirements of the role. The new rating categories asked the manager to judge where in the range of the role an individual was performing—in the top or bottom half of the role and at which of three steps in that half—high, mid or low.

The Manager-once-Removed (the manager's manager) reviewed the performance ratings and recommended merit increases prepared by his/her managers to ensure each was applying a standard, fair and accurate rating process to all employees.

Performance appraisals and merit increases, two highly emotionally charged issues, could now be handled more efficiently and effectively. Employees were fully aware that the changes in the compensation and performance management program meant the 'performance bar' had not been lowered but had been raised, and they agreed this exchange was fair.

The Requisite Principles and Roche Strategic Planning

The Requisite Organization principles had another important impact. Vic was interested in implementing Norton and Kaplan's Balanced Scorecard concept but wanted to ensure it was consistent with the Requisite Organization approach. He asked Elliott, Nancy and me to work out how to apply the Scorecard concept.

What needed to be worked out was how to apply the Scorecard concept in a multi-functional, multi-level organization.

The approach we developed strengthened the business planning process for managers who were already very adept at business planning. Scorecard deliverables or 'Key Goals' and 'Indicators' with targeted completion times appropriate for each organization level were developed. Goals were aligned and integrated, including appropriate time spans, from the level of the president down to the first organization level and horizontally across all functions. This process enabled every employee to have a 'Key Goals' card and see how his/her 'Key Goals' aligned with those at the next higher organization level. For example, function vice presidents working with the president were accountable for developing and achieving 'five year end goals or deliverables' which were integrated with the president's 'five year interim goals' which led to achievement of his '10 year vision' for the organization.

'Key Goals' would be updated annually or as dictated by events. A mid-course 'temperature reading' was planned for each six months. A periodic review of the Key Indicators would be used to reveal any deviations from course and determine satisfactory performance. In addition, the senior team would reflect upon the progress made and the soundness of the premises upon which the 'Key Goals' were set. Regardless of whether or not the Indicators showed progress to be on target, further reflection on emerging conditions and further changes might suggest that the original goals were too conservative, too optimistic, or in the wrong direction and therefore in need of modification.

The overall goal of the process was, of course, to ensure that every function and employee understood what individual and team contributions were necessary to help Roche Canada achieve its goals.

The comprehensive and scientific approach embodied in Requisite Organization to organization design and management provided Roche with a sharper understanding of the nature of the organization—just what sort of thing it is, how it is made up, how it functions, and some of the best ways of managing it. It added value by enhancing the decisions that depend upon or impact good organization and management. For example, Roche had better answers to questions such as:

- How do we retain our focus on customers, markets, and the competition?
- How can we better execute our strategies?
- What employee development investments will provide the greatest return for the company and the employee?
- How do we link our human resources to the company's strategy?

Requisite principles enabled Roche Canada to strengthen its organization structure, accurately assess employee capability, train and hold managers accountable for the best managerial practices, and clarify managerial and cross-functional accountabilities and authorities.

Lessons Learned at Roche Canada

I believe that many of the lessons learned at Roche Canada about organization and management could form part of the innovative and successful recovery strategies needed to address the continuing crisis in the pharmaceutical industry. While a wide variety of interdependent and complex solutions are necessary to steer the industry through a turbulent environment, one that has not been considered is a scientific and well-researched approach to organization and management.

The key lessons of organization and management for the pharmaceutical industry include:

1. Getting the number of organization layers right

Getting the number of organization layers right is paramount. Unless we got just the right number, sustainable organization growth and development would be greatly constrained.

2. Aligning organization levels and employee capability

Organization levels are categories of work complexity. The alignment of employee capability and compensation with these levels are necessary to obtain efficient and effective results and outcomes.

3. Alignment of the organization's spine

The correct number of vertical levels and the optimal grouping of functions form the backbone of the organization. Until the layers and groupings are optimal, all other initiatives will be sub-optimal (e.g., business planning, defining accountabilities and authorities, selection and development of employees, establishing and managing teams, etc.)

4. Vertical distance between managers and direct reports

Managers must be one level above the direct report in terms of capability and the level of complexity of work performed. When the relationship is too close, with manager and direct report working at the same organization level, the direct report is micro-managed and cannot use his/her initiative. When the relationship is too far apart, the manager feels the direct report lacks capability and initiative and the direct report feels the manager does not provide good context, direction and support for the work. Getting this working relationship right is the most powerful factor in organization structuring and design.

5. Clear and common understanding of what it means to be a manager and clearly defined managerial accountabilities and authorities

Effective understanding and implementation of these accountabilities and authorities ensure good governance, good leadership, and the development and maintenance of a trust-based organization.

6. Clear cross-functional accountabilities and authorities

Clear cross-functional accountabilities and authorities, rather than the vague and confusing definitions of 'dotted line or lateral relationships' and 'matrix organizations', are essential to reduce organization silos, 'turfs' and to create effective working relationships between functions, thus increasing the flow and quality of work across the organization.

The increasingly intense levels of interactions required between functions, corporate offices and country level affiliates and across the supply chain demands clear specification of accountabilities and authorities. Unclear accountabilities and authorities lead to extreme inefficiencies and acrimonious working relationships.

7. Effective managerial leadership practices

Capability or raw cognitive power is a necessary but not sufficient condition for effective managerial leadership. Clearly defined managerial leadership accountabilities, authorities and practices are essential for good organization governance and performance.

8. High-performing teams

Well-established project and coordinative teams can accomplish the intense collaborative work required within and between the major functions of organizations. To enable high performing teams requires:

- clear accountabilities and authorities for team leaders and members of both project and coordinative teams;
- clearly defined role relationships between teams and the rest of the organization;
- selection criteria and processes for team leaders and members;
- processes for delegation of authorities; and
- guidelines for applying human resource management policies— personal effectiveness appraisals, rewards and recognition, training and development, and other types of team support.

SUMMARY

With Requisite organization and management practices key initiatives, the pharmaceutical industry would be better positioned to regain credibility with customers, suppliers and other key stakeholders. The use of Requisite Organization principles could provide a critical strategic resource to create the robust future for the industry which must be created because of its critical role in health care solutions.

Chapter 10

EXPERIENCES IN IMPLEMENTING REQUISITE ORGANIZATION

In this chapter I discuss various aspects of working with clients in the implementation of Requisite Organization principles and practices gleaned from more than twenty-five years of consulting in this field. Observations, suggestions and techniques developed over those years are provided. It is my hope that some of these ideas and examples may prove useful to both Requisite consultants and to clients who are currently involved in, or interested in, implementing Requisite Organization.

Generally I have used the implementation process outlined by Dr. Jaques on page 131 in his book, *Requisite Organization,* when doing a full scale implementation, although each client assignment has required some adaptation of the basic procedure.

Introduction to Dr. Elliott Jaques and Requisite Organization

While working in a number of positions in organizations such as General Electric, AT&T and Macy's, I observed and experienced some very serious management problems. These issues caused unnecessary stress to employees and the loss of profit to the organization. This led me to pursue an MBA focusing on Organization Development. As a result, over a number of years, I had the opportunity to write a business book, *Targeting the Top*, and to present management development courses throughout the United States and worldwide.

In 1982 I was a speaker at the American Management Association conference in San Francisco. There I first heard Dr. Elliott Jaques who gave the keynote talk. His presentation was a revelation to me, despite my graduate work in the field and years of experience teaching management. He described what was then, and still is, **the only comprehensive system of principles and practices for structuring, staffing and managing organizations.** These concepts were at that time called Stratified Systems Theory (SST). Subsequent to the conference I contacted Dr. Jaques and reviewed with him a simplified version of his ideas. I planned to put these into practice, both through teaching and consulting. At that time his book, *A General Theory of Bureaucracy*, was the only one available that described his research and concepts in detail.

I urged him to write a book on his theories that was easier to understand and utilize. That began a 20-year relationship working with Dr. Jaques. During these years he collaborated with me on some of my projects that were of interest to him in further developing and testing his ideas. He called his method of doing this type of work 'consulting research'.

Dr. Jaques subsequently renamed his body of work Requisite Organization (RO). He chose the word 'requisite' because it refers to the nature of things and the nature of people. This comprehensive, science-based system evolved from studying the nature of people in completing tasks, and the nature of tasks to be completed, in managerial hierarchies. As he stated "Steps in complexity of mental processing correspond to the steps in the underlying natural pattern of organizational layers that appears to be universally requisite for managerial hierarchical systems."

In 1989 he published **Requisite Organization**: *A Total System for Effective Managerial Organization and Managerial Leadership for the 21st Century,* a book that provided more readily accessible information on his concepts. A second edition appeared in 1996. Over the next several years, while working with many clients and having access to discussions with Dr. Jaques, in 2007 I published the first edition of this book, *The Practice of Managerial Leadership.* It presents Requisite Organization in a simpler, more linear way than in Dr. Jaques' publications. Dr. Jaques edited the first five chapters of this book to ensure that they accurately represented his ideas.

The topics of Requisite Talent Pool Development and Requisite Compensation are included in this second edition as Chapters Six and Seven. I wrote these later after I had sufficient experience in these areas with clients to be able to do so. My continuing goal is to provide his concepts as accurately as possible in a way that is relatively easy to understand.

Over the years I have had clients that ranged from tens of thousands of employees globally to small, locally based companies, from start-ups and family-owned companies to those publicly traded. These organizations are in fields such as pharmaceutical, financial services, food and energy production, insurance and technology. I have found that Requisite principles achieve outstanding results equally well in all sizes and all types of organizations.

RO projects typically fall into two categories, no matter the size of the organization or the field in which it is operating. The first type of client is the one where the CEO has become familiar with Requisite Organization and has determined that it is the management system s/he wants to use. The other type of organization is one in which the head of Human Resources or a specific manager heading a unit chooses to implement Requisite concepts.

Richard Beckhard, who was a professor at MIT, is considered by many to be the founder of the field of Organization Development. He described the head of an organization as someone who can "**make** things happen, **let** things happen or **keep things from happening**". Where the CEO has been exposed to Requisite concepts and s/he decides to use them to **make** the organization more effective and leads the implementation process, this is the ideal situation. Many of my examples and comments will be drawn from experiences where the CEO has elected to implement RO principles and practices and has driven the project. However, I have also found that concepts in Requisite Organization can be effective in organizations where only some of the ideas are able to be introduced, and the CEO is willing to **let** these changes happen. In some instances this type of situation eventually becomes a full scale RO implementation.

IMPLEMENTATION DRIVEN BY THE CEO: MAKING IT HAPPEN

In all Requisite work the initial step is to gain an understanding of the strategic plan of the organization—where are they are seeking to go and how are they planning to move in that direction. It is especially critical to understand how far in the future the planning extends or needs to extend. This provides an initial indication of how many layers of management will likely be required in order to work most effectively toward achieving the desired results.

It is sometimes found that there is a fairly short term strategic plan of typically three years, because of concern with the rapid change being experienced. It these instances it is important to look for the longer term goals or requirements of the organization to establish how far planning needs to extend into the future, based on the desires of the owner or Board of Directors.

Something to keep in mind in researching an organization's goals and objectives is that the overall plan is always a work in progress. Strategic plans are not engraved in bronze but are outcomes being striven for. Information on the plan may exist in many differing forms ranging from elaborate written plans to ideas that exist only in the mind of the CEO. It is important to continue to be aware of the plans and their outreach into the future as any Requisite project continues since the strategy, and the goals and tactics for achieving them, will likely be changing and evolving over time.

The organization's values, vision, and mission are reviewed when starting the project. Requisite values are discussed with the senior management for a full awareness of the focus on fairness and justice achieved through clarity, resulting in a trusting and trustworthy environment.

The Time Horizon of the CEO

In addition to the outreach of the strategic plan into the future, it is essential to get a sense of the time horizon of the CEO. The fact that a plan is described with a five-year perspective does not automatically mean that the CEO is capable of envisioning and overseeing assignments that far into the future. Alternatively the CEO may have a time horizon that is substantially longer than that of the plan and, for example, may conceptualize results to be achieved a decade or more ahead while the strategy and plans only deal with the next five years. In either case a significant disconformity between the outreach of the strategy and the time horizon of the CEO is likely to cause serious problems.

For example, in one organization we dealt with the CEO felt strongly that the strategy and goals could not be longer than three years into the future, yet raw materials needed to be contracted for as far as eight years to ten years ahead. This appeared to be a situation where a person with the Complexity of Information Processing suitable for Stratum IV had to deal with Stratum V problems. In another organization the CEO's vision reached out more than a decade but most members of the senior team could envision no more than two or three years ahead. Therefore they often did not understand or agree with what the CEO described to them as her plans for the future.

The point here is that the complexity of the work of the organization, demonstrated by **the longest tasks that have to be accomplished for the strategy to be achieved, is the starting consideration for Requisite structure.** It provides a first indication of what the structure needs to look like in terms of managerial layers (strata). This is tested and possibly revised as the project continues.

It is also necessary to make an assumption about the level of the Complexity of Information Processing of the CEO to test over time as you work with him or her. The reason, of course, is that if the CEO's time horizon does not extend as far into the future as the strategic plans, they will not be achieved. The ideal is that the outreach of the company's strategy and the Complexity of Information Processing of the CEO are the same or that the CEO is no more than one level of capability higher than the strategy. More than one level creates the danger of the CEO pushing into activities of more complexity than can be coped with by the senior management team and, in Dr. Jaques' words, may "pull the top off the organization".

Once you have an understanding of the strategy and have made an initial judgment of the time horizon of the CEO, the plan for Requisite implementation can begin to be developed.

The Requisite Implementation Team

Whenever possible a strong internal project leader needs to be appointed and a team established to support the Requisite work. The number of persons on the team will depend upon the size of the organization and the speed at which implementation is desired. Often the project leader is a senior individual in Human Resources since the involvement of the HR function is essential in the facilitation of the project.

In a large organization the internal lead role often requires a full time commitment and maybe selected from an area other than HR. In a smaller organization the head of HR, if s/he has the right level of capability, can sometimes fill this role since the time demand is usually less. Team members typically consist of both individuals in HR and persons from other functions.

Having a number of employees from different functional areas who are closely involved in the project from the beginning is an important step in embedding Requisite principles and practices. Members of this group become the specialists who can help sustain the system. Participation in the RO implementation team often acts as a key development tool for individuals who have potential for moving up in the organization.

In one organization where the introduction of Requisite Organization took place over a number of years there have subsequently been three heads of Human Resources and one change in CEO. However, the Requisite system was well embedded. These individuals, as well as many managers throughout the organization, had participated in the in-depth education activities. Consequently Requisite principles continued to be utilized throughout this organization. Interestingly this project was one initially in which the original CEO **let** it happen. The next CEO directly oversaw the continuance of the use of Requisite concepts. Throughout, and despite challenging economic times, this organization continued to be outstandingly successful in its field.

The Involvement of Human Resources

The cooperation of the Human Resources staff is essential to introduce and embed RO effectively. The most successful projects are those where not only the CEO understands and drives Requisite Organization but the head of Human Resources does as well. Implementing Requisite Organization has a large impact on HR practices and processes. However, the implementation of Requisite Organization needs to be established as **the organization's management system** driven by the CEO and not seen as just another HR effort, too often regarded as the 'flavor of the month'.

Some of the human resources policies and practices that are directly affected by Requisite Organization practices are how:

- key tasks and general responsibilities are assigned by managers
- personal effectiveness appraisals take place
- organization charts are developed and used
- succession planning and talent pool review take place
- grading, titling and compensation are established
- cross-functional accountability and authority are established
- redeployment and de-selection take place

It is important for Requisite consultants to familiarize themselves with the policies and processes currently in use in the organization. Reading through policy manuals or statements, if such are available, is a necessary step early in the project.

In one large organization we found 72 different forms were being used for recording annual appraisals. In another we found that there were no written HR policies or organization charts. Up-front research with RO team members will help determine what currently exists in the organization so that this material can be reviewed prior to starting the implementation.

Practical Considerations

Because of the confidential nature of Requisite work, it is advisable to establish a secure on-site workplace that has locked office space and locked cabinets. Administrative Assistant support is essential since there is a good deal of written detail involved that is best recorded by someone internal who is familiar with the organization and who can be relied on to keep the work confidential. Once these issues are agreed upon and put in place the work plan can be developed and implementation can begin.

Beta Test

An important consideration in establishing a requisite organization is to determine whether or not a test area is advisable. In some client assignments it was decided to beta test the requisite planning and implementation process in a small segment of the organization. This has proved very useful in finding potential issues and opportunities before undertaking a full roll out. If this approach is decided upon, it is best done in a reasonably well functioning unit rather than a problem area. The same steps that are outlined below are followed in a beta test area.

INITIAL STEPS IN IMPLEMENTATION

Initial steps in introducing Requisite Organization are:

- providing education about RO
- gaining an understanding of the organization as it now exists
- developing an initial Requisite chart of the current (extant) organization

Education

Requisite implementation involves an extensive amount of education in Requisite principles and practices for all employees, customized to what is relevant to their work and roles. This process begins with three groups, the CEO and his/her immediate subordinates, the Requisite team members and relevant persons in Human Resources.

Senior management is the first to be provided with education in key concepts of Requisite Organization. It is also important to educate relevant members of Human Resources, such as business partners who are the liaison between HR and business functions, in aspects of RO in the early stages of the project. Once information circulates about the RO undertaking, these individuals are usually asked about what is happening and hence need be fully informed about Requisite Organization and the implementation process.

In one organization most of the educational topics were provided to the senior team by adding them one by one to the weekly staff meetings, taking about an hour each with time provided for questions. A written description of the topic was given out along with a reference to the pages in *Requisite Organization* by Dr. Jaques and in my book, *The Practice of Managerial Leadership.* The senior managers discussed their thoughts and concerns regarding these topics in subsequent meetings and individually with the consultant.

As was mentioned earlier, the organization's values, vision, mission and strategy are the starting point and foundation for any Requisite work. The beginning of Requisite implementation provides an excellent opportunity to review these topics as part of the education process. Requisite values of honesty, respect, fairness, integrity and trust are discussed. It is a good time emphasize that clarity and trust are fundamental elements of RO and to suggest that when making decisions managers will want to consider when the decision will enhance or erode trust.

Specific areas of Requisite Organization covered in the education process are often divided as follows:

- Structuring the Organization

- Staffing
- Accountability and Authority
- Working Relationships
- The Role of the Manager-once-Removed
- First Line Management (if relevant)
- Managerial Leadership Practices

Education on Talent Pool Development and Compensation can often be provided at a later time.

Involving Managers in the Education Process

Since Requisite Organization is a Management System it is strongly recommended that managers actively participate in the education programs. This happens best by having the senior management of a unit present the material assisted by the Requisite consultant. This is a practice we have used in most assignments. Providing in-depth education to senior managers as one of the initial undertakings enables them to take part in presenting this material to their subordinates. In global organizations a video of the CEO is often used to introduce the education series, providing context as to why this system is being introduced. In smaller organizations the CEO can do this in person.

Cascading RO Education

Once the senior managers at Stratum V and above and relevant HR staff are provided with the major concepts of Requisite Organization and an overview of plans for implementation, the second stage of the teaching can begin, focusing on employees at Stratum IV and III. Education is subsequently provided to those in Stratum II and I roles, also using their managers to assist in the teaching.

In some organizations high potential managers, who may or may not be part of the Requisite team, take part in the effort of conducting courses to managers at Stratum III and II such as Managerial Leadership Practices. (There is no better way to learn something than to have to teach it.) The practice of having these managers participate in teaching further reinforces that this system is a Managerial System and it is not simply a Human Resources undertaking.

I have found that persons in different strata in an organization require a somewhat different emphasis in the content of the material. Senior managers are interested in the conceptual ideas inherent in the system such as time-span measurement and organizational layering. Middle managers want to know how the changes that will be happening will affect the processes they use as well as when and how the changes are going to happen. They want to know what they are to do specifically that is different from what they have been doing. Employees at Stratum II and I typically want to know about changes to their work, their title, their compensations and their relationship with their manager.

In a large organization with several thousand employees where it was necessary to implement RO rapidly, courses were given two times a day for several months in work units. Each topic was covered in about 4 hours. These meetings were introduced by the senior manager of the function who was then available at the end of the sessions for questions and concerns.

Reviewing the Current Organization

At the same time as initial efforts in education are underway, an analysis of the organization as it currently exists is carried out. Dr. Jaques referred to this as the **extant** organization. Simultaneously with reviewing the extant organization, work begins on reviewing systems that need to be changed and designing them requisitely. These are usually HR systems as mentioned earlier such as task assignment, appraisal, de-selection and so on. Once systems are redesigned to be requisite, employees are educated about these changes and the new systems are implemented.

The process of understanding the extant organization starts by interviewing the CEO and his/her immediate subordinates and Subordinates-once-Removed. In preparation for these interviews organization charts are gathered and reviewed. Information on each role and employee is obtained, typically from enterprise or HRIS software including role title, any numerical designation attached to the role and the person, reporting relationships and the role incumbent's name, grade, birth date and total compensation for the past year. This information has a number of uses which were described in Chapter

Seven and in the Appendix article on Comprehensive Organization Charts.

One of the major contributions that Dr. Jaques made to management science is to determine the work that needs to be done in a role separately from thinking about the individual currently in that role. This is not easy to do. **Separating consideration of the work required in a role and the capability of the person filling it is essential step in first ensuring an effective structure and then filling roles with persons capable of carrying out the tasks in each role.**

The fundamental question is always, "What is the work that needs to be done in the role?" The **Requisite definition of work is the exercise of discretion and judgment in carrying out goal-directed activity.** Once decisions are made as to the tasks that need to be assigned to the role, then someone who is capable of doing that work is sought to fill the role. This is the way first to get the 'role right', then subsequently to consider who is the 'right person' to fill the role.

Initial Interviews

Initial interviews are typically scheduled for 1½ to 2 hours depending upon the number of subordinates that a manager has. In my practice I have personally conducted the interviews of the CEO and his/her immediate subordinates and in smaller organizations those of the CEO's SoRs as well. This provides me with a reasonably full picture of the work of the organization and of each of these management roles.

In these interviews I am seeking to find out what the person understands to be his/her most important assignments, what subordinate roles he or she has and what assignments the manager is giving to these roles. This questioning aims to understand the way functions are currently aligned and, very importantly, the time span of the longest tasks being given to roles.

The CEO Interview

The first interview is with the CEO focusing on his/her understanding of the major accountabilities given to him or her by the owner or

Board of Directors. Gathering this information from the CEO may take several meetings. I have found it useful to have CEOs (and other senior managers) first think about the Major Categories of Assignments (MCAs) that they are giving to each role rather than moving immediately to discussions of specific tasks. An aggregation of types of tasks seems to come to mind first when discussing roles at the senior management level, rather than specific tasks. This approach also helps to clarify the differences in functions. The use of MCAs was developed when working with my colleague Sandi Cardillo on several major projects.

The initial interview with CEOs starts by asking what they understand is expected of them by the Board of Directors or owner of the organization. I do this in the context of the organization's strategic plan. (Even when there is no written plan, CEOs will have some sort of overarching goals within which they are working.) The discussion then moves on to how they are delegating work to the various functions immediately subordinate to them.

Following these meetings a chart showing the Major Categories of Assignments of the CEO and of each immediate subordinate role is prepared and subsequently reviewed with the CEO, making any changes needed.

Sample Chart of Major Categories of Work

Manager
Vice President
Customer & Employee Relations
Susan Chavez

Division Manager	Division Manager	Division Manager	Division Manager
Human Resources	Customer Service	Sales & Service	Corporate Communications

Staffing & Recruiting	Billing/Collections	Customer Satisfaction	External Communications
Compensation & Benefits	Call Center	Sales Staff	Advertising
HR Legal & Compliance	Customer Systems Reliability	Product Sales/Service	Media
Training & Development		Service Development	Social Marketing
Employee Relations			Website
			Internal Communications

Using the MCA chart I meet with the CEO to ascertain important tasks s/he is undertaking and ask for specific examples of the longest assignments that the CEO feels accountable for. The same questions regarding key tasks in each immediate subordinate's MCAs are explored along with seeking information on longest task(s) the CEO is assigning. The description of the longest task(s) of the CEO and those s/he is assigning gives a strong indication of the level of work of the top two layers in the organization. Lists of these assignments are prepared and reviewed with the CEO for accuracy, as well as discussing issues that have been raised.

While it is possible to conduct these interviews by asking directly about specific tasks the CEO is giving immediate subordinates and skipping the step of first determining Major Categories of Assignments, I have found this extra step is useful both to the client and the consultant in getting a full and clear picture of roles and functions.

First Thoughts about the Future Requisite Organization

At some point during these interviews CEOs will often start thinking about how they would prefer to distribute MCAs to functions or about the roles they need reporting to them that are missing. Enabling them to think about their subordinate roles without taking into consideration the current role incumbents is quite liberating. These initial interviews provide CEOs an opportunity to explore the number and type of roles that are subordinate to them and any problems in aligning the functional work. They will frequently begin to think about and articulate changes they would like to make. These issues are made careful note of for review in later meetings.

In one organization when the CEO was asked about MCAs she found this approach so useful she began to examine how she wanted the organization to operate in the future. She went to the white board in front of the room and drew the roles she felt she needed subordinate to her in order to support the planned growth of the organization. She then allocated MCAs to these roles.

Interviewing the CEO's Immediate Subordinates

As part of the interview process it is important to give managers an assurance of confidentiality. In these discussions managers usually reveal the issues with which they are struggling and may initially hesitate to have that information shared with their manager. However, my experience has been that those being interviewed are generally eager to have difficult situations relayed back to the manager through the consultant, once a trusting relationship is established..

In individual meetings with the CEO's subordinates their understanding of their key tasks is discussed and the time that they believe they have been given to complete them. We have often found misunderstandings and point them out to both the subordinate and, with the subordinate's permission, to the CEO to be reviewed and reconciled.

We follow the same procedure with the CEO's immediate subordinates as that with the CEO, asking first about the Major Categories of Assignments they have been given and then those they are giving their subordinates and provide them with an MCA chart to review. In a second meeting we ask about specific tasks and ascertain the longest tasks they are assigning to their subordinates. We record this information and confirm it with the person who was interviewed.

We enquire about and take note of other issues and problems that the managers feel they are currently dealing with. Two questions that prove useful in this regard are to ask what important work they feel is not currently being adequately done and also where time and effort is being needlessly spent. The latter is often referred to as 'legacy work', something that is being done because it has always been done but is no longer required. A good deal of unnecessary legacy work is often eliminated as a result.

Time Span Information

Interviews with the CEO and his/her immediate subordinates are the starting point for eliciting and confirming information on time span of roles. I generally prefer to do the most senior level roles without anyone else present because I have found that the time span of an assignment is most accurately gained in one-on-one interviews.

As was described in Chapter One, the time span of a role can be found by understanding the time span of the longest task the manager is currently assigning to a role. It must be a real task, actually being assigned. There is sometimes more than one task with the longest outreach. Although managers sometimes try to use hypothetical tasks, these are of no use in determining the true time span of a role. Only the longest task that has *actually* been assigned provides a measure of the level of work of the role. For the most part I have found that a clear picture of role levels emerges that is consistent with Requisite theory.

I record the longest task or tasks assigned in detail since I subsequently refer to this information when discussing the picture of the current organization gleaned from these interviews.

Sometimes there is a situation where the role incumbent does not have the Complexity of Information Processing required by the role and the manager has to assign tasks of a lower level. For example, the manager feels this is a necessary developmental role and the person appears to be developing the CIP to be able to do the role in the near future. In some instances the role has to be filled with an individual less capable than the role requires because of shortage of suitable candidates or the work required in a role may have outgrown the candidate. (In these situations the necessary work that is missing is either being done by the manager or is not getting done.) I also find that occasionally that one or more of the managers being interviewed do not appear to have the CIP necessary for the work of the role, as evidenced by the time span of the longest tasks they are assigning to subordinate roles. These issues will need to be noted and explored later.

The time span of each role is the essential information from which the level of complexity of the work of roles in the extant organization is evidenced. Many find that becoming proficient at eliciting the time span of the longest task(s) a manager is giving to a role is not easy. It becomes easier in doing so by understanding the types of assignments that are typically given to specific functions and by extensive practice in helping managers articulate by when they need to have assignments completed. For many managers this is a new experience.

My recommendations with regard to becoming proficient with time-span interviewing are to:

- conduct the interview one-on-one
- take into consideration anomalies caused by the CIP of the manager or the subordinate
- read *The Time Span Handbook* by Dr. Jaques (referenced in the Appendix)
- role play the incumbent role as Dr. Jaques describes in *The Time Span Handbook*

In addition to ascertaining the time span of the longest tasks being assigned by the manager, you will want to confirm the role incumbent's understanding of that task and by when they believe it needs to be completed (its time span). Where the manager and subordinate do not have the same understanding, then a useful discussion between them needs to take place. I have found that quite often there is a lack of clarity in task assignments particularly with regard to the longest time the subordinate has to complete them.

After interviews with the senior management in the organization are completed, a first draft of the extant organization is created working closely with the internal RO project leader. The names of the role incumbents are not included on the first version of these charts. This is to help the managers think about what work they need done in a role and in what stratum and work band (high, mid or low) the role needs to be positioned without considering the present occupant of the role. Many, if not most, organizations become structured around the **persons** in roles. Hence the organization structure becomes based on who is occupying a role rather than considering the work that has to be done and to what role it is best assigned. Basing the work of a role on capabilities of the role incumbent has obvious problems which become readily apparent when there are changes in personnel.

The roles shown on the initial chart are in the first one or two layers below the CEO. They are also placed in the strata indicated by the time span information. It is sometimes possible at this point to place these roles only in the appropriate Strata without being able to be specific about the Work Band (Low, Mid and High) within the Stratum. More discussions of the longest tasks may be required in order to identify the Work Band. At other times the information obtained in the interviews with regard to time span is sufficiently precise that roles can be immediately placed within the Work Bands.

It is helpful to put the title of the role first on the organization chart rather than the name of the role incumbent. This is a way of becoming accustomed to think first of the role and then the person in the role. (This chart is the first step toward creating a Comprehensive Organization Chart which is discussed in detail in Chapter Seven and in an article in the Appendix.)

Follow-up meeting with the CEO

This initial chart showing the level of work of the roles of the first three Strata is reviewed with the CEO. Information gained in the interviews with his/her subordinates is also discussed. In particular, it is important to share details about any misunderstandings between what the CEO has assigned and what the role incumbent understands. The CEO can then determine what to do.

Modification of the chart occurs based on the CEO's input. The chart is then presented to senior management and reviewed for accuracy and agreement. It is used to observe where there are problems in compression between roles (two or more reporting roles in the same Stratum) or gaps (a missing layer of management). Issues in alignment of functions are also considered. At this point there is usually possible to have an understanding of the number of managerial layers that are requisitely needed.

My preference is to allow managers to observe the issues that become apparent (gaps and compression) and ask them to consider possible options that will enable the organization to be more effective. I ask leading questions and where the answers are not requisite I suggest what possible outcomes might occur, based on Requisite concepts, if the situation is not remedied. This is one of the reasons for providing extensive education early in the implementation.

Completing the Initial Interview Process

I have frequently used someone from the RO implementation team to assist me in interviewing the roles at the level of the CEO's SoRs. This individual captures the information gained in the interview that I conduct. This both frees me to focus totally on the questioning process and acts as a training session for the team member. This interviewing process is repeated down through the organization by trained members of RO team. In some large organizations where there are a number of similar roles only representative roles are interviewed.

Regardless of who is doing the interviewing a similar process is followed as that used with the CEO and Senior Management team. I have not found it necessary to create MCA charts below the level of the CEO's SoRs. Interviewees (who may or may not be managers) are asked about key tasks they have been given along with a time by when they believe the task must be completed. For individuals who are managers the same process takes place with regard to assignments being given to their subordinates and the time span of the longest task(s) they are assigning is sought. During these interviews problems, issues and opportunities arise which are carefully noted for further exploration at a later time. Interview results are reviewed with the relevant persons and corrected as needed. Several draft charts are often required. The final result is a Requisite organization chart of each area showing the stratum and work band of roles as they currently exist and a listing of MCAs and key assignments being given to each role.

OBTAINING INITIAL JUDGMENTS OF COMPLEXITY OF INFORMATION PROCESSING

Judgments of the Complexity of Information Processing (CIP) of each employee need to be gathered. This is done separately from discussions of the assignments being given to roles. Managers are asked to judge each of their subordinates. They then judge each of their subordinates-once-removed and anyone even further down in their unit with whom they are familiar.

The process for interviewing managers is outlined in detail in Chapter Seven. It is, of course, important to have a reasonably good idea of the judged level of Complexity of Information Processing (CIP) of the person being interviewed. For this reason interviews are done starting with the CEO and then cascading the process.

It is important to remember that these judgments provide an idea about where within a Stratum that a person is capable of working at the present time. Work Band designations of Low, Middle and High are helpful in this regard. For example one employee who is capable of working at Stratum I may have a time horizon of about one day and can do work in the Low Stratum I work band and another employee can conceptualize two months into the future and be judged in the High Band.

It is desirable to have someone assist you by writing down the judgments so you can focus on the questioning process. All of this information must be kept strictly confidential. In addition to the judgment of CIP a great deal of information about each person is usually provided in these interviews. This should be captured as part of ongoing talent pool work. For this reason these interviews are best done with the consultant assisted by someone on the Requisite team from Human Resources. It is particularly useful if that person is involved with Talent Pool Development activities.

The body language of the person being interviewed is especially important to observe. A manager may evidence discomfort in giving a judgment when the person under discussion has some serious behavioral issues. In these instances although the manager is aware of the subordinate's full CIP managers may be uncomfortable about providing a judgment because the subordinate is not seen as functioning at that level,. Managers are often hesitant in judging these individuals. This situation often shows in the person's facial expression and other body language. Upon closer questioning the current CIP can usually be elicited as well as a description of the negative temperament and its impact on that person's output and on the work of the unit.

Another situation where body language does not fully support the stated CIP occurs where there is what might be thought of as 'wishful thinking'. This is the situation where the manager has a good sense of the actual CIP but states the judgment as how s/he wishes or hopes the person could perform while being aware that it is not actually happening.

As part of the questioning about their judgments, managers are asked about where they believe their subordinates are working right now in terms of their CIP. For subordinates who are not judged capable of their role level some follow up questions to ask are:

What are the issues you have to deal with because of this?

Do the tasks assigned to the role get done satisfactorily? Do you have to do some of the work of this role yourself? Does some of the work not get done?

Would it be more comfortable if there was a manager between you and this individual?

What might you be considering doing to change this situation? When might that be able to happen?

The gearing chart illustrated in Chapter Seven is used to capture the information with regard to the judgment of each subordinate's current CIP. This is done in pencil so the manager can easily change judgments if desired. The completed gearing chart is reviewed by the manager so that s/he can compare the judgments. These judgments often become clearer to the interviewee by making these comparisons and changes are often made. It is helpful to point out that these are initial judgments and will be reviewed on a regular basis. Managers may want to change their judgments upon further observation. Also individuals mature in CIP over time.

Remind managers that MoRs will be discussing these judgments with the person involved for agreement and that the judged level of Complexity of Information Processing is **always** talked about using the titles common within the organization, **never** using numbers that designate Strata.

As was described in Chapter Seven, the *Potential Progress Data Sheet* is a chart that can be used as part of this process. These charts were initially developed by Dr. Jaques as a result of his research over the years in many organizations. They roughly reflect the typical progress of individuals at given points in their careers. These charts are copyrighted and available through www.CasonHall.com. This chart provides a picture of the various pathways that individuals appear to follow in their development based on Dr. Jaques' research. These pathways are called a person's Mode. Mode gives an indication of the highest level of Complexity of Information Processing an individual is likely to reach in their lifetime.

When a managers judge a person to have future potential I then ask when the believe the individual might be able to work at the next level higher. The answer is typically, one year or two or three years or five years. I next ask at what level role they judge this person might be able to work by the end of their career. Interesting enough I have found that most managers can reasonably easily and confidently make these judgments.

After a manager has made these judgments of an employee I plot the information on the Potential Progress Data Sheet to see if it appears to follow the trajectories indicated by Dr. Jaques' research. In almost all instances I have found that the information obtained in the interview does indeed follow the trajectories on the chart. Reviewing and comparing the Modes of individuals being judged also helps managers to refine and feel increased confidence in their judgments.

If the judgment is seriously different from what the chart indicates I point this out to the manager and we together explore what might be at issue here and possibly set aside a designation until the manager has been able to do further observations. Occasionally a young person who is highly articulate is over-judged. The chart will show that s/he would follow the trajectory to have a Mode of perhaps VII or VIII. In these instances I ask the manager if it seems that this person, in his/her opinion, would eventually be able to run a global corporation. Usually the answer from the manager is that "perhaps I have somewhat over-judged the person".

Designing the Requisite Organization

With clarity about the organization as it currently exists at the senior management levels, a requisite design for these layers (initially for the CEO's subordinates and SoRs) can be created and plans for implementation devised for having:

- the right number of layers
- the roles that are needed
- each role in its appropriate layer with a designation of low, medium or high
- functions appropriately aligned

This work is done by the CEO and the senior team working with the consultant and requires a number of meetings over a period often of weeks or months. When the plan is approved, implementation steps begin in restructuring and redeploying staff.

Cascading the Process

The process as described above of providing education, analyzing the extant organization, obtaining CIP, designing the requisite organization and planning implementation steps is cascaded to the next two layers which is typically IV and III. Implementation is begun. Extensive education about management leadership practices is provided and they are put in place and begun to be used. New processes needed are designed and introduced. With knowledge of the CIP of employees though level III, the talent pool process for senior management roles at IV and above can be started. All of this work is cascaded to Strata II and I. Appropriate education at those levels is carried out as well as for senior and middle management. When this work is completed the talent pool for mid-level management can begin since persons with Strata III and II potential have been identified.

At this stage in the project there are many activities going on simultaneously. It is important to have a method of following the status of these activities in order to provide regular progress reports to the client and to identify any issues or areas that are falling behind.

Requisite Compensation

As was discussed in Chapter Six, Requisite felt fair compensation comes late in the implementation process because requisite structure needs to be in place and roles need to be staffed appropriately. Nonetheless, early in the project it can be useful to review the salary structure as it currently exists. I have found that at least in strata I, II and III a pattern can often be found in the organization that is another indicator that can help confirm the level of work of roles. If the salaries that are outliers to the general pattern are eliminated, not only are demarcations for strata boundaries often found but sometimes rough boundaries of low, mid and high band within a stratum as well. This salary pattern may also help to confirm compression and gaps.

Titles and Grades

When the organization is ready in the Requisite implementation process to turn attention to compensation, modification of titles and grades needs to be done at the same time. In Novus International, discussed in Chapter Eight, the grading was simplified by simply using 1.1, 1.2 and 1.3 for Stratum I work at Low, Mid and High Work Bands and then 2.1, 2.2, 2.3 for Stratum II work and so on.

Titling roles is more complex because of the vexed word 'manager' with its many meanings. The problem usually arises at Stratum III. In one organization the solution was to use the title, People Manager for those who were managers in the requisite sense of the word, that is, for those who manage people, using titles such as People Manager, Tax Accounting and People Manager, Purchasing.

At Stratum II the title FLM is used for the First Line Manager role. At Stratum I the title FLMA (First Line Manager Assistant) is used indicating that the role is an assistant to the first line manager and does not have full managerial accountability and authority. The word 'supervisor' used in Stratum I often signals unclear role accountability and authority. Using a descriptive word here in titles can also be useful, for example: FLMA, Training or FLMA, Drafting.

Timing of Implementation

Dr. Jaques expressed the belief, somewhat tongue in cheek, that an organization where the Requisite work is driven by the CEO can change the way it operates over a weekend. Rapid implementation has not fully been our experience. We have found that it generally takes a minimum of two years, for example, to:

- provide education in Requisite principles and practices throughout the entire organization
- determine the desired changes to the extant organization structure and begin implementation
- decide changes in staffing that are needed and begin to implement them
- work through the changes needed in HR processes

We have further found that clearly specifying assignments as to quality, quantity, resources and completion time (QQTR) typically takes a year to be accepted. Experienced mid-level managers are a bit skeptical at first of the time and thought involved in providing complete assignments in writing including QQTR. However, by the time a full year has gone by and they are in the process of thinking about appraisals for the past year and assignments for the coming year, they realize the value of fully specifying tasks.

We have experienced the implementation process typically to take three to five years in order to embed Requisite fully in an organization. Two years has usually been the minimum. Of course, there are exceptions. We have also participated in an implementation in a very large organization that took place in under six months with daily direction by the CEO and a tremendous effort on the part of many persons.

COMPLETING THE PROJECT

By the end of a typical Requisite project implementation the requisite organization structure is designed and most roles are staffed with persons capable of the work of the role. In my experience at this point all changes are understood and planned for, but not all have yet taken place for various reasons. Some things are out of line such as the need to wait for a retirement or the inability to fill a role as desired because of a lack of suitable candidates. In a sense a complete Requisite Organization implementation is an ideal to be striven for and worked toward on a continuing basis. That said, I have come close to full completion a number of times.

Requisite Organization consulting includes teaching the system to managers so that they can make good decisions and take requisite steps at a time that is appropriate for the individuals involved. Roles and tasks are clearly spelled out and understood. Corporate policies are requisite in nature. Managerial leadership practices are being used throughout the organization. Comprehensive Organization Charts exist for each unit and are updated regularly so that anti-requisite issues can be readily seen and plans made for correction.

A critical part of completion is to ensure that the organization can carry out Requisite processes and practices after the consultant has left. This is a distinguishing feature of Requisite consulting. The goal is for the system to be fully embedded so that employees can carry forward the work. This is one of the reasons for extensive education about all expects of RO as part of implementation.

Comprehensive Organization Charts

Although Comprehensive Organization Charts will have been in the process of being developed during implementation, having the chart in final form is an important part of completion of the project. There should also be a procedure for updating the charts on a regular basis. As was mentioned earlier, these charts are an important tool to integrate much of the knowledge gained about the organization including the Stratum and Work Band of each role, the role incumbent's judged current CIP and Mode and the total compensation for the person in the role for the past year. These charts can also be coded to show gender, anticipated retirements and so on. With all of this information in one place, issues needing attention are clearly illustrated. Gaps and role compression are evident. Departments can be compared against each other. It is, for example, sometimes found that one area is more highly paid than another even where they are doing the same level of work. If differences in pay are found, based on gender, these become apparent.

In my experience these Comprehensive Organization Charts illustrate this information in a clear and fully consistent manner for managers for the first time, enabling them to see their opportunities and problems all in one place. I developed the concept of the Comprehensive Organization Chart while working with Dr. Jaques and perfected it over the years with my colleague Terry Seigel. I have found it to be a highly useful tool.

Continuing Education and Review

There are two essential activities that need to be in place to keep RO embedded in the organization and updated over time. One is a process in place for educating new hires and for providing education in managerial leadership practices to newly appointed managers. There also needs to be an annual review of Requisite principles and practices. This review is a time to deepen an understanding of RO and to reinforce managerial leadership practices. In a number of organizations this is done by the CEO at the annual meeting. This annual review embeds RO more deeply and keeps aspects of the system from eroding or being lost altogether.

LETTING REQUISITE ORGANIZATION HAPPEN

In a number of instances I have had senior managers who have learned about RO or have used RO while working for former employers who wish to implement this system, but the CEO has no particular interest in doing so. Even when a full scale project does not seem possible, aspects of RO can be effectively used if the CEO is willing to let it happen.

In one organization a business unit head decided to implement RO fully in his unit and over the next several years he not only did so but he also educated his colleagues on the senior management team on a continuing basis as to what he was doing and the results of the Requisite effort. Several years later he became the CEO and RO is now embedded in the total organization. In another example the senior vice president of HR used the four aspects of suitability for a role (CIP, skilled knowledge, values and required behavior) very effectively to help managers in a global organization consider both current employees and potential hires. This led to the introduction of Requisite managerial leadership practices.

Not all partial implementations are successful. The head of IT in a technology-based organization wished to implement RO in her area, but after the education of the executive team the CEO stated that he did not wish this to happen. In another somewhat similar situation the COO oversaw the introduction of RO in parts of the organization. However a senior manager fostered discontent among the senior leadership team as he was opposed to the changes that might potentially happen to his role. In time he and the team convinced the CEO to end the project.

Where the introduction and implementation is not driven by the CEO, I caution the client, in whatever role and area s/he is working, that the introduction of RO practices tends to act as a type of Trojan horse. No matter what aspects of RO are used or where in the system they are introduced, the implications of these concepts and their effects are quickly felt elsewhere in the organization and can cause some disruption. Nonetheless, I have found that regardless of the outcome for partial implementations the effort has proved worthwhile. Managers who are educated about RO principles cannot then unlearn what they have been educated about including such things as:

- considering the work to be done in a role separately from the person in the role
- the need for appropriate managerial layers, without gaps and compression
- having managers who are one level higher than subordinates in CIP
- the value of eliminating gaps and compression
- staffing with suitability for role concepts rather than using a complex, confusing and ill-defined list of competencies
- the need for role clarity and specifically defining assignments
- the value of the Manager-once-Removed role

I have found that once managers are fully introduced to Requisite principles and the logic of the system, it is as if they pass through a door which then shuts behind them on many of their former beliefs and traditional practices. They find a way to articulate many ideas that they intuitively knew but had no way of expressing. They also find new ways of thinking as well as new concepts and procedures. Some examples of this are the explicit concept of Complexity of Information Processing, the need for a manager one level of capability higher than subordinates, separating the consideration of the work needed to be done in a role from the suitability and capability of the role incumbent, the role of the Manager-once-Removed in ensuring fairness clearly defined task assignments with QQTR and generally understood definition of language used in the organization.

In one consulting assignment the CEO decided to implement RO fully and the project commenced with education of the senior management team who received a substantial amount of information about Requisite Organization. Tragically the CEO died quite suddenly. Two years later the need for reorganization was again raised. Several approaches were reviewed by the management team and the new CEO. Some members of the team recalled the ideas in RO and they urged the CEO to consider that approach. The result was one of the most complete implementations in which I participated.

THOUGHTS ON VARIOUS ASPECTS OF REQUISITE CONSULTING

There are a number of aspects of Requisite consulting that I will comment on in the balance of this chapter. These include:

- Linking Task Assignments to the Organization's Strategy and Goals
- Cross-Functional Working Relationships
- Personal Effectiveness Appraisal
- Change Management
- Educating Managers
- Stratum II and III Issues
- Bottom Up Analysis
- Common Assumptions
- Level and Stratum
- Temperament and Required Behavior
- Requisite Definitions
- Partial Solutions and Management Fads
- Family-owned organizations

Linking Task Assignments to the Organization's Goals

In order for an organization's strategy to be achieved it is essential to cascade task assignments that are directly derived from the corporate strategy. In this way the long-range plans and objectives are translated into desired results. This cascading takes place through the manager subordinate relationship using Requisite task delegation. It requires continuing communication of corporate goals and objectives throughout the organization. This linkage enables employees to understand how their work contributes to the overall goals of the organization. A method of linking corporate strategy and plans to key assignments, developed by Dr. Fred Mackenzie and myself, is described in the Appendix in the article entitled *Making Strategy Work*.

Cross-Functional Working Relationships

I have found defining Cross-Functional Working Relationships (CFWRs) also called Task Initiating Role Relationships (TIRRs) necessary between roles that do not report to the same manager to be one of the more difficult aspects of implementing RO. The basic structure of a managerial hierarchy is the vertical layering of manager-subordinate relationships in specialized functions such as production, marketing, accounting and so on. Managers have the accountability and authority to assign work to their subordinates and are held accountable for the results. However, work flow processes are often required to move laterally from one function to another. This flow brings roles into relationship with one another where there is no direct authority to give an assignment. This is often one of the biggest sources of interpersonal stress and conflict in managerial organizations.

An important contribution of requisite structuring is that it enables functions to be correctly aligned in each layer which is an important first step in passing partially completed outputs between functions appropriately. There are, however, many instances where it is essential to clearly specify accountability and authority in specific situations between roles where there is no direct managerial authority to assign work. To do this I have found two approaches that are particularly effective in defining essential cross-functional working relationships.

One approach is to start the process by having the MoR and his/her immediate managers meet to talk about their key assignments. This results in revealing where there were difficult issues between SoR roles reporting to different managers. (Lack of clarity in functional alignment and clarity of assignments also becomes apparent.) Participants generally find this type of open discussion and sharing is both enlightening and constructive. It is useful to hold CFWR meetings at regular intervals. Another approach is to have the managers of roles where problems exist and their manager, the MoR, meet to discuss situations where clarity is needed to have smooth horizontal work flow. In both types of meetings the six CFWRs described in Chapter Three are reviewed and the specific managers involved suggest which one might be most effective. If there is disagreement, the MoR makes the final decision.

It is useful to keep in mind that the CFWR decided upon can be changed whenever the situation seems to warrant it. For example in one company there was a problem with the safety of the elevators. The inspector role was initially given Monitoring authority and accountability with regard to maintenance roles. When problems continued this was increased to Auditing accountability and authority since the person in the role had to have the authority to require that the elevators be immediately stopped when he observed them to be outside the margins of safety. This avoided the potential for serious accidents. The problem was then referred to the relevant managers and their MoR where a decision could be made about getting the additional resources needed for adequate maintenance on a continuing basis.

There is a sample Key Assignment Document (KAD) in the appendix of this book in the article entitled *Establishing Key Assignments*. In that KAD there is a place to specify Cross-Functional Working Relationships including a description of the specific situation and the accountability and authority assigned to the relevant roles. Doing so adds greatly to role clarity and minimizes ongoing interpersonal difficulties. Cross-Functional Working Relationships are spelled out in detail in Chapter Three.

Personal Effectiveness Appraisal

In working with a number of clients there were several concerns about having only three designations: 'meets expectations', 'below expectations' and 'does not meet expectations', as set forth by Dr. Jaques. It was suggested by a number of my clients that another designation be added, that of, 'working toward expectations'. I have added that category to the appraisal form and process.

Another area of some disagreement was that Dr. Jaques felt that it was only necessary to have the top designation in appraisal as 'meeting expectations'. He felt that in instances where the individual exceeded expectations those situations would be taken care of by mentoring meetings with the Manager-once-Removed and the talent pool process. Some of my clients have felt strongly about including an Exceeds Expectations category on the appraisal. When this is the situation, 'exceeds expectations' is added to the appraisal with the following description:

Exceeds Expectations

- Performing at a higher level than that required by the role
- Suggesting alternatives or solutions to issues that could impede achievement of business goals
- Consistently going above and beyond expectations of the tasks assigned
- Adding substantial value to the role

If an Exceeds Expectations designation is used, it generally is an indication that the individual is ready to move to a new role.

Similar details on the other personal effectiveness appraisal designations are shown on the sample Key Assignments Document provided in the article on *Establishing Key Assignments* in the Appendix.

Change Management

Implementing Requisite Organization usually involves a fair amount of change in policies, systems, procedures and so on. Using a change management process while implementing RO will substantially assist in the implementation process. In particular it acts as a reminder to continually communicate what is happening and why the changes are important. One approach we have found especially effective is Dr. John Kotter's eight-step change model found in his book, *Leading Change.* Reference to a doctoral thesis written by Dr. Paul Lynch can be found through www.globalro.com. This thesis describes in detail how Kotter's steps in change management were used in a long-term major project at CRA, an Australian mining company. This thesis also gives insight into how Requisite theory developed in that organization as a result of Dr. Jaques' method of consulting research.

Stratum II and Stratum III Issues

In many organizations there is a substantial amount of roles and people at Stratum II and III in both managerial and often individual contributor roles as well. This is particularly true in technology and engineering organizations where much of the output is also the result of the work of teams. We have often found that it not easy to sort through these roles which may contain work of both strata. And we find that many times Stratum III roles are filled by individuals who are only Level II capable, further confusing the situation. We have also found organizations with Stratum I direct output that are missing Stratum II first line manager roles. In these organizations the first line of management is a Stratum III which can result in some quite serious problems. Nonetheless with careful application of requisite understanding and analysis it is possible to determine the extant organization and uncover the problems within it.

Bottom-Up Review

In addition to the process of top down examination of the extant organization we have found it most useful often to conduct a bottom up review. This happens by looking at the roles where the direct output occurs—where the product or service is produced, and then seeing how this is managed by the next stratum up, and so on. Bottom up review can be a help in sorting through the difficulties of determining Stratum II and III work and roles. And this approach will continue to be especially useful in the future as more of the direct output is produced at Stratum II or even Stratum III.

Educating Managers

The work of educating clients in all aspects of the system is one of the most crucial aspects of Requisite consulting. In enables the consultants to then ask questions of managers based on Requisite principles. In RO consulting, managers are the ones to make the decisions. It is the managers' organization and the decisions are theirs. The consultant has informed them of the logical, integrated and science-based way to proceed but each decision is theirs to make. When what they choose is anti-requisite, the consultant can give them one or more scenarios, based on Requisite practices, as to what is likely to be the results of that decision.

For example, in one client organization, the CEO decided to retain one member of her senior leadership team despite the fact that she stated on numerous occasions that this individual was only capable of Stratum III work and probably had a time horizon not much longer than a year. The other members of the team were capable of working in Stratum IV roles. She felt it would not be fair to put that person in a lower role although she realized that he was not capable of his present position. This individual often worked late at night after others had finished their work and gone home. He made frequent requests for more help in his department. In meetings his colleagues often grimaced or rolled their eyes when he spoke up.

The consultant described to the CEO several possible outcomes from leaving this anti-requisite situation in place. This included such things as:

- Much work in his area was not being completed or not completed to her satisfaction
- Her time being taken in having to do some of his work
- Difficulties with other areas in dealing with processes that involved his unit

- Possible stress-related impact on his health (It is stressful when you and others know you are not fully capable of doing the role you are in.)

In fact the CEO came to see that most of these issues existed. This employee eventually had a stress-related health problem, resigned and eventually took a lower level role in another company. After several similar instances where the consultant predicted probable results using Requisite concepts, the CEO much more quickly based her decisions on Requisite principles.

In providing education I present Requisite ideas as propositions to be considered. I find CEOs and senior managers do not like to be told what to do. I point out that in decades of doing this work, my colleagues and I have found that these propositions prove out. However, I like to give managers the time to think about these concepts and to assimilate them without pressure. As a result of in-depth education in Requisite principles managers gain an understanding of this total system and generally make some fundamental changes in their thinking. They gain a deeper understanding of effective management practices and how organizations can operate most effectively.

Common Assumptions

Some Requisite practices fly in the face of 'conventional wisdom' that often has no basis whatsoever. Three examples of this are:

- all managers should have a successor ready so that they are able to be promoted
- a manager should only have about four to six direct reports
- managerial roles are determined by the number of subordinates and budget control

To refute the first belief requisitely the following questions can be considered:

"Is the person selected by the manager capable of filling a role at the next higher level?"

"Does the MoR of the role feel the person selected by the manager is qualified to fill the role who will then be his/her subordinate?"

With regard to the second belief (that there is an optimum number of subordinates) I discuss the situation that in organizations lacking requisite concepts, subordinate roles are very often at different levels of work and the individuals filling them at a variety of levels of capability. This seriously limits a manager's ability to delegate work, much of it then having to be done by the manager, hence the number of subordinates that can be handled is also limited. In an organization that is requisitely structured the number of subordinates will vary considerably from six to eight or nine for senior managers to 60 or 70 for some first line managers depending upon such considerations as location, type of work and assistance given the manager. First line work is discussed in Chapter Four.

Regarding the third belief (that role level should be based on a given number of subordinates and budget accountability) I have managers consider senior advisory or specialist roles. These roles do not require any subordinates or only a few subordinates to assist them with their work. In some organizations such a role would not qualify for a Stratum IV, V or VI role even though that is the level of work required. An example is a Chief Economist in a financial services organization. In Requisite structure, roles are placed by the longest tasks that need to be assigned to the role and by the complexity of the work that needs to be done in the role, not by how many subordinates the role has or by the amount of resources for which it is accountable.

Level and Stratum

One misunderstanding in Requisite work that I have occasionally found has to do with the spread of time between Stratum boundaries. For example, a person who has the Complexity of Information Processing to fill a Stratum IV role, who can think and make decisions using parallel processing, may have a time horizon anywhere from just over two years up to as long as five years. While each Stratum has a spread between boundaries, any given individual is capable of working at a certain **level** within those boundaries. One person might be capable of parallel processing time horizon and have a time horizon a little more than two years into the future while another judged Stratum IV capable could carry out a four-year assignment or yet another could complete a task of almost five years duration. There is a great deal of difference in the assignments that can be successfully given to someone who is at the beginning stage of being able to use the parallel processing required for Stratum IV work and someone who is fully developed in this regard. The same is true with the time horizon an individual possesses currently within any Stratum. At any given time s/he will be at a given level within the stratum. A person's capability does not encompass the range of the Stratum but rather a specific point within it.

In one of my client organizations an experienced Stratum IV manager was perplexed because her subordinate, Jim, whom she judged capable of working at Stratum III, was unable to complete the two-year plan she had assigned him. Repeatedly Jim came back with an incomplete plan and was clearly stressed trying to do this work. He normally did his work well and on time. I explained to Linda that his time horizon might be closer to one year than two years and explored Linda's judgment of Jim. I asked her if she felt that Jim was able to do Stratum III tasks at the lower level of the Stratum or perhaps somewhere in the middle range. It seemed clear that Jim could not do a task at the high end of Stratum III. Linda judged that Jim was likely working at the low end of Stratum III and probably could only think a little more than a year into the future. Yet she had given him a task that she thought of as a three-month assignment but she now understood that to do it he was required to conceptualize two years out. She realized that she had to create that plan herself and that Jim could help by filling in details.

Managers will sometimes give an example of a planning assignment as the longest task being given to a role. Planning assignments are not good examples for considering the time span of a role. The time span of a planning assignment is not the length of the plan, but the length of time the manager is giving the person to complete the plan. In the earlier example, Linda thought that she had given to Jim only a three-month assignment, hence, she did not understand why he could not complete the task. However, as Linda's example illustrates, in tasks involving creating plans managers need to take into account the length of time horizon that someone is able to conceptualize as well as how long they are giving that person to do the task.

Temperament and Required Behavior

This area of capability has been approached by Dr. Jaques at various times with different words and concepts. In early publications he used the word temperament to describe a person's behavior. He referred to negative temperament as minus T (-T). This referred to behavior that interfered with getting work done. He was opposed to the use of competencies to describe personality characteristics that made someone more or less suited to various types of roles. In his last edition of *Requisite Organization* (1996) he did away with negative temperament as one of the fours aspects of suitability for role. Instead he discussed 'expected' behavior. This he sometimes referred to as 'required' behavior. Fundamentally he believed that if an organization was fully requisite people would demonstrate reasonable behavior and negative temperament would not be evidenced at work. He stated that it is a manager's accountability to note failure to behave reasonably and "to discuss such problems with subordinates as part of personal effectiveness assessment and coaching."

I have found that there is almost always some aspect of negative temperament to be dealt with in certain employees even when almost all requisite conditions are in place. Individuals are complex: sometimes there are compromises that need to be made. These behavioral issues are difficult and this is one area where many managers prefer to avoid addressing the situation. However, managers are accountable for making subordinates aware of unacceptable behavior and the consequences for continuing it.

As mentioned earlier, I have found that using 'required behavior' in discussing temperament and personality opens the door for the attempt to use competency analysis to be used where specific kinds of behavior, which are ill-defined, are required for certain types of work. I have found competencies to be a somewhat useless and wasteful exercise. (Later in this chapter I discuss Dr. Jaques issues with competencies and other management fads.) What I do find helpful with regard to **temperament** is to think of it as **any behavior so extreme that it gets in the way of work getting done** which is something that can be described using specific examples.

The four aspects of suitability for role I use are:

- Complexity of Information Processing
- Skilled Knowledge
- Values/Commitment
- No extreme behavior that interferes with work getting done

Requisite Definitions

Dr. Jaques spent more than 60 years seeking to make the management of employment hierarchies science based. This required having clear definitions that everyone understood. His book, *Requisite Organization,* has a glossary as does this book, in an attempt to move in that direction. He spent a great deal of time and effort in clarifying definitions and naming concepts.

Generally I have found difficulties arise when trying to substitute another word or phrase for the one that Dr. Jaques settled on and defined. An example of this is Manager-once-Removed. Some organizations prefer to use Manager's Manager. When trying to explain concepts or to write policies and procedures it is generally clearer to stay with the requisite terms. As an example, Manager's Manager doesn't lend itself to the use of Subordinate-once-Removed which is easily understood if the designations of Manager-once-Removed and Subordinate-once-Removed are used consistently.

Dr. Jaques discovered some specific distinctions that help in doing this work. For example in examining the current organization which is an early critical step in understanding how it is now operating, Dr. Jaques determined that there were several versions that could be uncovered and gave a name to each. There is the **manifest** organization which is the one shown on the organization charts. There is an **assumed** organization which is how different people believe the organization operates and there are many versions of the assumed organization. Finally, there is the **extant** organization which is how the organization actually functions. It is the extant organization that is sought to be uncovered in order to work on designing the organization requisitely.

In an attempt to become more descriptive Dr. Jaques sometimes changed the terms used for some of his concepts over the years. As an example Dr. Jaques changed Complexity of Information Processing (CIP) to Complexity of Mental Processing (CMP). He defined this as "the maximum scale and complexity of the world that one is able to pattern and construe and function in, including the amount and complexity of information that must be processed in doing so". He further described it as "the processes by which one takes information and analyzes it, puts it together, recognizes it, judges and reasons with it, arrives at conclusions, makes plans and takes action". In Requisite work practitioners use either term.

He at one point used the term Cross-Functional Working Relationships (CFWRs) instead of his earlier designation of Task Initiating Role Relationships (TIRRs) to describe relationships where one does not have task assigning authority. He later returned to using TIRRS which is a useful and memorable way to distinguish these lateral role relationships from Task Assigning Role Relationships (TARRs). TARRS are vertical role relationships in which the manager does have the authority to assign tasks to subordinate roles. I have continued to use CFWR in this book and leave the choice to the client of which umbrella term to use for this critically important group of horizontal accountabilities and authorities. One client simply called them Cross Functional Relationships (CFRs).

Often organizations resist certain words or prefer to use the words familiar to their cultures. For example, the word 'subordinate' is disliked in a number of companies and in some countries. A great deal of clarity is lost when trying to substitute another word. I explain early in educational sessions that there is no other word in the English language for this concept. It denotes that someone is paid in an employment organization for carrying out tasks assigned by their manager and that this applies to all employees up to and including the CEO who is subordinate to the owner or Board of Directors.

Nonetheless, 'subordinate' is one of the words often resisted and the preference is to use 'direct report' instead. Dr. Jaques did not like the use of 'direct report' and said that "one could report to any number of people but needed to have only one manager". However, direct report is a commonly used term to designate an immediate subordinate and the word 'subordinate' has a certain amount of negative connotation. If an organization chooses to use direct report I find that acceptable as long it indicates only <u>immediate</u> subordinates. I have found it often easier to use words that are clearly understood and in common usage in the client organization, rather than always trying to substitute the requisite term—'direct report' being a prime example. While it is generally better to use Dr. Jaques chosen designations, using another term for a concept does not change its definition. The important consideration is that the words chosen are clearly defined, understood and used consistently.

Some of my client companies are uncomfortable with the term Requisite Organization as the defining title words for the entire system. In some organizations I have substituted the title of 'The Accountable Management System' or used the name of the organization, for example, the Novus Management System. Changing the over-arching title does not change any of the underlying principles.

Partial Solutions

Dr. Jaques observed, as many of us have experienced, organizations typically have:

- too many layers
- undefined working relationships
- unclear accountability and authority
- work being done at the wrong level
- chaotic compensation systems
- unfair incentive schemes
- processes needing updating and improvement
- a lack of understanding of human mental capability and its growth
- poor career development procedures

Because most organizations do not recognize and address the two core issues—that **they are not structured and staffed requisitely**—they make continual attempts to solve their problems. Certain processes and fads recur regularly or remain in place to try to address issues that arise and new attempts at solutions are devised. Some of the myriad examples include self-managed teams, balanced score cards, roles described by competencies, various quality control methods and various approaches to re-engineering.

Methods to improve people, communications and teams surface and resurface such as the Myers Briggs and Spiral Dynamics. Some of the personality exercises are helpful in understanding others and improving communication, but they do not address the underlying problems.

The use of self-managed teams seems to recur every decade or so to attempt to resolve the problems where managers are not at the right level of capability and do not have clear accountability and authority. Yet these teams continually fail after a few attempts because there is no one manager providing resources and accountable for the output of the team. As Dr. Jaques pointed out the nature of the employment contract is that the employees will make their individual capability available to achieve assigned outputs. Although employees are also expected to work cooperatively with others, self-managed teams and other attempts to make individuals feel bound together in an autonomous group have proven dysfunctional.

The use of competencies in selecting someone for a role was first undertaken in the 1970's on a government contract from the Navy. This approach seems to wander in and out of favor in an attempt to make good placements in addition to interviewing for skill, knowledge and experience. What is missing is the understanding brought about by Dr. Jaques of Complexity of Information Processing that people have different mental capability (CIP). Using various ill-defined words to describe the personality type needed for a given role does not act as a substitute for selecting someone with the judgment and decision-making ability to be successful in a specific role.

It is this continual improvement of all aspects of the processes over which a manager has control that precludes the need to use separate Total Quality Management (TQM). quality circles and other quality control methods that are added outside direct managerial accountability and authority.

Re-engineering introduced in the 1980's as a solution to improving processes remains and also appears under different names. While continually improving processes is absolutely essential in the rapidly changing environment, it is the accountability of <u>all</u> managers in a Requisite organization. In a Requisite organization functions are divided vertically so that they are correctly aligned at each layer and Cross-Functional Working Relationships are clearly articulated. This provides the basis and the clarity for moving processes horizontally across functions to complete output. Reengineering efforts can undermine the accountability and authority of managers for continually improving processes as outlined in Requisite procedures (covered in Chapter Three).

Many reengineering projects have failed largely because they are not lead by an accountable manager who has the needed level of Complexity of Information Processing. Some organizations that are working toward implementing Requisite concepts may need to institute a re-engineering process to improve processes that have not been formerly attended to. In these situation it is critical to have the project led by a person capable of working at Stratum IV and sometimes Stratum V depending on the work to be done. Once the organization is requisitely organized and the improved processes are in place, reengineering consulting will generally no longer be needed nor will any of the attempts to overcome the lack of clear and required managerial accountability and authority.

Some of these attempted solutions may resolve some of the organizations issues for a period of time but none of them fully address the foundational issues of having the right number of layers, people in roles capable of the work of the role and value adding managers in place. Additionally, none of them require full-scale managerial leadership practices that enable clear task assignment linked to corporate goals and objectives.

Family-owned Organizations

While all types of employment organizations have outstanding results in increased productivity and profitability, one type is often particularly successful and that is the family-owned organization. The reasons for this is that they very often have a much longer time frame than publicly traded companies and they do not have to have a quarterly results focus.

Often their vision extends generations into the future. By contrast many corporate CEOs have a tenure of only three to five years. The lack of a requirement for a continual very short term focus and the long time horizon of the family is an especially appropriate environment for the use of Requisite Organization.

Evolving Requisite Organization Theory and Practice

Dr. Jaques believed that "the development of scientifically based and requisitely organized and led managerial hierarchies is one of the central socio-political issues of our democratic world for the 21st century." During his lifetime he continually researched and sought to extend an understanding of how organizations could most effectively operate-—effectiveness defined as productive, profitable and healthy places for people to work. He was constantly testing existing tenets of Requisite Organization and seeking full and clearer elaboration.

I observed an example of Dr. Jaques' continuing discernment of useful distinctions when he had been interviewing managers about their subordinates. He commented that he just realized that managers were talking about two kinds of potential in their subordinates. One was the potential that someone had right now, that is, the most complex role they could handle at the present time. This he discovered was different from the manager's judgment of that person's potential at some point in the future. Thus, since there were two different aspects of any individual's potential, he named each one so that they could be distinguished when discussing someone. The terms he chose were Current Potential Capability and Future Potential Capability. This distinction is particularly useful in talent pool work. Subtle distinctions such as this can continue to be made that further extend Requisite concepts.

Building on the Basic Concepts of Requisite Organization

There are activities continually going on throughout the world that are using and evolving Dr. Jaques' fundamental concepts of the natural stratification of managerial layers in employment organizations and the differences in individuals' complexity of information processing to do the work in the different layers.

While the basic tenets underlying Requisite Organization appear to be universal and timeless, their application can have many different approaches that integrate the tenets and continuing evolution is possible and necessary. Some key tenets of Requisite Organization are:

- There is a requisite number of layers needed in an organization based on its strategy and the complexity of the work required to achieve it.
- Layers (strata) in an organization differ in the complexity of the work that needs to get done.
- The complexity of a role can be measured by the longest tasks being assigned to it (time span).
- Individuals are placed in roles who are capable of the work required in the role.
- Each strata needs to be managed by a role at one higher level of complexity.
- Managers are accountable for the outputs and working behavior of their subordinates, for sustaining a team capable of producing those outputs and for giving effective leadership to that team.
- All employees are accountable to bring their best efforts to work every day.

Requisite consultants and organizations are finding new types of problems and new ways to apply RO concepts. An example of where the continuing evolution of Requisite thinking is needed is observed with regard to five strata business units. Initially Dr. Jaques found that full scale business units appeared to be most effective when made up of five layers, Strata I through V, and that these five-level business units were best aggregated under a Stratum VII CEO with a Stratum VI leadership team. With the growth of information technology and globalization, a number of consultants find organizations where the direct output work is at Stratum II as technology is taking care of the Stratum I work. The full implications of how these business units are best structured is being observed and tested.

A number of efforts are being made to automate some of the research required in uncovering the extant organization such as the ability to do a rough initial analysis of gaps, compression and span of control and also the ability to produce comprehensive organization charts, both by using information contained in an organization's HRIS or enterprise software. Information on these methods is available from www.orgcapitalpartners as well as a fuller description of aspects the complexity of management layers, especially senior management roles, that looks at a variety of indicators in addition to time span. Resources exist and are being expanded to provide RO education. Education in the basic concepts of RO is available on the www.globalro.org as well as an extensive bibliography of RO references. RO books and readings are available from www.casonhall.com as well as from www.globalro.org.

It is hoped that Requisite concepts will be more widely understood and will be used to help in solving serious societal issues such as the increasing lack of employment opportunities at Strata I and II as technology becomes ever more capable of handling work at Stratum I and rapidly at Stratum II as well. Until the differences in level of capability (CIP) and how individuals solve problems in getting work done are widely understood, the rapid reduction in the number of Stratum I and II roles cannot be satisfactorily addressed, because the problem cannot be fully and clearly articulated.

Another difficult issue that benefits from the application of Requisite principles is that of CEO compensation. In Chapter Six I have described how to consider Requisite compensation that is felt to be fair for the weight of the responsibility for which the role is accountable. This issue is important to understand as the compensation of certain CEOs has escalated to unreasonable amounts even in situations where the organization failed to thrive.

Dr. Jaques stated that "the aims of Requisite Organization are to provide accountable managerial leadership for highly effective organizations in which people can rest secure in the knowledge that they can trust each other in an honest straight-forward manner and they can use their personal capabilities to the full, both to their own satisfaction and to contribute to the successful functioning of the organization.".

Requisite Organization is the only comprehensive, science-based system that will allow that to happen and that will result in optimum productivity and profitability, competitive advantage and a socially healthy workplace. We look forward to the continuing successful application of Requisite principles and their adaptation as organizations evolve over the coming decades in support of the advancement of democratic societies.

Glossary

Accountability

Accountability is a situation where an individual can be called into account for his/her actions by another individual. See Managerial Accountability.

Aided Direct Output (ADO)

Aided Direct Output is Direct Output carried out with the assistance of subordinates. The subordinates are providing Direct Output Support (DOS).

Alignment

Alignment in an organization is getting the right function at the right level.

Association

An association is a social institution where the members of the group come together for a common purpose. There are non-voluntary associations, such as nations, whose citizens do not have free choice of membership. There are voluntary associations, such as companies, trade unions, and clubs in which the individuals have chosen to become members.

Authority

Authority is the power vested in a person by virtue of role to expend resources: financial, material, technical and human.

Business Unit

A business unit is a profit and loss account unit. It may stand alone or be within a corporation.

Capability

Capability is the ability of a person to do work.

Coaching

Coaching is the process through which a manager helps subordinates to understand the full range of their individual roles, what they need to do to perform the work of that role effectively, and what they need to do in order to develop in that role. The coaching of subordinates is an ordinary and necessary part of every manager's regular activities and an integral part of a manager's continuing review of each subordinate's personal effectiveness.

Complexity of Information Processing (CIP)

A person's complexity of information processing (CIP) is the complexity of mental activity a person uses in carrying out work. Complexity is determined by the number of factors, the rate of change of those factors and the ease of identification of the factors in a situation.

Compensation

The total remuneration granted to an employee in exchange for work and comprising all forms of payment including money and the financial equivalent of non-monetary payments.

Counseling

Counseling by the manager or Manager-once-Removed is done when someone asks for advice with a personal problem.

Cross Functional Working Relationship (CFWR)

Cross Functional Working Relationships are lateral or horizontal relationships that define the accountability and authority in a role in relation to other role(s) across functions. They are relationships in which A is authorized to initiate B's doing something but where it is B's manager and not A who is held accountable for whether or not B does it and for B's output. Dr. Jaques earlier called these Task Initiating Role Relationships (TIRRS). CFWRs include:

> *Advisory Accountability and Authority:* A is accountable for providing advice to B and trying to persuade him/her to take the advice. B is accountable for deciding whether or not to take the advice and, if B decides not to, then A does nothing further.

> *Auditing Accountability and Authority:* A is accountable for inspecting B's work and deciding if it is acceptable within prescribed limits. If it is not within limits B must stop until the matter is referred higher.

> *Collateral Accountability and Authority:* A and B are subordinates of the same manager and are accountable for making mutual adjustments in their work so that the best over-all result is achieved in the light of the context set by their manager. If they cannot agree, they see their manager.

> *Coordinative Accountability and Authority:* A has monitoring authority with respect to specified individuals and also has the authority to bring them together and try to persuade them to take a common course of action.

> *Monitoring Accountability and Authority:* A is accountable for keeping abreast of what B is doing and for taking opportunities to persuade B to take alternative courses of action which A thinks might be better. If B does not accept A's persuasion

and A considers the matter to be serious, then A must report to higher authority.

Prescribing Accountability and Authority: A has the authority to instruct B to carry out particular activities, and B is accountable for doing so, including carrying out the activities at the time prescribed.

Service-Getting and Service-Giving Accountability and Authority: The service-getter, A, has the authority to go to the service-giver, B, and to instruct B to provide an authorized service. B is accountable for providing the service unless s/he does not have the resources to do so, in which case B must indicate to A whether and when it will be possible to provide the authorized service.

Current Applied Capability (CAC)

Current Applied Capability is the capability someone has to do a certain kind of work in a specific role at a given level at the present time. It is a function of his/her complexity of information processing, how much s/he values the work of the role, his/her skilled use of knowledge for the tasks in the role, and the absence of temperamental characteristics that get in the way of getting work done.

Current Potential Capability (CPC)

Current Potential Capability is a person's highest current level of complexity of information processing. It determines the maximum level at which someone could work at the present time, given the opportunity to do so and provided that the work is of value to him/her, and given the opportunity to acquire the necessary skilled knowledge. This is the level of work that people aspire to have and feel satisfied if they can get. When people have work at their CPC, they feel they have an opportunity for the full expression of their potential.

Decision

The making of a choice with the commitment of resources.

Delegation

Delegation is the act of assigning a task to a subordinate.

Delegated Direct Output (DDO)

Delegated Direct Output is output which is assigned to be produced and sent out at subordinate levels.

Direct Output (DO)

Direct Output is output that is sent out directly by the individual producing it and not sent up for approval.

Direct Output Support (DOS)

Direct Output Support is the assistance a subordinate provides to a manager in completing the manager's own direct output.

Discretionary Content

The Discretionary Content of a task are those aspects of a task about which a subordinate must exercise his/her own judgment in order to fulfill the manager's instructions. Discretion always contains judgment with regard to both pace and quality of work to ensure that the work is done on time and to quality standards.

Equilibration

Equilibration is the balancing by managers of the standards being used by their immediate subordinate managers in appraising and managing their own immediate subordinates.

Equitable Pay Differentials

Equitable Pay Differentials are differences in payment between work at different levels that are experienced by the incumbents as fair and just.

Functions

Functions are main types of activity which are required by the objectives of an organization. There are functions that can be generalized for all managerial hierarchies. Functions must be aligned at each organizational level.

Future Potential Capability (FPC)

Future Potential Capability is the maximum level at which a person will be capable of working at some time in the future.

Gearing

Gearing for Talent Pool is the process whereby the Manager-once-Removed and immediate subordinate managers check their judgments with each other regarding the levels of current potential capability of individuals in the next two layers down.

General Responsibility

A General Responsibility is an instruction which applies indefinitely that specifies conditions which, whenever they arise, require an employee to make decisions or take actions within prescribed limits. The task content of a general responsibility lies in the activities that have to be carried through at the times prescribed. The content of these activities may sometimes be prescribed or may sometimes be left to the discretion of the subordinate.

Information Processing Methods

There are four methods of information processing that recur at different Orders of Information Complexity:

> *Declarative*—reasoning by bringing forward a number of reasons that are separate with no connection made to any other reasons

> *Cumulative*—reasoning by bringing together a number of different ideas

Serial—reasoning by constructing a line of thought made up of a sequence of ideas, each one of which leads to the next

Parallel—reasoning by examining a number of possible positions, each arrived at by means of serial processing that can be interlinked

Individual Contributor

An individual contributor is anyone who is mainly engaged in producing direct output. These persons do not delegate their work but complete the final output themselves. Individual contributors' work may occur at any level in the organization based on the level of work of the role. Individual contributors may be managers of subordinates who provide them with direct output support.

Induction

Induction is the process a manager uses to provide subordinates new to the role with the information necessary to do the work of that role.

Knowledge

Knowledge consists of facts, including procedures, that have been learned and can be reproduced.

Level of Work

The Level of Work in a role is the complexity of what needs to be done. This results in the weight of responsibility felt in that role. The level of work in any role can be measured by the time span, which is the targeted completion time of the longest tasks in that role.

Manager

A manager is a person in a role in which s/he is held accountable not only for his/her own personal effectiveness but also for the work and the working behavior of subordinates.

Managerial Accountability

The accountability managers have for their own personal effectiveness; the output of their subordinates; exercising effective managerial leadership of their subordinates; and, building and sustaining an effective team of subordinates capable of producing the assigned outputs.

Managerial Authority

A manager has the minimum authority with regard to immediate subordinates to decide: assignment of tasks, personal effectiveness appraisal, to veto the selection of an unsuitable candidate and to initiate removal from role of a subordinate judged not capable of the work of the role.

Managerial Hierarchies

Managerial Hierarchies are organizations used for employing people to get work done. They are employment systems organized into accountability hierarchies of manager and subordinate roles. It is a vertical organization for getting work done with clearly specified accountabilities.

Manager-once-Removed (MoR)

The manager of a subordinate's immediate manager is that subordinate's manager-once-removed.

Maturation

A maturation process is one in which a given aspect of a person is biologically innate and grows in a regular way to a predictable end state, so long as the individual does not encounter any severely limiting environmental conditions, especially in infancy.

Measurement

Measurement is the quantification of a property of an entity by means of an objective measuring instrument.

Mode

Mode is the highest level of Complexity of Information Processing to which an individual will finally mature.

Mentoring

Mentoring is a periodic discussion by a Manager-once-Removed to help a Subordinate-once-Removed to understand his/her potential and how that potential might be developed to achieve as full a career growth in the organization as possible.

Mutual Recognition Unit (MRU)

A mutual recognition unit is a unit which is small enough (under 250 people) for all of its members to be able to recognize one another.

Orders of Information Complexity

There are four methods of information processing that have been found to recur at higher and higher orders of complexity of the information that is being processed, giving a recursive hierarchy of categories.

> *Pre-Verbal*—Expressed in infancy by gestures and physical contact with objects
>
> *Concrete Verbal*—Thinking and language used in childhood tied to physical pointing out of things referred to that are present or have recently been present
>
> *Symbolic Verbal*—The form of thinking and language used by most adults (Stratum I through IV) that does not have to have specific tangible items present but can represent them by symbols

Conceptual Abstract—Thought and language used at Stratum V and above that refers to other thoughts and words rather than to tangible things.

Universals—Thought and language used at Stratum IX and above to create new universal theories, new types of society, new systems of values, ethics, morality and culture.

Organization

Any system with an identifiable structure. The focus in this book is on employment organizations that are managerial hierarchies.

Assumed Organization—the pattern of connections between roles as it is assumed to be by the different individuals who occupy positions in the organization.

Extant Organization—the pattern of connections between roles as shown by systematic research to be actually operating.

Formal/Informal Organization—these terms are not used in this book; they are replaced by the concepts of manifest, assumed, extant, and requisite organization

Manifest Organization—The structure of an organization as it appears on the organization chart

Requisite Organization—the pattern of connections which ought to exist between roles if the system is to work efficiently and to operate as required by the nature of the work to be done and the nature of human nature.

Organizational Culture

Organizational Culture includes: rules and regulations; resources; customs and practices; shared values; language; belief systems; economics; policies and procedures; and traditions and assumptions.

Organization Process

Organization process consists of practices and procedures that enable the organization to function effectively.

Organizational Structure

Organizational structure is a system of roles and role relationships that people have when they work together. These role relationships establish the boundaries within which people relate to each other.

Output

Output is the product/service produced in a given period of time.

P, Pr and T

The three specialist staff functions are Personnel (P), programming (work flow and business modeling) (Pr) and production technology (T).

Project Team

A project team is an ad hoc group of individuals brought together under a team leader to complete a particular assignment. There is always a specific manager accountable for the team output.

Responsibility

Something one is depended upon or trusted to carry out.

Role

A role is a position within an organization.

Role Complexity

Role complexity is the complexity of tasks in a role as measured by time-span.

Role Relationships

Role relationships are connections between roles that define working relationships between individuals who occupy those roles in term of accountability, authority and content. Role relationships include both vertical task assigning relationships and cross functional working relationships.

Skill

A skill is an ability, learned through training, experience and practice, to carry out a given procedure without having to pay attention, i.e., what a person has learned to do without thinking through the steps involved.

Stratum (plural: Strata)

Managerial strata are organizational layers in a managerial hierarchy. The work in a given stratum is characterized by a specific range of complexity.

Subordinate-once-Removed (SoR)

The subordinate of a manager's immediate subordinate is that manager's subordinate-once-removed.

Talent Pool Development (TPD)

Talent Pool Development is a system for the development of a population of employees who have a distribution of current and future potential capability to discharge the company's current and future human resourcing requirements. The system includes talent pool mapping, selection, recruitment, mentoring, lateral transfers and other methods of individual career development. It embraces all aspects of Succession Planning and Succession Management.

Target Completion Time

The time a manager has in mind by when s/he needs a specific task to be completed.

Task

A task is an assignment to produce a specified output. Tasks have a specified quantity (Q) and quality (Q), and a targeted completion time (T) and are carried out with allocated resources (R) and within specified limits (policies and procedures). A manager assigns a **task** and the subordinate **works** to complete it. A task is a "what by when" or a QQT/R.

Task Assigning Role Relationships (TARRs)

Task Assigning Role Relationships are relationships in which A is not only authorized to get B to do something, but is also held accountable by his/her own manager for B's output (and its quantity, quality and delivery time, within resources and procedures). These are vertical role relationships.

Task Complexity

Task complexity is the complexity of information that has to be handled in carrying out a task. No measure of task complexity has yet been developed, yet managers have a good sense of the differences in complexity of tasks.

Task Initiating Role Relationships (TIRRs)

See Cross Functional Working Relationships

Teaching

The term **teaching** is used to describe the imparting of knowledge to individuals by lectures and discussions.

Temperament

Temperament is the tendency a person has to behave in given ways. Minus T (-T) refers to temperamental qualities in an individual that are dysfunctional in the sense of preventing that individual from carrying out the work required.

Time Horizon

The requisite method of quantifying an individual's potential capability by using the time span of the longest task he or she can handle.

Time Span

Time Span provides the level of work of a role in a simple, objective type of measurement of the weight of responsibility in that role. The longer the time span of a role, the higher is the level of complexity of the work in that role. The time span of a role is measured in terms of those tasks that have the longest target completion time as specified by the immediate manager of the role.

Training

The term training is used to describe the process of helping individuals to develop or enhance their skills through practice, either on the job or in learning simulations.

Trust

Trust is the ability to rely on other to do as they say, to follow established rules, procedures, customs and practice and to be fair and just.

Values

Values are those things to which an individual will give priority or wants to do. Values direct our actions and enable commitment.

Work

Work is the exercise of judgment and discretion in making decisions in carrying out goal directed activities.

USEFUL DEFINITIONS

There are a group of words used that are used somewhat interchangeably which lack clear definition. This leads to misuse and misunderstanding. The definitions that follow clarify the distinction between these words in an organizational setting.

Guideline

A statement of the preferred method of doing and completing an activity.

Examples: Guidelines for the selection interview
Guidelines for preparing an expense report
Guidelines for an effective meeting

Policy

A written statement describing an organization's commitment to a specific value, standard or goal.

Examples: Our safety policy
Our environmental policy
Our anti-discrimination policy

Practice

An activity in the organization designed to provide managerial leadership and bring accountable management concepts to the operational level.

Examples: Task assignment
Context setting
Continual improvement

Procedure

A step-by-step description of what is required (and what role is to do it) to reach a desired outcome

Examples: The de-selection procedure
The security check procedure
The federal tax reporting procedure

Process

A series of sequential actions designed to produce an outcome.

Examples: The employment process
The strategic planning process
The personal effectiveness appraisal process

System

A collection of related procedures, processes and policies that result in work output

Examples: The accounting system
The management system
The production system

Appendix

Requisite Organization Articles

The appendix contains six articles on Requisite Organization topics as listed below. These articles may be reproduced for educational purposes by requesting permission from nmrlee@aol.com or requisiteorganization@gmail.com.

Article 1: **Requisite Organization Overview**
This is a brief introductory description of Requisite Organization.

Article 2: **Making Strategy Work—The Linkage Process**
This article describes how to link the strategy, goals and objectives of an organization to key assignments given to employees.

Article 3: **Determining Role Level and Judging Suitability for a Role**
The differences in complexity of work at the eight Requisite strata in organizations are described in this article as well as differences in capability of individuals suitable for roles.

Article 4: **Establishing Key Assignments**
Giving appropriate and clear assignments is critical as is keeping track of the output and the personal effectiveness of employees. This article explains how to do this and provides a model for a Key Assignment Document.

Article 5: **Teams and Team Working**
Teams are critical to cross functional integration of work. Different types of teams are described in this article.

Article 6: **The Comprehensive Organization Chart**
This article describes how to develop Comprehensive Organization Charts. They are one of the most useful tools in integrating critical aspects of the knowledge gained as a result of the RO consulting process.

Requisite Organization Overview

By Nancy R. Lee

Requisite Organization (RO) is a comprehensive and integrated set of principles and procedures that enables organizations and the people who work in them to be fully effective. The use of these common sense ideas results in an organization that is a good and healthy place for people to work and one that substantially increases its productivity and its profit.

This System enables an organization to:

1. *Structure* appropriately to achieve its mission, strategy, goals and objectives
2. *Staff* with employees fully capable of doing the work in their roles
3. *Establish* accountable managerial leadership practices

ORGANIZATIONAL STRUCTURE

The structure of an organization is provided by the roles that are established and the relationship of the roles to each other. An organization that uses Requisite Organization Management principles can determine and establish the correct number of managerial levels, and place roles at the right level for the complexity of the work that needs to get done.

The relationships between roles are clearly spelled out both for the vertical relationship between manager and subordinate and for the lateral role relationships so essential for working across functions. Roles and role relationships that are clearly defined and understood provide the foundation for an effective organization.

When roles and their relationship to each other are confusing there is uncertainly, conflict and wasted effort. *Role clarity coupled with clear accountability builds personal confidence and generates trust between individuals and between individuals and the organization.*

STAFFING THE ORGANIZATION

Tasks given to different roles vary in complexity, and the capability of each individual to do the tasks differs as well. Therefore, one of the challenges in building and maintaining an effective organization is to select the right person for each role.

Requisite Organization provides procedures for selecting a person capable of handling the complexity of the work in the role and for ensuring that each employee has a manager who can work at one level of complexity higher. This provides everyone with a manager who can add value to, and set context for, the work to be done.

REQUISITE PRACTICES AND ROLE RELATIONSHIPS

There are explicitly defined practices in this System that enable work to get done effectively including managerial leadership practices, three-level management, cross-functional working relationships and talent pool development.

Managerial Leadership Practices

The performance management process includes managerial planning, context setting, task assignment, feedback, coaching, appraisal and continual improvement.

Three-Level Management

The establishment of a working relationship between each manager and his/her subordinates and the manager's manager enables more effective communication. It also provides each employee with someone to assure fairness of treatment and to assist him or her in consideration of long-range career opportunities.

Cross-Functional Working Relationships

People who must interact with each other but who are subordinates of different managers are frequently very unclear about what accountability and authority they have with regard to each other. All the necessary work processes and work systems are integrated through the use of clearly-defined working relationships. What has previously appeared to be a clash of personalities disappears when working relationships are clearly specified between roles in different functions.

Talent Pool Development

Provision is made to regularly review the entire pool of talent in the organization to ensure that each employee is fairly considered for developmental and promotional opportunities and that employees are available with the necessary capability and knowledge to meet current and anticipated staffing needs.

Managerial Accountability

Managers are held accountable for the output and the working behavior of their subordinates. This accountability is central to Requisite Organization. It is the manager who decides what each subordinate is to do and with what resources they are to be provided. It is also the manager who revises plans and priorities if a task cannot be completed as originally specified.

All managers must exercise managerial leadership. Managers are accountable for:

- Maintaining a team of qualified and capable subordinates
- Leading subordinates to agreed-upon goals
- The results of their subordinates' work
- Their own personal effectiveness

Managers do not delegate all of their work. They do some of their work themselves, they get assistance with their own work from subordinates, and they delegate some of their work.

Managers are accountable to coach each of their subordinates regularly to help them increase their knowledge, skills and experience so they can effectively carry out all of the requirements of their individual role.

Managerial Authority

In order for managers to be held accountable by their manager for the work of subordinates, they must have certain authority with regard to their subordinates. They must have the authority to judge how they will get the work of their unit done and to decide how effective any given subordinate is in doing his or her work. Managers also need to be able to veto the selection of someone to be their subordinate, as well as to be able to initiate the removal of a subordinate from a role if they do not believe the individual is capable of doing the work.

Subordinate Accountability and Authority

Subordinates are accountable for working to achieve the tasks they are assigned. They are accountable and have the authority to discuss task assignment with their manager and review any problems they anticipate or that may develop. They are also accountable for providing their manager with ideas as to how processes might be improved.

When a task is in progress, a subordinate is accountable to inform his or her manager if what has been assigned cannot be completed as specified and do so in time for the manager to take adaptive action. This might, for example, happen because circumstances have changed or certain aspects of the task were not fully understood or initially anticipated.

When a task needs to be modified, the subordinate is expected to make useful suggestions as to what might be done about the situation. It is the manager, however, who adjusts the task, its priority and the resources available. Working in this way assures that there are no surprises and that everything is done as assigned.

The manager-subordinate relationship is a two-way working relationship between adults where the best ideas of each are applied, recognizing that the manager has a broader perspective and the final say if there is not complete agreement.

TEAMS

Teams are an essential component of organizational success. In order to be fully effective, each team must have a manager who is accountable for the work of the team. The manager may or may not choose to appoint someone else as team leader to direct the work of the team. Team members are accountable as individuals for their work as contributing participants.

THE BASIS OF THE REQUISITE ORGANIZATION MANAGEMENT SYSTEM

The principles and practices that make up this System are adapted from the work of Dr. Elliott Jaques. Dr. Jaques held an M.D. degree from Johns Hopkins Medical School and a Ph.D. in Social Relations from Harvard University. He studied effective organizations for more than 50 years and developed the comprehensive system that is called Requisite Organization. Dr. Jaques referred to his body of work in management as Requisite Organization. He chose the term 'requisite' to describe his integrated theory of how organizations work best because the word means 'as required by the nature of things'. The concepts of Requisite Organization flow from the nature of things—the nature of people, the nature of work and the nature of the relationship between the two.

Making Strategy Work – The Linkage Process

By Nancy Lee and Fred Mackenzie

The Linkage Process is a method of converting an organization's long-term Strategy into actual work output. It involves a logical and systematic procedure in which employees, at all levels, actively participate.

There are two compelling reasons for implementing this process. The first is organizational and the second is individual. Organizationally, it establishes a step-by-step way of ensuring that long-range plans and objectives are translated into desired results. Individually, it creates an understanding of how each employee's work output contributes to the overall goals of the organization. This enhances the motivation of each person since output becomes personal goal accomplishment, not just ongoing day-to-day activity.

Aligning individual assignments with organizational objectives is a win-win opportunity. It is both logical and essential that the sum total of the employees' work achieves the overall objectives of the organization. *The better the fit between work output and corporate strategy, the more outstanding will be the results, where the ordinary becomes the extraordinary.* Agreeing with this conclusion is easy. Implementing it takes effort.

For objectivity and skill in facilitating the Linkage Process, it is helpful to use an external consultant, at least for the initial cycle.

Linking Long-Term Strategy to Key Assignments

337

Communicate the Corporate Strategy and Determine Critical Success Factors

As in life itself, little progress on anticipated results can be made without first having a mission and a plan. Having an explicit Strategic Plan is the first step. The Linkage Process begins with Senior Management determining, and then communicating, the organization's Vision, Mission, Values and overall Strategy.

Senior Management then meets to decide four to six key factors to be focused on that will make the difference in whether or not the organization is successful in achieving its Strategy. These are called Critical Success Factors (CSFs). They are subjects, not action phrases.

Typical examples are Growth, Profitability, Technology, Human Resources, Manufacturing, Acquisitions/Divestitures, Access to Capital and Product Development.

Identify Corporate Objectives for Each Critical Success Factor

Each of the identified CSFs is broken down into long-range Corporate Objectives (COs), typically with a three-year horizon. When doing this is the first time, three years appears to be the most effective to use. Some organizations find they later use this process with a five-year time horizon. There are usually about four objectives for each CSF. Here, numbers, percentages, milestone dates, and other metrics are included. These are organizational objectives; individual assignments are not delineated at this time.

The formulation of these long-range Corporate Objectives is generally accomplished in a meeting of Senior Management where the group is divided into subgroups working within the CSF of their expertise. The findings of the subgroups are then shared with the larger group for understanding and modification. This activity typically results in 16 to 24 Corporate Objectives which all of Senior Management has participated in formulating. The role of the CEO in this process is paramount as he/she will be held accountable for the end results.

An example of a Corporate Objective is: "Complete two acquisitions within three years, one in the USA and one in Europe."

Develop Corporate Short-Term Goals for each Corporate Objective

From these Corporate Objectives, Corporate Short-Term Goals (STGs) are developed. These are usually 9 to 18 months in duration. On average, there are about three to five short-term goals for each of the longer-range objectives yielding anywhere from 50 to 100 Corporate Short-Term Goals.

To determine these Short-Term Goals, Senior Management decides who should work on creating them for each of the Corporate Objectives. Teams are created to address each of the objectives. Each team develops specific goals from the objective(s) assigned to them and submits the draft to a Planning Facilitator for consolidation into a list of goals by CSF and Objective. All goals are assigned to a functional manager who is accountable for achieving the goal. (When a goal is corporate-wide in scope, this functional manager may create a cross-functional ad hoc team for implementation and acts as the team leader). This list is then distributed to all members of Senior Management for review prior to meeting as a group.

A group meeting is held to discuss, clarify and modify as necessary the Corporate Short-Term Goals. This meeting may include members of the working teams who are not part of Senior Management. It is important not to have more goals than Senior Management believes can be accomplished during the designated time frame of either three or five years.

The end result is a <u>Master Corporate Document</u> showing Corporate Short-Term Goals, how they relate to longer-term Corporate Objectives and how the Objectives relate to the Critical Success Factors derived from the Strategy.

An example of a Corporate Short-Term Goal is: "Within 15 months identify four potential acquisitions, two in the USA and two in Europe."

Senior Management has now participated in formulating, developing and understanding the organization's specific goals for the near term as well as the longer term objectives. The process has now moved from the strategic (planning) stage to the tactical (operational) stage.

Determine and Cascade Key Assignments

The last step in this process is the linkage of Corporate Short-Term Goals to Key Assignments. The CEO works with his/her immediate subordinates individually to determine their Key Assignments. Many times a Corporate Short-Term Goal (and sometimes a Corporate Objective) becomes a Key Assignment for one of the CEO's immediate subordinates who, in turn, may delegate all or part of it to their immediate subordinates. Each of these assignments then gets broken down and cascaded into Key Assignments for Vice Presidents, Directors, Managers and their subordinates.

Some education is initially required for proper crafting of the Key Assignments by the managers at all levels. This would include the use of a customized Key Assignments Document specifying each employee's work output for a given time period. An example of a Key Assignment is: "By July 1, 20xx, establish an Acquisition Task Force, have members agree on a plan to proceed and submit this plan to the CEO for approval."

Linking Corporate Long-Range Strategy to individual Key Accountabilities transforms broad strategic plans into focused operational plans where all employees are able to understand and feel part of the overall direction and thrust of the organization, both in the short term and long term.

The Steps in Linking Strategy to Key Assignments

Following is an outline of the seven-step process for linking long-term Strategy to Key Assignments.

1. **Meeting One:**   Describe Long-Range Strategy (seven to ten year outlook)

Determine 4 to 6 Critical Success Factors (CSFs) needed to achieve the strategy.

In small groups, draft 4 to 6 Three-Year Corporate Objectives (COs) for each of the CSFs; if time permits, review and refine in large group.

2. Meeting Two: Complete preparation of 4 to 6 Three-Year Corporate Objectives for each CSF, a total of 20 to 30 Objectives.

CEO and Leadership Team decide who should develop 4 to 6 Corporate Short-Term Goals (STGs) for each of the Three-Year Corporate Objectives.

3. Team Member Work: Those people designated prepare the Corporate Short-Term Goals and submit them to the Planning Facilitator who combines them into one consolidated list by Objective. There will be a total of 100 or more goals. This list is distributed to all group members for review prior to step 4.

4. Meeting Three: The Corporate Short-Term Goals for each Three-Year Corporate Objective are reviewed, discussed and modified as necessary.

5. CEO Work: The CEO works with his Senior Leadership Team individually to determine each of their Key Assignments linked to the Corporate Short-Term Goals.

6. Team Member Work: Team members work with each of their subordinates to establish their Key Assignments.

7. Vice President's, Director's and Manager's Work: Key Assignments and team assignments relating to the Corporate Short-Term Goals are developed for their subordinates and cascaded.

Determining Role Level and Judging Suitability for Role

By Nancy R. Lee

In this paper, the focus is on providing a brief description of the different types of work complexity found in roles within organizations where tasks are aggregated. Indicators of the different types of thinking used by individuals suited to the various strata are also described. This material reflects Requisite Organization concepts and assumes that the reader is familiar with basic RO principles and practices. Particularly relevant is the clear separation of establishing the complexity of work required by a role and considering the suitability of a given individual to fill that role. Common practice is often to have roles reflect the abilities of the person occupying the role rather than focusing on the work that is required to be done in that role.

In organizations tasks differ to a large extent depending on different requirements for acquiring, understanding and processing information. Tasks are clustered into roles that need to be filled by individuals with the appropriate capability to make judgments and decisions required by the work of the role. Roles are places in layers in an organization (strata) based on the complexity of the tasks and work required in a role.

The complexity of information that any individual can handle at a given time has to do with such things as:

- the number, rate of change and ease of identification of factors in a situation
- the clarity or ambiguity of factors
- the amount of information that can be dealt with
- how far into the future one can envision (referred to as the individual's time horizon)
- the ability to pattern, order, categorize and generalize information

There is a vast difference in difficulty among such tasks as being directed to make 100 copies on a copy machine, planning how to increase sales for next year by 15% and deciding whether or not to sell a unit of the company.

Virtually everyone would agree that tasks differ in complexity and individuals differ in the ability to complete different tasks and that individuals are most happy, healthy and productive when they are suited to the work they are doing. Therefore, it is desirable for both employees and their organizations to have a good fit.

The idea of more complex, more difficult or higher levels of work does not refer to more work in quantity but to work that is greater in scope. Although everyone has a sense of what these ideas mean, until the concepts and definitions of Requisite Organization were developed there was no clear language to describe or discuss them.

When considering someone to do the work of a role there are four areas to consider:

- Knowledge, skill, experience and any necessary educational qualifications
- Whether the individual values the work of the role and will give full commitment to it
- The complexity of information processing necessary for the complexity of the work
- No issues of behavior that interfere with accomplishing the work

In the selection process the focus has most often been on knowledge, skill and experience. However, it is also useful and necessary to understand whether or not the person will value the work of the role and if he or she has any issues of behavior that will have an impact on getting the work done. In addition, it is important to understand the different levels of mental capability required to undertake work of differing complexity. This is called the Complexity of Information Processing (CIP). All of the four areas are necessary and none alone sufficient for a given individual to be suitable for a specific role.

In order to assist managers to confirm and feel more confident about their judgments of the level of complexity of work required by a role and of the CIP required of a person to perform a specific role, following are descriptions of typical work at each organizational level and of the different types of reasoning that is used by individuals best suited to each Strata.

Strata are further divided into work bands of Low, Mid and High. Individuals capable of work at the Low Band need a time horizon at the lower end of the time span for the role. Those capable of work in the High Band will have a time horizon toward the high end of the time span of the Strata.

Stratum I: First Line Work
(Time Span: 1 Day to 3 Months)

This work is direct output work where the employee is given a clear pathway to follow. It is work that usually involves direct contact with something physical such as a lathe or a postage machine. For this type of work individuals are given or trained in a procedure to follow. When employees encounter a problem they use direct judgment as to what is prescribed to do when that particular problem is encountered. If there is no such solution already set out, employees generally must ask their manager how to solve the problem and what should be done next. The focus here is upon correctly performing procedural tasks. Direct physical feedback indicates whether the work is being done correctly or not. First line work does not include management of others although a person at this level might assist his/her manager in some aspects of the manager's work. In this Stratum work largely results in a direct output. The emphasis is on accuracy and quality.

The work in the Low Band of Stratum I often involves doing one task at a time, completing that task and then moving on to another task. For example, "stuff this group of envelopes and then move on to the next group" or, "clean off these tables in this room and then move to the next room to clean those tables". The work is usually completed within a day. Work in the High Band of Stratum I can be highly complicated work requiring substantial skilled knowledge and experience. An example would be the work of an electric power lineman. Although this type of higher level Stratum I work can be short in nature, such as repairing a downed electrical line, the training to do the work often requires as much as three months to become initially skilled in the work. Stratum I Low band work is sometimes referred to as unskilled, Mid-level as skilled and High level as multi-skilled work.

Declarative Information Processing

Individuals who are best suited to Level I work tend to explain their position by bringing forward a number of separate reasons for their decision or action. Each reason is stated on its own. No connection is made with any of the other reasons that may be mentioned. For example: "I can't make the copies you requested because the copy machine is not working. It wasn't working very well yesterday. There is an indicator flashing that says a new toner is needed. I have replaced the toner as directed. It still is not working. What should I do next?"

To the observer the use of information has a declarative quality and the points that are being made seem to lack unity or a sense of being connected. Each of the reasons stands alone in support of the conclusion. The conclusion is supported by this reason 'or' that reason, 'or' this other reason. The individual may frequently provide a response that appears to be 'either' this 'or' that.

Stratum II: First Line Management, Analyst, Technician, Programmer
(Time Span: 3 Months to One Year)

Work at Stratum II in an organization is diagnostic or analytical in nature. The first line manager establishes tasks, the pathway and the boundaries for Stratum I first line workers. S/he diagnoses the problems encountered by the first line worker and, if necessary, determines a new procedure to be followed. This work is concerned with monitoring of operational processes and managing to standards. It is also the work of individual contributor analysts who review data, draw conclusions and manage deviations. Diagnostic patterns and models may be learned through training and experience, for example in financial analysis, engineering and nursing. Work at this level requires the ability to draw conclusions from information without direct hands-on contact, although the managerial work involves overseeing such work. The work often is directed at one task at a time.

In the Low Band of this Stratum the manager may oversee relatively simple direct output work of, for example, some types of technicians. In the High Band there are roles such as financial analysts and nurse practitioners who diagnose quite complex situations.

Cumulative Information Processing

A person who is suited to work at Stratum II explains his or her position by bringing together a number of different ideas none of which is sufficient alone to make the case, but do so when taken together. An example is the investigator who says, "if we consider that the thief knew when the payroll would be delivered, knew when the guard was on break and was able to use the alarm code to turn it off, we can conclude that this was probably an inside job." The reasons are accumulated and explicitly connected. This type of processing has an 'and' this reason, 'and' that reason to support the conclusion.

Stratum III: Middle Management
(Time Span: One Year to Two Years)

At this level the work continues to be operational in nature and involves developing pathways and systems to achieve a goal. Often a number of pathways need to be conceptualized as possible methods for dealing with actual or anticipated problems. Design of work processes, best practices development, process redesign, and the re-engineering of systems takes place at this level. A fixed pathway or system is selected and the manager oversees work step by step toward each goal. If a problem arises, the manager moves from that pathway to another pathway and proceeds in a fixed manner toward the goal. Stratum III is the first level where a manager may manage other managers. Work here often relates to a specific discipline or profession such as that of a lawyer or an accountant. Level III work may also be that of individual contributors such as college professors and physicians.

In the Low Work Band of Stratum III work may require creating one or two pathways toward a goal and may rely on knowledge that already exists. As the work complexity at this level increases the ability to create more optional pathways to deal with the projected future is required. Managers who are capable of working in the High Band of Stratum III will have in mind many pathways they have used over time. Work here is typically conceptualized on an annual basis and as the complexity increases it is done so in the context of perhaps 15 to 20 months. An example would be a 15 month rolling annual budget forecast or carrying out a plan to secure an identified customer within 18 months.

Serial Information Processing

Work at Stratum III requires serial processing. A person using serial processing explains his/her position by constructing a line of thought consisting of a sequence of reasons, each one of which leads on to the next, creating a chain of linked reasons. For example, "I think we should do A because it will result in B which will cause C to happen". This method of thinking has both a serial and a conditional quality in the sense that each reason in the series sets the conditions that lead to the next reason. That is, 'if' this happens 'then' that will happen which will lead to something else happening.

Stratum IV: Functional Managers
(Time Span: Two Years to Five Years)

Work at the level of Functional Managers deals with a number of pathways in relation to each other. Interactive projects are undertaken and adjusted to each other with regard to resources and timing as work proceeds in order to keep the total program on target. Various disciplines are integrated to achieve overall business performance. Patterns are developed here in order to establish policies and guidelines for Stratum III. This is where critical path analysis is done in which a number of processes have to be controlled in relation to each other. This is also the area of change management and of review and correction of business strategy. Decisions and actions demonstrate the ability to be flexible and to adapt to unanticipated obstacles. Strata I, II, and III are operational in nature. Stratum IV is the first level which has future strategic planning aspects to the work. Typical roles in a Stratum V business unit manage Stratum IV functions such as Sales and Marketing, Human Resources, IT, Engineering and so on. Depending on the organization these are often Director or Vice President level roles.

Parallel Information Processing

A person capable of using parallel information processing explains her/her position by examining a number of positions, each arrived at by means of serial processing. Several lines of thought are held in parallel and are interlinked with each other. Additional information is taken into consideration. Reasons or points are selected from these parallel sequences, and a new sequence is described that support the position chosen. Often alternative sequences are described, acknowledging two sides of an issue and two possible strategies, with reasons being given for the selection of one of them.

An illustration of parallel process thinking is: "We could do A which would then lead to B and we could get to S. Or, we could do M which would lead to N and we would arrive at another desired end, Y. But we might get to a better outcome, W, by modifying the first plan with M and adding S, but on balance I think we should do M to get to Y because that seems a more desirable result." The individual combines reasons or points from one or more chains to reach a desired conclusion. The nature of this, the most complex type of information processing, is bi-conditional, meaning that only if particular consequences could be met then another series of conditions could be put into place. Parallel reasoning has an 'if, then but only if' quality to it.

Stratum V: Business Unit Head or Vice President of a Stratum VI Company
(Time Span: Five to Ten Years)

Work at Stratum V deals with a unified whole system and is concerned with the overall nature of the organization. There is a wide variety of issues that have to be worked on in the context of the relationship between the business unit and the outside marketplace. This is most often where profit and loss accounting takes place. There are financial, human resourcing, production, technology and product research issues to be dealt with which continually interact with each other. The business unit head has to handle problems such as a shortage of raw materials, strikes, rising costs, new product issues balancing the whole range of complex variables against each other. This is the first area of total strategy for the organization as opposed to strategy for a function or operational tactics. The focus of the Business Unit head is vertical, downward to integrate the business and upward to connect the unit with the corporate entity.

Declarative Information Processing.

The individual capable of a Stratum V role uses direct judgment, but the information that now has to be used is at a higher order of complexity than the information used in roles at Level I through IV. The person is capable of using and understanding universal principles and theories. They use ideas that are abstract and conceptual in nature. In describing a decision this person will have discrete reasons to support the action but the reasons will consist of complex Level IV bi-conditional units. It is interesting to note that while persons operating at Level IV are often very articulate in describing all aspects of why they are making a particular decision, individuals at Level V sometimes sound less so, because they are now using more abstract concepts in thinking about and in making decisions. A number of these complex reasons are involved, more by a person capable of working in the High Band in this level than the Low Band.

Stratum VI: Executive Vice Presidents of Level VII Corporations or CEO of a Stratum VI Organization
(Time Span: Ten Years to Twenty Years)

The Stratum VI Corporate CEO enables Stratum V, or fledgling Stratum IV business units to be created and flourish. Work at this level focuses on global networking in all areas likely to be significant to the organization, including political, legal, economic, social, technological and international concerns. Here again it is a diagnostic type of work but at a higher order conceptual abstract type of information complexity. The CEO of a Stratum VI corporation (or Executive Vice Presidents of a Stratum VII) sponsor and encourage research, liaison and other activities at the top level of stakeholder organizations, seeking to ensure a common knowledge base and understanding. They act to influence the larger global environment in ways favorable to their organization.

They are concerned with corporate social responsibility as well as corporate performance. Work includes overseeing business units and assessing their needs for increases in investment, while balancing resource allocation. This level recommends investment in or divestment of technologies, lines of business or business units and, if operating as the CEO, makes these decisions. The CEO role deals on a continuing basis with the complexity of financial market issues, balance sheet value of the business units, issues of major competitors, the culture of the organization and what is happening in the world.

Cumulative Information Processing

Abstract conceptual concepts are used by these individuals capable of working at Stratum VI to diagnose and analyze issues affecting the business units and the entire corporation. They are able to understand and deal with intangible concepts like balance sheets, treasury policies, the Pacific Rim, the European Union and so on. With a horizontal, outward focus, their interests are in world-wide issues and how they affect the organization. They screen information for the Stratum V unit leaders. Executive Vice Presidents provide relevant information to the Stratum VII corporate CEO. Problems are anticipated and envisioned many years into the future, often a decade or more, so current planning and actions can take place understanding possible downstream consequences.

Stratum VII: Corporate CEO
(Time Span: Twenty Years plus)

Serial Information Processing

The work of the CEO of a Stratum VII corporation is similar to that of a Corporate CEO at Level VI described above. Stratum VII corporations are generally global, have a longer strategic outreach (more than two decades) and require a number of functions whose purpose is to oversee the work of groups of business units and to enhance their asset value while maintaining a profitable balance sheet for the business as a whole. Here serial information processing is used but at the abstract conceptual level using complex bi-conditional units in serial pathways.

Stratum VIII: Corporate CEO of a Mega-Corporation
(Time Span: Fifty years plus)

Parallel Information Processing

This CEO oversees a Stratum VIII organization that is made up of a number of Stratum VII corporations. The CEO manages a number of Level VII CEOs as well as a holding company staff. General Electric is an example of this type of organization. There are few of them and they have not been studied in detail. This CEO uses parallel processing at an abstract conceptual level.

Three Methods of Judging Stratum and the Work Band within a Stratum

Comparing roles within an organization has always been very difficult. Using Requisite concepts, this task becomes both easier and more accurate. There are three ways to make this judgment. Organizations often use two or more of these methods in combination.

- All or Key Roles are reviewed and measured as to Time Span
- The roles within an organization are compared against one another with regard to Stratum and Band
- The Manager and Manager-once-Removed agree the Stratum and the Band within the Stratum that is required by the complexity of the work of the role

Time-Span Measurement

The most accurate way to judge the Stratum and Work Band within the Stratum is to question the immediate manager of the role with regard to the longest tasks s/he assigns to that role. This provides an objective measure of the Stratum and Work Band. Sometimes certain key roles are time spanned and other roles compared to it. Roles in the Low Work Band will be toward the lower end of this spread in the time span and in the High band will be toward the upper end.

Stratum I has a time span of 1 day to 3 months.

Stratum II has a time span of 3 months to 1 year

Stratum III has a time span of 1 year to 2 years

Stratum IV has a time span of 2 years to 5 years

Stratum V has a time span of 5 years to 10 years

Stratum VI has a time span of 10 years to 20 years

Stratum VII has a time span of more than 20 years

For an in-depth discussion of Time Span see *The Time Span Handbook* by Dr. Elliott Jaques and *The Practice of Managerial Leadership* by Nancy Lee.

Roles are Compared across the Organization

A Manager meets with his subordinate managers and compares all Subordinate-once-Removed roles. The group discusses any roles where there are disagreements as to the complexity of the work. The Manager makes the final decision. This process takes place throughout the entire organization. (Note that occasionally a role must be placed below the true level required of the role because it is not deemed possible for financial considerations or because there is a scarcity of people of the right level to fill the role. This is an example of the type of conscious compromise that must be made from time to time in an organization, but with the full recognition that a compromise is being made.)

Although this paper has largely focused above Stratum II on managerial roles, it is possible to have roles at all levels up to VI that are individual contributor roles. The level of work of a Research Scientist for example would be based on the longest tasks being assigned to that role; it could be a level IV role. The role of a Chief Economist in a Stratum VII financial services organization could be a Stratum VI individual contributor role.

The Manager and Manager-once-Removed Agree on a Stratum and Work Band

The immediate manager of a role compares the roles subordinate to him/her and determines if a given role is in Work Band Low, Mid or High. This is discussed with the Manager-once-Removed who compares

354 DETERMINING ROLE LEVEL AND JUDGING SUITABILITY FOR ROLE

it with other Subordinate-once-Removed roles and agrees or changes the Work Band. The decision is based on a sense of the complexity of the work of the role relative to other roles.

Considering the Work Band within a Role

Managers generally have a good sense of the Work Band within a Stratum. The Low Work Band requires someone with entry level ability for the work of the role. The High Band requires someone who is highly developed in their ability to do the work and the type of reasoning required and Mid Band requires someone in the middle.

Judging the Complexity of Information Processing of an Individual

Managers also have a good sense of the relative mental capability of each person subordinate to them, their Complexity of Information Processing (CIP). This comes from assigning tasks and observing how each individual completes tasks of differing difficulty. Managers are usually quite confident of their judgments after someone has been working for them for three to six months. As part of this judgment process managers can ask themselves the following question:

> *Do I feel this person is capable of being my immediate subordinate?*
>
> If the answer is no, ask yourself if you feel another manager is needed between you and this subordinate, in which case they would function best in a role two levels (or even more) below yours.
>
> If the answer is yes, then ask if you feel this person can handle the work you delegate at an entry level, in a highly developed way or somewhere in between?

Once you have judged someone to have the necessary CIP for a role, be sure to consider the other critical aspects of suitability for a role, that of valuing the work, having the necessary skilled knowledge and having no work behavior issues.

Bear in mind that the level of complexity of a role in a given Stratum and Work Band are separate issues from the CIP of a given individual.

A role may be filled by a person with more capability than required by the role or by someone who does not have the necessary CIP for the role. Persons may choose, for example, to work below their level of capability because of heavy family responsibilities or there may not be a suitable role available for them at the present time. Or, a role may have to be filled with someone not yet capable of the required level because there are no fully qualified candidates. In the first instance that is the person's choice and the organization is benefiting from having someone in the role with additional CIP.

Value-Adding Managers

Establishing roles requisitely with each Stratum in the organization managed by fully capable persons in the next higher layer will provide each employee with a value-adding manager who can plan and delegate tasks appropriately, set context, coach, solve problems and integrate the work of the unit in a productive manner.

Summary

The information provided in this paper is aimed at helping managers feel confident in determining the complexity of a role as to Stratum and Work Band and in considering the four factors of Suitability for Role of a given individual to do the work of a specific role.

Establishing Key Assignments

By Nancy Lee and Fred Mackenzie

Introduction

Key Assignments are the most important tasks a manager gives to each subordinate in order to achieve the unit's goals. Clearly describing each employee's Key Assignments (KAs) is the crucial step in linking corporate strategy to real-time work output. Key Assignments are actions and outputs for which an employee is held accountable. When delegated properly, KAs offer a clear description of the major achievements each employee is expected to accomplish within a specific time frame.

Basic Principles

- Delegating Key Assignments and discussing them with each subordinate is not a once-a-year exercise. It is a continuing process through which ongoing progress can be gauged of employees' effectiveness in their role.
- Key Assignments include both specific **tasks** with targeted completion times and **general responsibilities** that are ongoing in nature with no specific closure. Together, they define the most *important* assignments—but not all of them. They are the ones to be focused on during the time period involved. **Tasks** are an output the manager needs to have completed by a specific time in the future. **General responsibilities** are outputs that are needed but are ongoing in nature.
- There is a distinct difference between **position descriptions** and **Key Assignments.** As the name implies, **position descriptions** cover the activities encompassed in the entire role on an ongoing basis. They are useful in the employment process, developmental planning and determining role level. **Key Assignments** are created by the manager and given to a specific subordinate. They are used as part of the personal effectiveness appraisal, compensation considerations and the coaching process.

Attachment A describes in detail the differences between the two documents.

- Managers decide what tasks they will give subordinates to do. The manager's manager is not to by-pass the manager and give assignments since subordinates are the manager's resources to get the work of the unit done.

Delegating Key Assignments

Thinking through the most important work that has to be done in a role and discussing it with a subordinate is fundamental to managing. It is this process that helps all employees understand what they are to do. These discussions provide the basis of role clarity for subordinates. Committing the results of these discussions into a Key Assignments Document (KAD) further defines for both manager and subordinate what is expected to happen within a given time frame.

Not all assignments are key and some need not be listed. In preparing an Accountability Document for the person in a role, typically about 6 to 8 assignments should be identified. These are the most important work to be done within the role in the short-term. To achieve full clarity in first line roles and first line managerial roles it may be necessary to include a few additional KAs.

Key Assignments should cover the major thrust of the role for a designated period of time. Typically, 70% to 80% of all work would be covered. The priority and list of Key Assignments changes from year to year, and during the year as well, depending upon overall unit and corporate targets.

Having clear definitions of Key Assignments helps an employee decide where his or her time should be spent each day. For this reason, it is also helpful for the manager to list KAs in order of their importance where possible.

Preparing Key Assignments

Key Assignments should be planned and established by the person's immediate manager. They are then discussed with the subordinate for agreement as to the achievability of the assignments and any needed revisions are made. These Key Assignments are next reviewed by the manager with his/her manager to provide an understanding of how the work is being delegated within his/her unit.

Key Assignments should be developed and assigned by the immediate manager to each subordinate role. This is by far the preferable method. However, sometimes the subordinate is asked to develop the Key Assignments in <u>draft</u> form for editing and approval by the manager. Although it is not recommended, given the time pressure many managers are under, this latter procedure can be made to work providing the manager does the important tasks of:

- having an initial discussion with the subordinate on the content,
- reviewing the draft and changing the list to be compatible with other subordinates' KAs and, most importantly, with the manager's own Key Assignments, and
- reviewing the document with the Manager-once-Removed for overall consistency.

The final Key Accountability document should reflect assignments that are challenging, measurable where possible, attainable and in line with the manager's Assignments and the corporate goals.

Having the employee actively participate in the process provides clarity and has important motivational and commitment factors. Employees should feel comfortable asking for clarification on any aspects of the assignment that they do not fully understand.

Assigning Tasks and General Responsibilities

Managers plan the work of their unit and decide what they will give subordinates to do. They may delegate an assignment completely to a subordinate or may assign a subordinate to assist in one of the manager's own tasks.

Managers decide on and communicate a task having in mind an output that is expected to be generated when the task is completed, e.g. a report to be written, a research project to be completed, calls on customers to be made, a sale to be closed, a rating to be achieved, a percentage to be reduced, a meeting to be conducted. Output can be a finite product or a service rendered. Output, whether a product or service, is both visible and observable.

When writing a task assignment, the text should begin with a verb that denotes closure, not one that describes an activity.

Some closure verbs are: achieve, complete, conduct, identify, obtain, sell. Attachment B is a list of sample closure verbs. Activity verbs, e.g. assure, investigate, analyze, support, assist, monitor are not suitable for defining a task. They can, however, be used in describing a general responsibility which is described below.

In simple terms, a task assignment has three parts: the closure verb, the subject with metrics where possible, and the timing. Attachment C illustrates the format and gives examples.

QQTR

A task can be defined as a quantity (Q) of things within given quality (Q) limits to be produced by a target completion time (T) within specified resource limits (R). Key tasks should follow the QQTR format.

The manager and subordinate can discuss these parameters to agree on an outcome that is satisfactory to the manager and that the employee believes can be accomplished as assigned. This discussion is an important part of the two-way manager-subordinate working relationship.

Quantity (Q)

There is usually a quantity involved in an output, hence the quantity needs to be specified or understood in the assignment of the task. It may be a number, a percentage or an item such as a report, proposal or plan.

Examples of task quantity include: reduce air travel by 10% in 20xx, increase use of on-line education programs by 20% in 20xx, conduct three safety drills by 7/1/20xx.

Quality (Q)

The manager specifying output has a quality in mind. There are always quality standards to be met. If a subordinate is to produce a given quantity to that quality, it is necessary to ensure that the quality needed is understood. Too low a quality and the output is unsatisfactory; too high and more resources are used than necessary. The output needs to be provided within certain quality standards, and these standards must be set clearly enough that everyone knows what they are.

Time (T)

A task is not only a 'what' but is a 'what-by-when'—that which is to be completed by a targeted completion time. This should be made explicit when assigning a task. The manager plans this target completion time to fit with the other tasks that the manager needs to get done toward achieving the unit goals.

One of the reasons for making the time explicit when assigning a task is that the subordinate can discuss with the manager any problems anticipated in meeting the timing given the resources, quantity and quality specified. If no target completion time is defined, it is difficult both to plan and to evaluate task accomplishment.

Tasks can be of any length—a day, a month, 6 months, a year, 15 months, 18 months, 2 years, etc. Too often managers focus only on what has to be done each year since appraisals are generally done annually. It is more effective to think of when the most important tasks need to be completed and then to discuss the results with the subordinate at the time of completion. Tasks of longer than a year in duration can have milestone discussions that help the manager evaluate how things are progressing. The annual appraisal then consists of a review of these completion and milestone discussions and contains no surprises.

Resources (R)

Tasks need to be assigned in terms of resources that are available, e.g. the amount of money that can be spent, how many man-hours can be used, what equipment and materials are available. The resources that are available are often not explicitly discussed but the manager must ensure that the employee understands what they are since R*esources* directly affect the other three parameters (*Quantity, Quality, and Time*). The employee should be clear about what resources are available and, if there are concerns, to negotiate available resources with the manager.

An example of QQTR is a report that needs to be written. The manager sets context by describing to the subordinate why the report is needed and the topic of the report. The manager specifies that an overview of the literature needs to be carried out resulting in a survey of at least 80% of all identified writing on the subject published in the last two years. This provides both the *Quantity* and *Quality* expected and a way to consider how effective the employee was in completing the task.

The manager states that the researcher has three months to complete the report *(Time)*. The manager tells the subordinate that there is a budget of $900 to cover research expenses and that an intern will be provided to help compile the bibliography (*Resources*).

The manager expects the subordinate to work on this report along with other ongoing work in such a way that the report will be completed on time as well as all of the subordinate's other assigned tasks.

Policies and Procedure

Although quality standards, policy and procedure limits are not always explicitly stated, they always exist and are implicitly assumed by both manager and the subordinate. It is a manager's responsibility to familiarize subordinates with these parameters and to see that they are adhered to in working on tasks. This is critically important with policies that involve safety or legal liability.

Prioritization and Changing Circumstances

The manager sets priorities for the work of subordinates. Where possible it is useful to list Key Assignments in order of priority, adding additional clarity to the document. When a subordinate is not able to complete a task as defined, s/he should go to the manager in time for adjustments to be made. This is often caused by a change in circumstances or prevailing conditions. When this occurs, the subordinate meets with the manager to discuss the situation and, when possible, makes suggestions as to changes that might be made. It is the manager who then makes the decisions and reprioritizes, often adjusting the QQTR of that or other tasks. The goal is to have all tasks completed to QQTR with no unpleasant surprises for the manager.

If There is Need for Speed

There is an important point that needs to be understood. Both managers and subordinates generally have a good idea of what is a **reasonable** time needed to complete an assignment. If the manager assigns a task that is to be completed in three months, it is a different task than if the subordinate is given one month to do it. Some people have difficulty with this point and think that it cannot be a different task just because the time allowed is two months less—but, it is a different task. The subordinate will have to make different decisions and behave differently. The manager may have to adjust some of the other parameters such as quality or quantity and perhaps assign more resources, or revise other tasks that the subordinate has been assigned.

With only one month to do the report, the subordinate may decide to do much less research and the literature review may have to be much more cursory. The employee will have to decide to adjust his/her work on other tasks in quite a different way, because of the allotted time s/he has been given to complete the report.

Here, for example, the employee who now must complete the report very quickly, may ask the manager for temporary clerical help to be assigned to assist with certain aspects of producing the report and also ask to have the date on another task postponed for several weeks.

Depending upon how much time the employee has to spend on the report, s/he will have to consider what can be set aside for now and what cannot, while still completing all of the assignments on time. Where these decisions impact other key assignments the employee will need to discuss these issues with the manager. It is the manager who is the one to adjust some of those other assignments if necessary.

What—Not How

In establishing key tasks it is neither necessary nor desirable to describe <u>how</u> to accomplish the task. That is for the subordinate to decide and is part of the subordinate's work. As long as they remain within the boundaries set by the organization, allowing employees to get on with their work in their own way is what is empowering, creative and rewarding for employees. When a manager describes how to do a task in great detail (micromanaging) it may indicate:

- the employee may not be of the right level to do the task or the work of the role
- coaching the employee is required to help growth in the job
- being hesitant to delegate (fear of failure) or not knowing how

An example of too much 'how': "By working with the Business Units discussing their concerns and reviewing the last five years of statistical data, create charts on an excel spreadsheet and analyze trends to determine future actions regarding the avoidable and unavoidable turnover situation. After reviewing the results with the Business Units, revise and submit a report with recommendations by 10/31/xx".

Although the manager and subordinate may wish to discuss some of the methods to be used, the task might be stated more simply: "By 10/31/xx, submit a report on the present status of employee turnover rate and recommend actions to be taken to reduce future avoidable turnover."

General Responsibilities

As mentioned earlier, Key Assignments that are <u>ongoing</u> are called General Responsibilities. They are closer to the things typically described in position descriptions and do not have a specific date by when they must be completed. However, they often have specific tasks that are imbedded in them which have target dates involved.

General Responsibilities should:

- be directly related to the goals of the unit and the strategy of the organization

- be specific to the role (not universal items e.g. control the budget, build the team, support corporate strategy, develop subordinates, manage the unit, etc.)

Sometimes it is desirable to include certain generic statements as part of every employee's Key Accountability document to support legal requirements or place emphasis on a particular concern such as safety.

> All managers are accountable to use requisite managerial leadership practices.

> All employees are to adhere to the safety standards at all times.

Writing General Responsibilities

General Responsibilities should begin with an action verb such as: monitor, oversee, provide, participate, maintain, assist, support, etc. Examples of a general responsibility statement are:

> Revise the company organization charts each time there is a change in personnel

> Remain current with changes in the OSHA regulations regarding...........

> When changes occur, update the Policy & Procedures Manual quarterly except for safety issues which need to be updated and distributed within one week of approval.

Summary

The foundation of the manager-subordinate relationship is the clear specification of the Key Assignments to be carried out. Clarity of the most important assignments given to subordinates, both key tasks and key general responsibilities, is critical to enhancing trust and achieving the overall success of the organization.

Attachment A

Comparison of a Position Description compared to a KAD

A role description describes the role in general and a Key Assignment Document provides specific assignments from the manager to the person in the role.

	Role Description	**Key Assignment Document**
Focus	The role	The person in the role
Scope	Everything in the role	Key assignments for specific time period
Origin	Human Resources	Managers' Assignments for specified period of time
Strategy	Not Related	Supports Corporate Goals
Description	Activities	QQTR
Updating	Seldom	Often, sometimes twice a year or when KAs are completed
Performance	Not Related	Dynamic
Verbs	Open-Ended	Closure
Time	Ongoing	Specific and varies with the assignment

Note: It is possible for two incumbents with the same Position Description to have two different Key Assignment Documents for the same time period.

Attachment B

Sample Closure Verbs

Important Key Words	Also Usable	Usable with added Closure Verb
Achieve	Appraise	Advise and ...
Audit	Approve	Analyze and ...
Close	Assign	Apply and...
Complete	Attend	Arrange and ...
Conduct	Authorize	Assure and ...
Consolidate	Classify	Check and ...
Eliminate	Construct	Consolidate and ...
Establish	Create	Describe and ...
Evaluate	Design	Determine and ...
Generate	Deliver	Develop and ...
Identify	Distribute	Inspect and ...
Implement	Execute	Interview and ...
Initiate	Issue	Perform and ...
Manage	Open	Prepare and ...
Obtain	Provide	Review and ...
Recommend	Select	Revise and ...
Schedule	Summarize	Transmit and ...
Sell	Test	Update and ...
Submit	Train	Verify and ...

Attachment C

Describing an Assignment

Use a closure verb, describe metrics (%, #, subject) and target completion or milestone date.

Examples

Execute	newly approved XX plan	by 7/31/xx
Submit	recommendations for XX	by 8/31/xx
Reduce	avoidable turnover by 20% compared to average for the years 20xx through 20xx	by 12/31/xx
Increase	20xx customer satisfaction ratings by 15% over 20xx	by 12/31/xx
Implement	two LEAN process reviews and submit results	first by 7/31/xx second by 11/30/xx
Achieve	profit of minimum $ 200K from P&S projects	by 12/31/xx
Conduct	CPI/Lean training for 50% of all employees	by 11/15/xx
Provide	up-to-date budget information to XXX for use in managing the budget throughout the year	by end of each month

Attachment D

KEY ASSIGNMENTS DOCUMENT (KAD)
PERSONAL EFFECTIVENESS APPRAISAL (PEA)

(EMPLOYEE NAME)
FY (YEAR)

Name	
Title	
Role Level & Grade	
World Area/Country/Department	
Manager	
Manager Once Removed (MoR)	
Email address	(Employee Name) @company.com

ROLE DEFINITION

Provide brief description of this role	
List key knowledge/skills required	
Additional Role Remarks and academic requirements (if essential to the role)	

KEY TASKS

	Mid-Year Results	Rating	Year-End Results	Rating	Comments
List the key tasks (typically 6 to 8) for this fiscal year. These are specific assignments that have a stated or understood Quality, Quantity, a targeted completion Time and designated Resources (QQTR). They may be longer or shorter than the fiscal year.					

GENERAL RESPONSIBILITIES

	Mid-Year Results	Rating	Year-End Results	Rating	Comments
List the ongoing key assignments (typically 6 to 8)					

Effectiveness Level Ratings:

ME = Meets/Exceeds Expectations
WTE= Working Toward Expectations
BE = Below Expectations
U = Unacceptable

Page 1 of 3

KEY ASSIGNMENTS DOCUMENT (KAD)
PERSONAL EFFECTIVENESS APPRAISAL (PEA)

(EMPLOYEE NAME) FY (YEAR)

TEAMS (PROJECT OR COORDINATIVE)

List the teams in which this role participates.	Accountable Team Manager, Team Leader if different	Time Commitment	Team type (Project or Coordinative) Team Purpose	Mid-Year Results	Rating	Year-End Results	Rating

CROSS FUNCTIONAL RELATIONSHIPS (CFRs)

List significant working relationships with others outside the role's functional base and identify type: Collateral, Advisory, Monitoring, Auditing, Prescribing, Service and Coordinative relationships

Situation Requiring CFR	Type of CFR

MANAGER'S OVERALL RATING AND COMMENTS

Give the employee an **Overall Rating** based on all the above categories:	Comments

DEVELOPMENT PLANS

List employee strengths (characteristics and behaviors against role expectations).	
List improvement areas (behaviors that are below what is expected in this role) and also describe relevant opportunities for growth within the role.	
List specific actions to be taken by employee to improve in a deficient area and/or growth opportunities to be undertaken including dates, costs, results expected and follow up plans.	

Effectiveness Level Ratings:
ME = Meets/Exceeds Expectations
WTE = Working Toward Expectations
BE = Below Expectations
U = Unacceptable

Key Assignments Document (KAD)
Personal Effectiveness Appraisal (PEA)

(Employee Name)

FY (Year)

Signatures

Reviewed by MoR _____ Date _____

Discussed with employee by manager _____ Date _____

Read by employee _____ Date _____

Employee's Comments

Changes to Key Assignments during the fiscal year:

Send completed KAD to HR

Effectiveness Level Ratings:

ME = Meets/Exceeds Expectations
WTE= Working Toward Expectations
BE = Below Expectations
U = Unacceptable

Teams and Team Working

By Nancy R. Lee

A 'team' can be defined as a group of people who work together to achieve a specific output for which there is an accountable manager. Teams and team working are essential to work effectively across functions to achieve the organization's Objectives and Goals.

There are three types of teams: project, coordinative and managerial. **Project** teams have an accountable manager for whom they produce an output. This, like the manager-subordinate relationship, is a task-assigning relationship. **Coordinative** teams consist of a number of people representing different functions whose work needs to be synchronized. Coordinative teams are especially important to coordinate the work of different functions.. The third type consists of all of a manager's immediate subordinates, who can be thought of as a **Managerial** team.

Project Teams

All project teams should have a manager for whom the work is carried out and who is accountable for the output of the team. These teams are resources that managers use to help them solve problems or accomplish tasks.

The accountable manager specifies the tasks with regard to the target completion time and the quantity and quality desired and also secures and provides resources for the team. Project teams may be made up of people chosen from a manager's own unit, or people selected from across several units when specific expertise is needed. The manager accountable for the project team may or may not appoint a team leader. When the work of the project team is completed the team is disbanded.

Project Team Leader

The accountable manager may choose to assign a project team leader rather than head the work of the team directly. When this is the case the person appointed has the same task-assigning role relationships and managerial authority as the manager except for that of appraising the effectiveness of team members. Project team leaders can:

- veto the appointment of a person to the team s/he considers unsuitable
- request removal of a team member judged not capable of the required work
- call meetings
- assign tasks to team members
- coordinate and integrate the work of the team

Project team leaders are accountable for the output of the team and for getting the collaboration and confidence of their team members. The team leader discusses with the immediate manager of each team member that person's effectiveness as a member of the team, or provides this information via email where necessary. The immediate manager carries out the appraisal.

Project Team Members

Individuals are requested to participate on a team by the team's accountable manager. An estimate of the time required is provided since the individual's manager may need to modify some of that person's task assignments. By agreeing to make any given subordinate available for work on a team, the immediate manager of that person demonstrates that s/he values the work of the team.

If subordinates find that the time needed for the work of a team they are on is interfering with their ability to get the work done on their regular assigned tasks, they discuss this with their immediate manager and resolve the issue.

Team members are to bring their full capability to bear on the work of the team. They are to attempt to resolve any team and departmental conflicts with the team, the team leader and the team's accountable manager. Any conflicts that cannot be resolved are to be referred to the team member's immediate manager who then discusses it with the team's accountable manager.

Project Team Output

Teams are often formed to provide direct output support (DOS) to the accountable manager who has decided s/he needs the help of several people who may be within his or her own unit, or from across several units. It is also possible for the accountable manager to delegate direct output to a team. If this is done, the accountable manager must appoint a project team leader so that there is a person accountable for the team's direct output.

Individual contributors may also need a team to provide them with direct output support. The individual contributor then becomes the manager accountable for the output of any team that s/he forms. An individual contributor would not delegate direct output to a team. Output of individual contributors is their own.

Coordinative Teams

Coordinative teams differ from project teams because the coordinative team leader does not have task-assigning authority. The team participants represent their functions and carry out work on the team as assigned by their own managers. Coordinative teams are used in situations where the work of a group of people representing a number of functions must be coordinated and synchronized over a period of time.

The manager who is accountable for the output of the coordinative team discusses the purpose of the team with the manager of each function to be represented on the team and the anticipated amount of time that will be required. The manager of the each function decides who will represent that function on the coordinative team.

Coordinative Team Leaders

The manager who is accountable for the output of the coordinative team may lead the team or may appoint a coordinative team leader, usually an immediate subordinate. The function of the coordinative team leader is to persuade the team of people to work together in a joint undertaking.

The coordinative team leader has the accountability and authority to:

- propose how tasks should be approached
- keep the group informed of progress in carrying out the tasks
- help overcome setbacks and problems encountered

In order to carry out this work, the coordinative team leader has the authority to:

- try to persuade the others to act together to plan and to implement plans for action
- arrange meetings
- obtain necessary information from team members
- take issues an disagreements to his/her own manager if persuasive efforts fail to settle the problem

A coordinative team leader does not have the authority to issue overriding instructions when there are disagreements. If a coordinative team member is not participating as fully as needed, the leader reports the problem to his/her manager who takes up the issue with the manager of that function who resolves any problems.

The coordinative team leader provides the team member's manager with a report on that person's participation on the team prior to the manager's preparation of the annual personal effectiveness appraisal.

Managerial Teams

Because the use of the concept of a 'team' is so pervasive in organizations, a manager's subordinates can be thought of as a manager's team. They are permanently part of the manager's team by virtue of the role they occupy. There are several types of managerial teams including:

- all of a manager's immediate subordinates
- three stratum teams made up of immediate subordinates and subordinates-once-removed
- all of a manager's subordinates at all levels

No Team Decisions

In working together as a team, subordinates are actively encouraged to express dissent, to explore pros and cons and to engage in debate with the manager or team leader and with each other. But, if there are decisions to be made in the case of serious disagreement, the team's accountable manager or the accountable project leader makes them. Where the disagreement exists on a coordinative team, the accountable manager and the manager of the function involved resolve the issue.

Summary

In a managerial hierarchy, decisions are made by individuals. People are employed as individuals, not as groups, and are held accountable for decisions as individuals. For this reason, there should be no group decisions and no self-managed teams.

Comprehensive Organization Charts

By Nancy R. Lee

Developing Comprehensive Organization Charts (COCs) for each unit in the organization is one of the most useful outcomes of a Requisite Organization consulting project. These charts provide a single place where the structure, staffing and compensation can be viewed in totality. They are a critical diagnostic tool for all managers to use on a continuing basis.

Sample Box for Comprehensive Org Chart

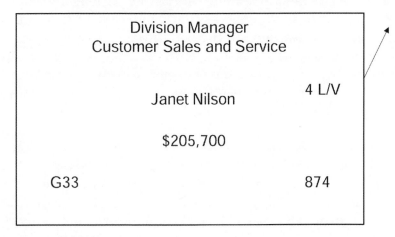

Most organization charts show only the title of the role, the name of the role incumbent and the reporting relationship. These charts are often out-of-date, frequently inaccurate and do not give any true indication of the level of work of the role.

As part of the Requisite consulting process when analyzing the existing (extant) organization each role is placed on the Comprehensive Organization Chart showing its Stratum and Work Band without the name of the role incumbent. This is the first step in developing these charts. At this point each unit in the organization is reviewed for gaps (a missing role level) or compression (one or more reporting roles in the same layer), as well as issues of functional alignment and span of control.

The names of the role incumbents are then added to the charts along with any identification numbers that relate to the role or the individual. A double line is used around the box if the role manages subordinates. These charts can also contain other useful information by means of color coding such as anticipated retirement, individuals considered at risk, geographical area, special skills, etc. This information is helpful in determining who might be moved between units, who is ready to move to a higher level role and who needs to be redeployed.

When employees have been judged as to Complexity of Information Processing (CIP), this is shown on the chart next to the employee's name, as well as the Mode indicated by their CIP. If the employee is judged capable of working in a stratum higher than that of the role, an up arrow is shown next to the box. If the employee is judged at a stratum or more lower than that of the role a down arrow is placed next to the box. This shows the manager where employees are being underutilized or overstretched. Issues of this type are reviewed and plans for needed changes are considered.

Total compensation for the past year is indicated on a version of the chart that is only seen by the manager and Manager-once-Removed (MoR). This information clearly shows whether or not the individual in the role is being fairly paid for the level of work of the role and identifies individuals who are overpaid or underpaid. It further enables comparison of compensation between individuals within a unit, and between units, and shows where there is inequity.

Comprehensive Organization Charts are developed throughout the process of requisite implementation. They can also be used to show how a future organization might look with requisite roles shown in the appropriate stratum with the anticipated compensation.

A version of the Comprehensive Organization Charts without the compensation being shown is used in talent pool meetings.

Comprehensive Organization Charts are one of the end results of a completed Requisite Organization project. It is critical to have these charts kept up to date on a regular basis (at least quarterly) by someone assigned to do so and to have unit managers and their MoRs regularly review the charts and discuss and resolve the issues that are identified.

These charts are to managers and HR professionals what schematic drawings are for engineers and technicians. When managers are presented with their total organization in a complete and consistent manner they can identify issues to be solved and anticipate future problems. Not only do gaps and compressions become immediately obvious graphically, so also do compensation and titling issues, span of control issues and excessive concurrent retirements —all in one document.

Following is an example of a Comprehensive Organization Chart showing total compensation. As mentioned above, there would also be a version of this chart for use in talent pool discussions without the compensation information.

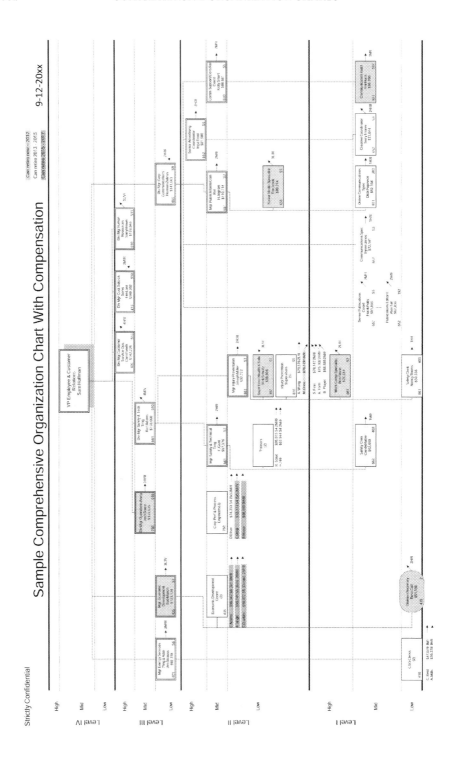

Sample Comprehensive Organization Chart With Compensation

9-12-20xx

Strictly Confidential

Readings on Requisite Organization

All of the books on this list are available through Amazon. All of the books listed, except *Requisite Organization* by Dr. Elliott Jaques, are also available in a Kindle version.

Requisite Organization: A Total System for Effective Managerial Leadership (Revised Second Edition 2006) Elliott Jaques

This is the essential reading on Requisite Organization. After reviewing the entire book a useful approach is to reread any topics of particular interest. This is a deep and complex book worth much study.

Social Power and the CEO: Leadership and Trust in a Sustainable Free Enterprise System (2002) Elliott Jaques

This is also critical reading on Requisite Organization. It is a much more linear book aimed at senior management but essential reading for anyone interested in Requisite Organization.

It's All About Work: Organizing Your Company to Get Work Done (2013) Stephen Clement and Christopher Clement

An easy-to-read in-depth description of Requisite Organization written by Dr. Stephen Clement, a long-time associate of Dr. Jaques on numerous projects.

Optimizing Organization Design: A Proven Approach to Enhance Financial Performance, Customer Satisfaction and Employee Engagement (2013) Ronald G. Capelle

This book includes not only a complete description of Requisite Organization but many research studies conducted by Dr. Capelle's consulting company.

Systems Leadership: Creating Positive Organizations (2006)
Ian MacDonald and Catherine Burke

A very complete description of Requisite Organization written by two associates of Dr. Jaques who worked with him on many projects.

7 Paths to Managerial Leadership: Doing Well by Doing it Right (2016)
Dr. Fred Mackenzie

A practical application of Requisite principles for all levels of management.

How Dare You Manage: Seven Principles to Close the CEO Skill Gap (2013)
Nick Forrest

A brief and useful description of Requisite principles.

Organization Design, Levels of Work and Human Capability: Executive Guide

This book is available for download at no charge from www.GlobalRO. org. It is compendium of a group of articles on Requisite Organization written by a variety of clients, consultants and academics.

Requisite Organization Resources

---

www.requisite.org

The website of the Requisite Organization International Institute was established to provide support to organizations engaged in implementation and further development of the work of Requisite Organization. ROII provides access to books and readings written by Elliott Jaques published by Cason Hall.

www.GlobalRO.org

This is the website of the Global Organization Design Society. It provides a great deal of background on Requisite Organization including videos, in-depth information on organizations that have used RO and results they have obtained, readings and books that can be downloaded at no charge, an introductory educational program on RO, and much more.

Bibliography

A bibliography developed over many years by Ken Craddock providing reference to Requisite Organization and Dr. Elliott Jaques. The bibliography is several hundred pages long and is available on line at GlobalRO.org.

www.orgcapitalpartners.com

Research and articles on Work Levels related to corporate governance, organization design, talent management and equitable executive compensation and pay for performance are found at this website.

www.requisiteorganizationassociates.com

This is the website of my company. E-learning modules on Requisite Organization and related desk references are available through this website at no cost on topics such as structure, staffing, accountability and authority and managerial practices. Details about how to access these modules are available on the website or by contacting requisiteorganization@gmail.com or nmrlee@aol.com.

NMRLEE@aol.com or requisiteorganization@gmail.com

If you wish further information on Requisite Organization contact me via email.